EXPLORERS & DISCOVERERS

EXPLORERS & DISCOVERERS

From Alexander the Great to Sally Ride

Volume A-Ca

Peggy Saari
•
Daniel B. Baker

U·X·L

AN IMPRINT OF GALE RESEARCH INC.,
AN INTERNATIONAL THOMPSON PUBLISHING COMPANY

I(T)P

NEW YORK • LONDON • BONN • BOSTON • DETROIT • MADRID
MELBOURNE • MEXICO CITY • PARIS • SINGAPORE • TOKYO
TORONTO • WASHINGTON • ALBANY NY • BELMONT CA • CINCINNATI OH

Explorers and Discoverers

From Alexander the Great to Sally Ride

Peggy Saari and Daniel B. Baker

Staff

Carol DeKane Nagel, *U·X·L Developmental Editor*
Thomas L. Romig, *U·X·L Publisher*

Shanna Heilveil, *Production Associate*
Evi Seoud, *Assistant Production Manager*
Mary Beth Trimper, *Production Director*

Pamela A. E. Galbreath, *Page and Cover Designer*
Cynthia Baldwin, *Art Director*

Margaret A. Chamberlain, *Permissions Supervisor (Pictures)*

The Graphix Group, *Typesetter*

Library of Congress Cataloging-in-Publication Data
Explorers & Discoverers : from Alexander the Great to Sally Ride
   / by Peggy Saari and Daniel B. Baker.
       lxxx, 886 p. : ill., maps, ports. ; 25 cm.
   Includes complete index in each volume.
   Contents: v. 1. A-Ca — v. 2. Ch-He — v. 3. Hi-Pi — v. 4. Po-Z
   ISBN 0-8103-9787-8 (set); 0-8103-9787-6 (v. 1); 0-8103-9799-4
(v. 2); 0-8103-9800-1 (v. 3); 0-8103-9801-X (v. 4)
   1. Explorers—Biography—Encyclopedias, Juvenile. 2. Discoverers in
     Geography—Encyclopedias, Juvenile. 3. Travelers—Biography—
     Encyclopedias, Juvenile. I. Saari, Peggy. II. Baker, Daniel B.
   G200.S22   1995
   920.02—dc20   95-166826
                                                              CIP

This publication is a creative work fully protected by all applicable copyright laws, as well as by misappropriation, trade secret, unfair competition, and other applicable laws. The editors of this work have added value to the underlying factual material herein through one or more of the following: unique and original selection, coordination, expression, arrangement, and classification of the information. All rights to this publication will be vigorously defended.

Copyright © 1995   U•X•L   An Imprint of Gale

All rights reserved, including the right of reproduction in whole or in part in any form.

∞™ This book is printed on acid-free paper that meets the minimum requirements of American National Standard for Information Sciences—Permanence Paper for Printed Library Materials, ANSI Z39.48-1984.

Printed in the United States of America

10 9 8 7 6 5 4 3 2

Contents

Preface xiii

Introduction xv

Picture Credits xix

Maps xxi

Biographical Listings

Volume 1: A-Ca

Delia Akeley (1875-1970) 1
Alexander the Great (356-323 B.C.) 5
Roald Amundsen (1872-c. 1928) 14

Antonio de Andrade (1580-1634) 23

Apollo (1957-1972) 26

Neil Armstrong (1930-) 34

Vladimir Atlasov (b. 17th century-1711) 40

Samuel White Baker (1821-1893)
and Florence Baker (1841-1916) 43

Joseph Banks (1743-1820) 52

Pedro João Baptista (lived 19th century)
and Amaro José (lived 19th century) 57

Aleksandr Baranov (1746-1819) 61

Rabban Bar Sauma (c. 1220-c. 1294) 65

Heinrich Barth (1821-1865) 69

Abu Abdallah Ibn Battutah (1304-1369) 75

Jim Beckwourth (1798-1867) 81

Gertrude Bell (1868-1926) 86

Fabian Gottlieb von Bellingshausen (1778-1852) ... 90

Benjamin of Tudela
(b. early 12th century-d. after 1173) 94

Hiram Bingham (1875-1956) 98

Isabella Bird (1831-1904) 103

Anne Blunt (1837-1917)
and Wilfrid Scawen Blunt (1840-1922) 107

Sidi Mubarak Bombay (c. 1820-1885) 112

Daniel Boone (1734-1820) 117

Louis-Antoine de Bougainville (1729-1811) 122

Louise Arner Boyd (1887-1972) 129

Pierre Savorgnan de Brazza (1852-1905) 133

Hermenegildo de Brito Capelo (1841-1917)
and Roberto Ivens (1850-1898) 137

Étienne Brulé (c. 1592-1633) 141

Robert O'Hara Burke (c. 1820-c. 1861)
and William John Wills (1834-1861) 144

Richard Burton (1821-1890) 150
Richard Evelyn Byrd (1888-1957) 158
Álvar Núñez Cabeza de Vaca (c. 1490-c. 1560) 164
John Cabot (c. 1450-c. 1499) 169
Sebastian Cabot (c. 1476-1557) 172
João Rodrigues Cabrilho
  (b. 16th [possibly 15th] century-d. 1543) 176
René Caillié (1799-c. 1838) 179
Giovanni da Pian del Carpini (c. 1180-1252) 183
Philip Carteret (1734-1796)
  and Samuel Wallis (1728-1795) 187
Jacques Cartier (1491-1557) 193

Chronology of Exploration 197

Explorers by Place of Birth 205

Index xli

Volume 2: Ch-He

H.M.S. *Challenger* (1872-1876) 209
Samuel de Champlain (c. 1567-1635) 212
Chang Ch'ien (c. 160-114 B.C.) 218
Cheng Ho (c. 1371-c. 1433) 221
Médard Chouart des Groselliers (1625-1698)
  and Pierre Esprit Radisson (c. 1636-c. 1710) 225
James Chuma (c. 1850-1882) 231
Christopher Columbus (1451-1506) 238
James Cook (1728-1779) 255
Francisco Vásquez de Coronado (c. 1510-1554) 268
Hernán Cortés (1485-1547) 274
Jacques Cousteau (1910-) 282

Pero da Covilhã (1450-1545) 287

Charles Darwin (1809-1882) 292

Alexandra David-Neel (1868-1969) 306

Bartolomeu Dias (c. 1450-1500) 311

Francis Drake (c. 1540-1596) 315

Paul Du Chaillu (c. 1831-1903) 321

Jules-Sébastien-César Dumont d'Urville (1790-1842) . . 325

Amelia Earhart (1897-1937) 330

Lincoln Ellsworth (1880-1951) 336

Erik the Red (c. 950-c. 1004) 341

Estevanico (c. 1500-1539) 345

Explorer 1 (1958-1970) 351

Edward John Eyre (1815-1901) 355

Matthew Flinders (1774-1814) 359

John Franklin (1786-1847) 364

John Charles Frémont (1813-1890) 370

Vivian Fuchs (1908-) 375

Yury Gagarin (1934-1968) 378

Aelius Gallus (lived first century B.C.) 383

Vasco da Gama (c. 1460-1524) 386

Francis Garnier (1839-1873) 393

John Glenn (1921-) 400

Glomar Challenger (1968-1980) 406

Isabel Godin des Odonais (1728-1792) 409

Abu al-Kasim Ibn Ali al-Nasibi Ibn Hawkal
    (c. 920-c. 990) 415

Sven Hedin (1865-1952) 418

Henry the Navigator (1394-1460) 424

Matthew A. Henson (1866-1955) 428

Herodotus (c. 484-c. 425 B.C.) 433

Chronology of Exploration 437

Explorers by Place of Birth 445

Index xli

Volume 3: Hi-Pi

Edmund Hillary (1919-) 449

Cornelis de Houtman (c. 1540-1599) 454

Hsüan-tsang (602-664) 460

Hubble Space Telescope (1990-) 464

Henry Hudson (c. 1565-1611) 469

Alexander von Humboldt (1769-1859) 474

Wilson Price Hunt (1782-1842)
 and Robert Stuart (1785-1848) 483

Willem Janszoon (1570-d. 17th century) 486

Amy Johnson (1903-1941) 489

Louis Jolliet (1645-1700) 494

Mary Kingsley (1862-1900) 499

Johann Ludwig Krapf (1810-1881) 502

Jean François de Galaup, Comte de La Pérouse
 (1741-c. 1788) 508

René-Robert Cavelier de La Salle (1643-1687) 512

Michael J. Leahy (1901-1979) 519

Leif Eriksson (b. late 970s-1020) 524

Meriwether Lewis (1774-1809)
 and William Clark (1770-1838) 528

Charles Lindbergh (1902-1974) 538

David Livingstone (1813-1873) 543

Luna (1959-1976) 555

Alexander Mackenzie (1764-1820) 560

Ferdinand Magellan (c. 1480-1521) 566
Thomas Manning (1772-1840) 574
Jean-Baptiste Marchand (1863-1934) 578
Mariner (1962-1975) 585
Beryl Markham (1902-1986) 589
Abu al-Hasan 'Ali al-Mas'udi (c. 895-957) 595
Robert McClure (1807-1873) 599
Fridtjof Nansen (1861-1930) 604
U.S.S. *Nautilus* (1954-1980) 610
Vasco Núñez de Balboa (1475-1519) 614
Peter Skene Ogden (1794-1854) 618
Alonso de Ojeda (1465-1515) 623
Francisco de Orellana (c. 1490-1546) 627
Mungo Park (1771-1806) 632
Edward Parry (1790-1855) 638
Robert Edwin Peary (1856-1920) 644
Annie Smith Peck (1850-1935) 653
Auguste Piccard (1884-1962)
  and Jacques Piccard (1922-) 657
Zebulon Pike (1779-1813) 661
Fernão Mendes Pinto (c. 1510-1583) 665
Francisco Pizarro (c. 1475-1541) 669

Chronology of Exploration 675

Explorers by Place of Birth 683

Index xli

Volume 4: Po-Z
Marco Polo (1254-1324) 687
Juan Ponce de León (1460-1521) 695

Wiley Post (1899-1935) 699

Nikolay Przhevalsky (1839-1888) 704

Pytheas (c. 380-c. 300 B.C.) 709

Walter Raleigh (1554-1618) 712

Johannes Rebmann (1820-1876) 718

Sally Ride (1951-) 723

Susie Carson Rijnhart (1868-1908) 727

Jacob Roggeveen (1659-1729) 731

Friedrich Gerhard Rohlfs (1831-1896) 735

Dick Rutan (1939-) and Jeana Yeager (1952-) 739

Ernest Shackleton (1874-1922) 744

Nain Singh (c. 1832-c. 1882) 750

Jedediah Smith (1799-1831) 757

John Smith (1580-1631) 762

Hernando de Soto (c. 1500-1542) 767

John Hanning Speke (1827-1864) 772

Sputnik (1957-1961) 778

Hester Stanhope (1776-1839) 783

Henry Morton Stanley (1841-1904) 788

Will Steger (1944-) 800

Aurel Stein (1862-1943) 806

Abel Tasman (1603-1659) 809

Annie Royle Taylor (1855-d. 20th century) 813

Valentina Tereshkova (1937-) 817

David Thompson (1770-1857) 821

Joseph Thomson (1858-1895) 825

George Vancouver (1757-1798) 830

Giovanni da Verrazano (1485-1528) 836

Amerigo Vespucci (1454-1512) 839

Viking (1975-1983) 843

Voyager 1 and *2* (1977-1990) 847

Charles Wilkes (1798-1877) 852
Hubert Wilkins (1888-1958) 856
Fanny Bullock Workman (1859-1925) 861
Saint Francis Xavier (1506-1552) 864
Xenophon (c. 431-c. 352 B.C.) 867
Chuck Yeager (1923-) 871

Chronology of Exploration 875

Explorers by Place of Birth 883

Index xli

Preface

Explorers and Discoverers: From Alexander the Great to Sally Ride features biographies of 171 men, women, and machines who have expanded the horizons of our world and universe. Beginning with ancient Greek scholars and travelers and extending to twentieth-century oceanographers and astronauts, *Explorers and Discoverers* tells of the lives and times of both well-known and lesser-known explorers and includes many women and non-European explorers whose contributions have often been overlooked in the past. Who these travelers were, when and how they lived and traveled, why their journeys were significant, and what the consequences of their discoveries were are all answered within these biographies.

The 160 biographical entries of *Explorers and Discoverers* are arranged in alphabetical order over four volumes. Because the paths of these explorers often crossed, an entry about one explorer may refer to other explorers whose biographies also appear in *Explorers and Discoverers*. When this occurs, the other explorers' names appear in bold letters and are followed by a parenthetical note to see the appropriate entry for further information. The 176 illustrations and maps bring the subjects to life as well as provide geographic details of specific journeys. Additionally, 16 maps of major regions of the world lead off each volume, and each volume concludes with a chronology of exploration by region, a list of explorers by place of birth, and an extensive cumulative index.

Comments and Suggestions

We welcome your comments on this work as well as your suggestions for individuals to be featured in future editions of *Explorers and Discoverers*. Please write: Editors, *Explorers and Discoverers,* U·X·L, 835 Penobscot Bldg., Detroit, Michigan 48226-4094; call toll-free: 1-800-877-4253; or fax: 313-961-6348.

Introduction

Explorers and Discoverers: From Alexander the Great to Sally Ride takes the reader on an adventure with 171 men and women who have made significant contributions to human knowledge of the earth and the universe. Journeying through the centuries from ancient times to the present, we will conquer frontiers and sail uncharted waters. We will trek across treacherous mountains, scorching deserts, steamy jungles, and icy glaciers. We will plumb the depths of the oceans, land on the moon, and test the limits of outer space. Encountering isolation, disease, and even death, we will experience the exhilaration of triumph and the desolation of defeat.

Before joining the explorers and discoverers, however, it is worthwhile to consider why they venture into the unknown. Certainly a primary motivation is curiosity: they want to find out what is on the other side of a mountain, or they are intrigued by rumors about a strange new land, or they simply enjoy wandering the world. Yet adventurers often—indeed, usually—embark on a journey of discovery under less spontaneous circumstances; many of the great explorers were commissioned to lead an expedition with a specific mission. For instance, Spanish and Portuguese states sent **Christopher Columbus, Vasco da Gama,** and the sixteenth-century *conquistadors* on voyages to the New World in search of wealth.

Explorers also receive support from private investors. Prince **Henry the Navigator** financed expeditions along the coast of Africa. The popes of Rome sent emissaries to the Mongol khans. The Hudson's Bay Company, through the development of fur trade, was largely responsible for the exploration of Canada. **Joseph Banks** and the Royal Geographical Society backed the great nineteenth-century expeditions to the African continent. In each of these cases the explorer's discoveries resulted in lucrative trade routes and increased political power for the investor's home country.

Religion has been another strong motivating force for exploration. Famous Chinese travelers such as **Hsüang-tsang,** who was a Buddhist monk, went to India to obtain sacred Buddhist texts. **Abu Abdallah Ibn Battutah,** a Muslim, explored the Islamic world during a pilgrimage to Mecca. The medieval travel writer and rabbi **Benjamin of Tudela** investigated the state of Jewish communities throughout the Holy Land. Later, Christian missionaries **Johann Ludwig Krapf, Annie Royle Taylor,** and **Susie Carson Rijnhart** took their faith to the indigenous peoples of Asia and Africa.

Explorers have been inspired, too, by the quest for knowledge about the world. **Alexander von Humboldt** made an expedition to South America that collected a wealth of scientific information, while **James Cook** is credited with having done more than any other explorer to increase human knowledge of world geography. **Charles Darwin**'s famous voyage to South America aboard the Beagle resulted in his revolutionary theory of evolution.

Perhaps the foremost motivation to explore, however, is the desire to be the first to accomplish a particular feat. For instance, for nearly three centuries European nations engaged in a competition to be the first to find the Northwest Passage, a water route between the Atlantic and Pacific oceans, which the Norwegian explorer **Roald Amundsen** successfully navigated in 1903. Similarly, in the 1950s the United States and the Soviet Union became involved in a "space race," which culminated in 1969 when **Neil Armstrong** became the first human to walk on the moon.

Sometimes the spirit of cooperation can also be an incentive. During an 18-month period of maximum sunspot activity, from July 1957 through December 1958, 67 nations joined together to study the solar-terrestrial environment. Known as the International Geophysical Year, the project resulted in several major scientific discoveries along with the setting aside of Antarctica as a region for purposes of nonmilitary, international scientific research.

Although daring individuals throughout history have been driven by the desire to be first, the achievement began to take on special meaning with the increasing participation of women in travel and exploration during the nineteenth century. Pioneering women such as **Hester Stanhope, Mary Kingsley,** and **Alexandra David-Neel** broke away from rigid social roles to make remarkable journeys, but their accomplishments have only recently received the recognition they deserve. Since the advent of the aviation age in the early twentieth century, however, women have truly been at the forefront of exploration. **Amelia Earhart, Amy Johnson,** and **Beryl Markham** achieved as many flying "firsts" as their male colleagues; Soviet cosmonaut **Valentina Tereshkova** and U.S. astronaut **Sally Ride,** the first women in space, have made important contributions to space exploration.

By concentrating on biographies of individual explorers in this book we seem to suggest that these adventurers were loners who set out on their own to singlehandedly confront the unknown. Yet possibly the only "one-man show" was **René Caillié,** the first Westerner to travel to the forbidden city of Timbuktu and return alive. As a rule, explorers rarely traveled alone and they had help in achieving their goals. Therefore, use of an individual name is often only shorthand for the achievements of the expedition as a whole.

Famous explorers of Africa like **Richard Burton, John Hanning Speke, David Livingstone,** and **Henry Morton Stanley,** for instance, were all accompanied by large groups of servants and porters. In fact, the freed African slave **James Chuma,** who was the caravan leader for Livingstone and several other explorers, has been credited with the success of more than one expedition. Similar stories occur in other areas of exploration. For example, **Robert Edwin Peary** is considered to be the first person to reach the North Pole, yet he was accompanied by **Matthew A. Henson,** his African American assistant, and four Inuit—Egingwah, Seeglo, Ootah, and Ooqueah.

Explorers and Discoverers tells the stories of these men and women as well as others motivated by a daring spirit and an intense curiosity. They ventured forth to rediscover remote lands, to conquer the last frontiers, and to increase our knowledge of the world and the universe.

A final note of clarification: When we say that an explorer "discovered" a place, we do not mean she or he was the first human ever to have been there. Although the discoverer may have been the first from his or her country to set foot in a new land, most areas of the world during the great periods of exploration were already occupied or their existence had been verified by other people.

Picture Credits

The photographs and illustrations appearing in *Explorers and Discoverers: From Alexander the Great to Sally Ride* were received from the following sources:

On the cover: John Smith; **The Granger Collection, New York:** Beryl Markham and Matthew A. Henson.

UPI/Bettmann: pages 1, 129, 306, 375, 406, 489, 555, 611, 657, 699, 733, 742, 817, 856; **Norwegian Information Service:** page 14; **NASA:** pages 26, 30, 31, 34, 351, 400, 588, 723, 779, 844, 847; **The Granger Collection, New York:** pages 43, 44, 52, 61, 81, 86, 107, 122, 133, 141, 144, 145, 150, 164, 179, 187, 193, 209, 225, 282, 285, 311, 321, 325, 330, 334, 336, 345, 355, 359, 393, 424, 428, 433, 449, 460, 474, 499, 508, 512, 524, 560, 578, 589, 632, 638, 704, 744, 757, 772, 783, 806, 811, 830, 836, 852, 864; **The Bettmann Archive:** pages 169, 176, 268, 303, 341, 464, 494, 528, 623, 653, 695, 735, 767, 809, 828, 867; **Novosti Press Agency, Moscow:** page 378; **Hulton Deutsch Collection Limited:** page 418; **AP/Wide World Photos:** pages 538, 800;

NASA/Jet Propulsion Laboratory: page 585; **UNHCR:** page 604; **Archive Photos/American Stock:** page 610; **UPI/Bettman Newsphotos:** pages 739, 871.

Maps

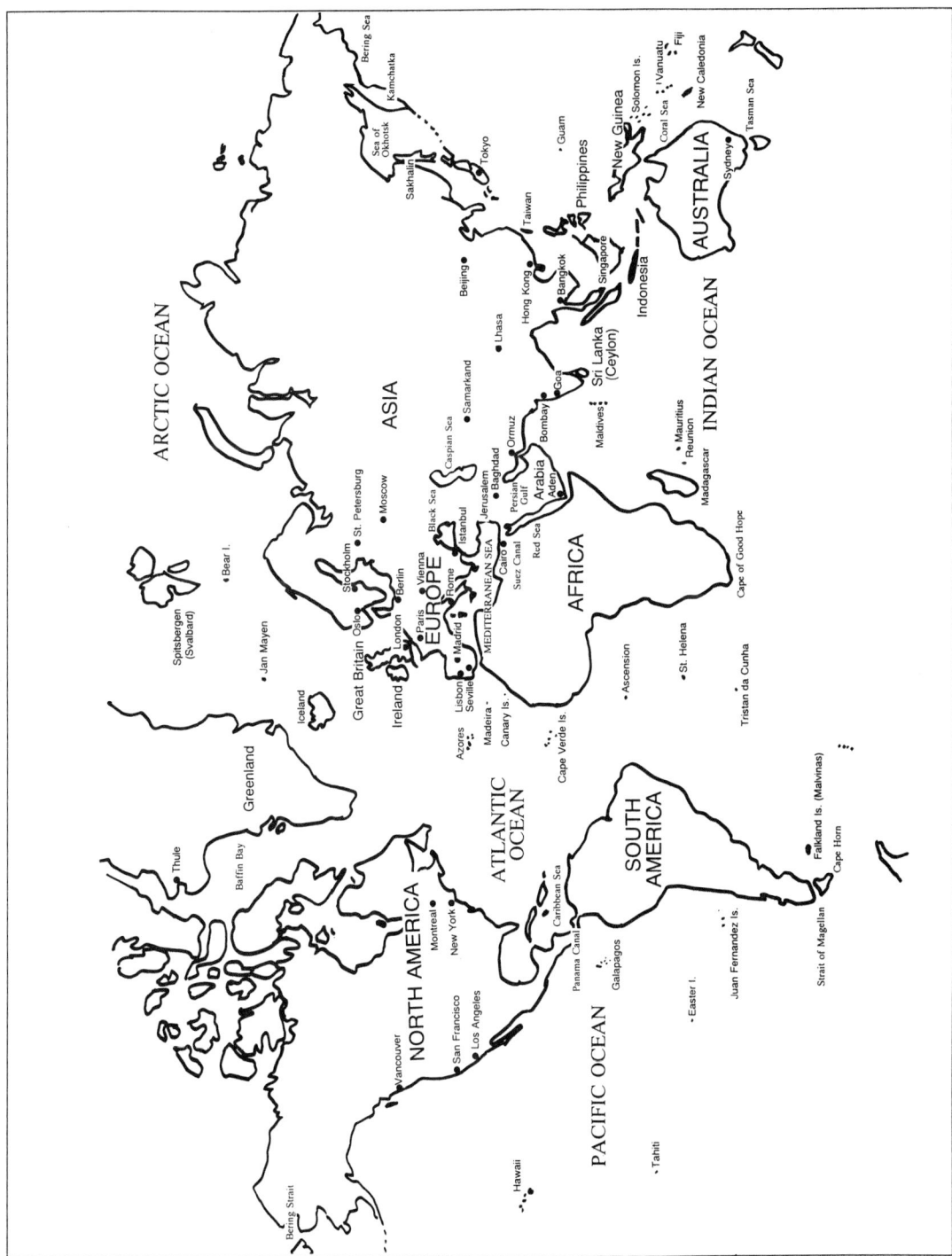

The World

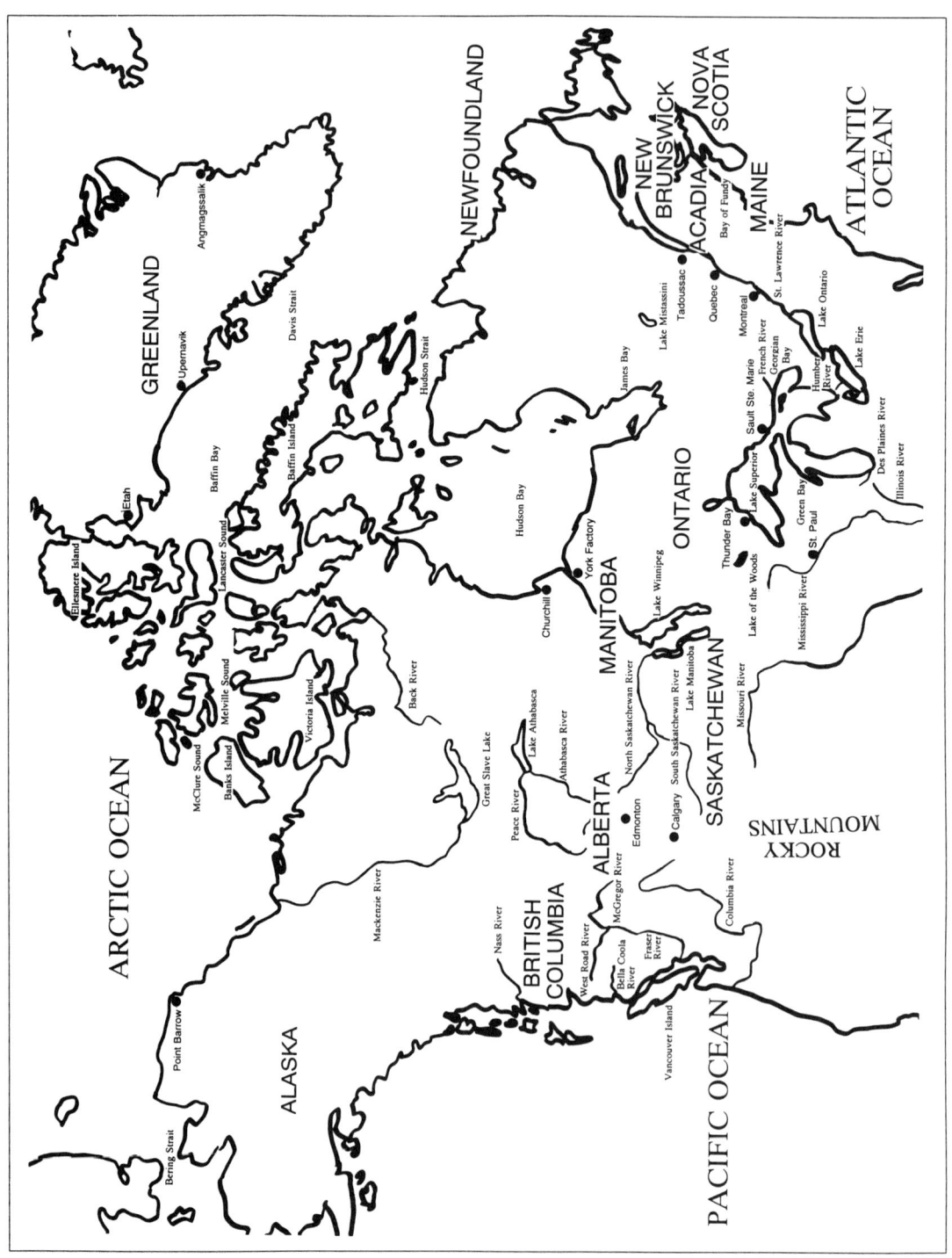
Americas–Canada.

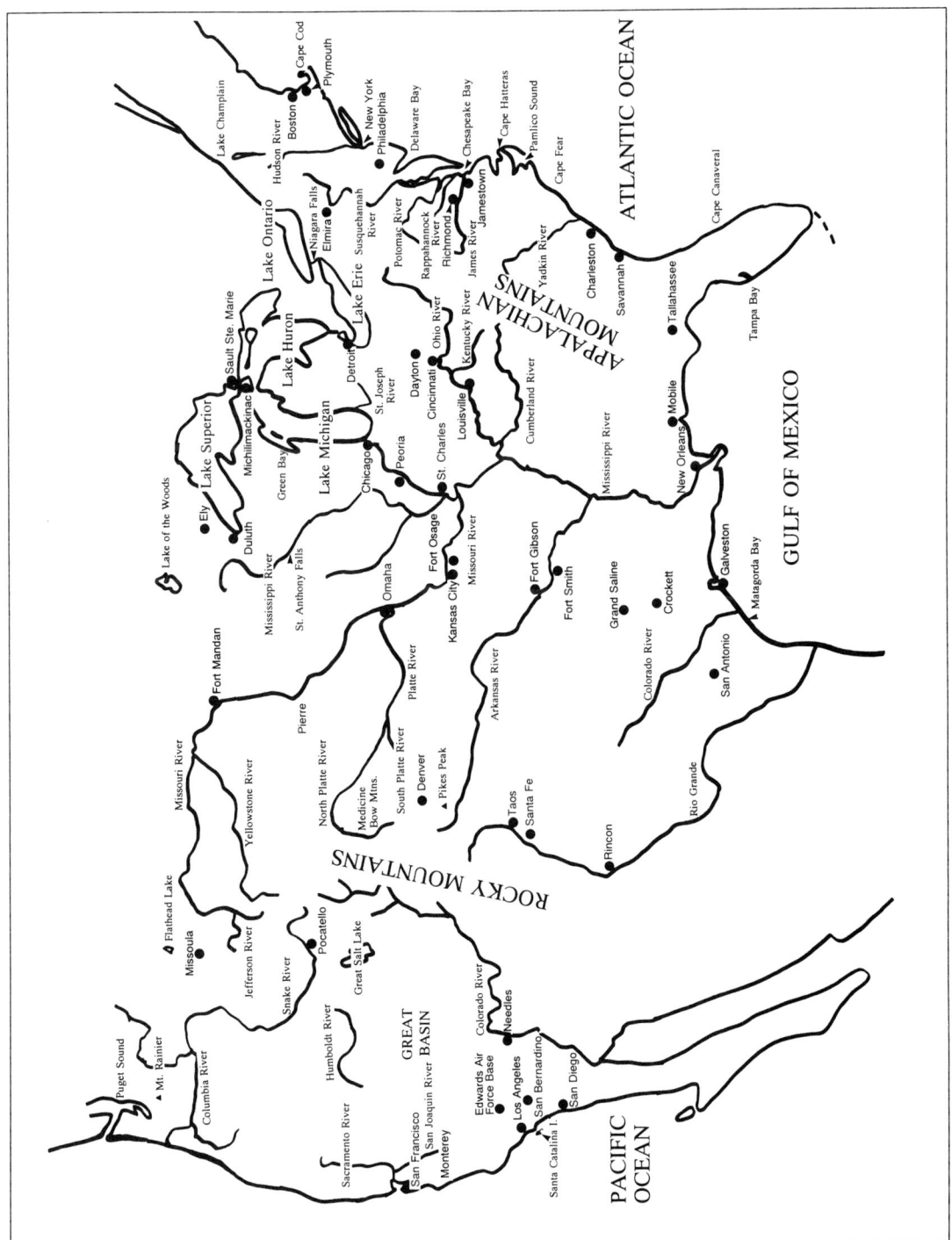

Americas—United States of America.

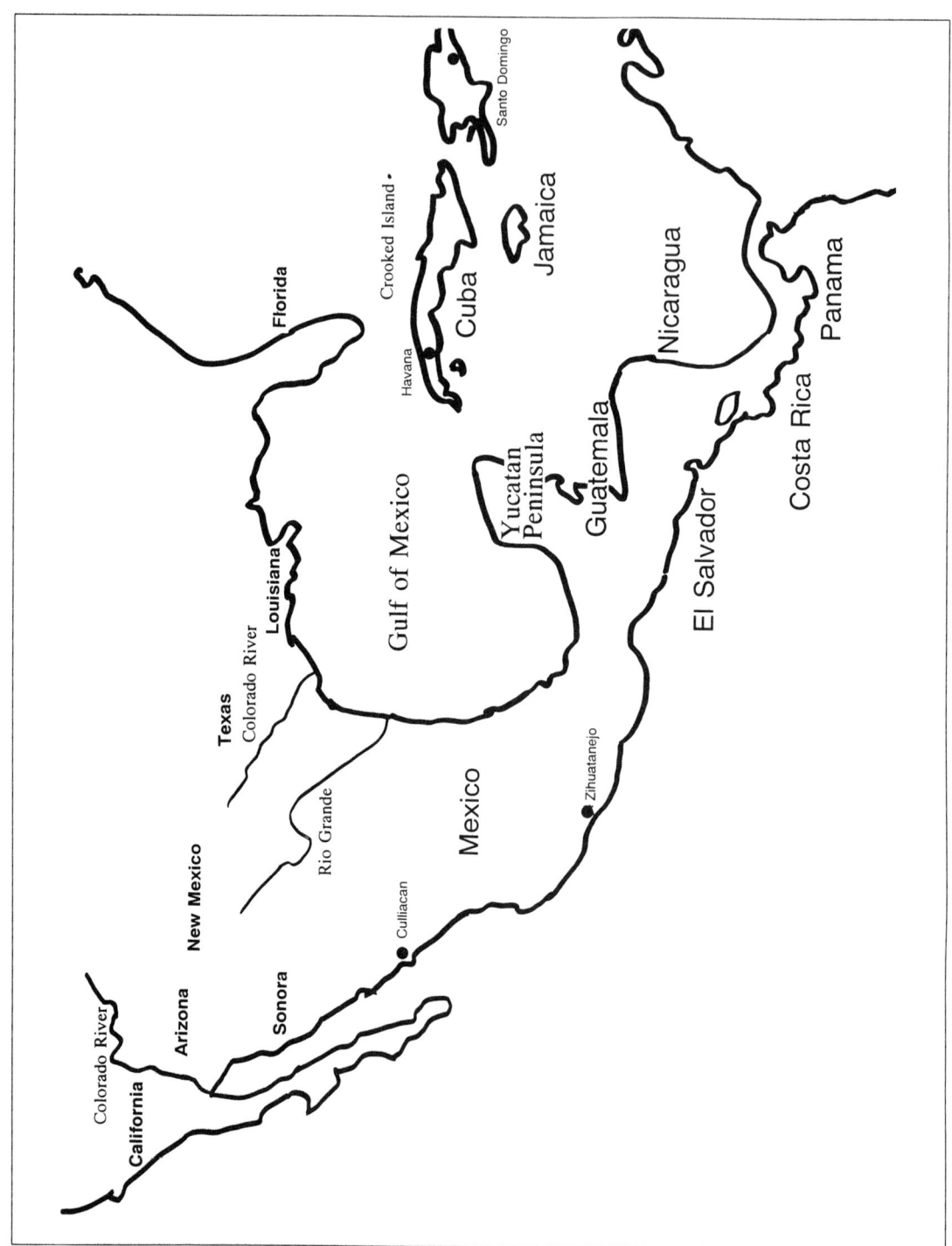

Americas—Mexico and Central America.

Americas—South America.

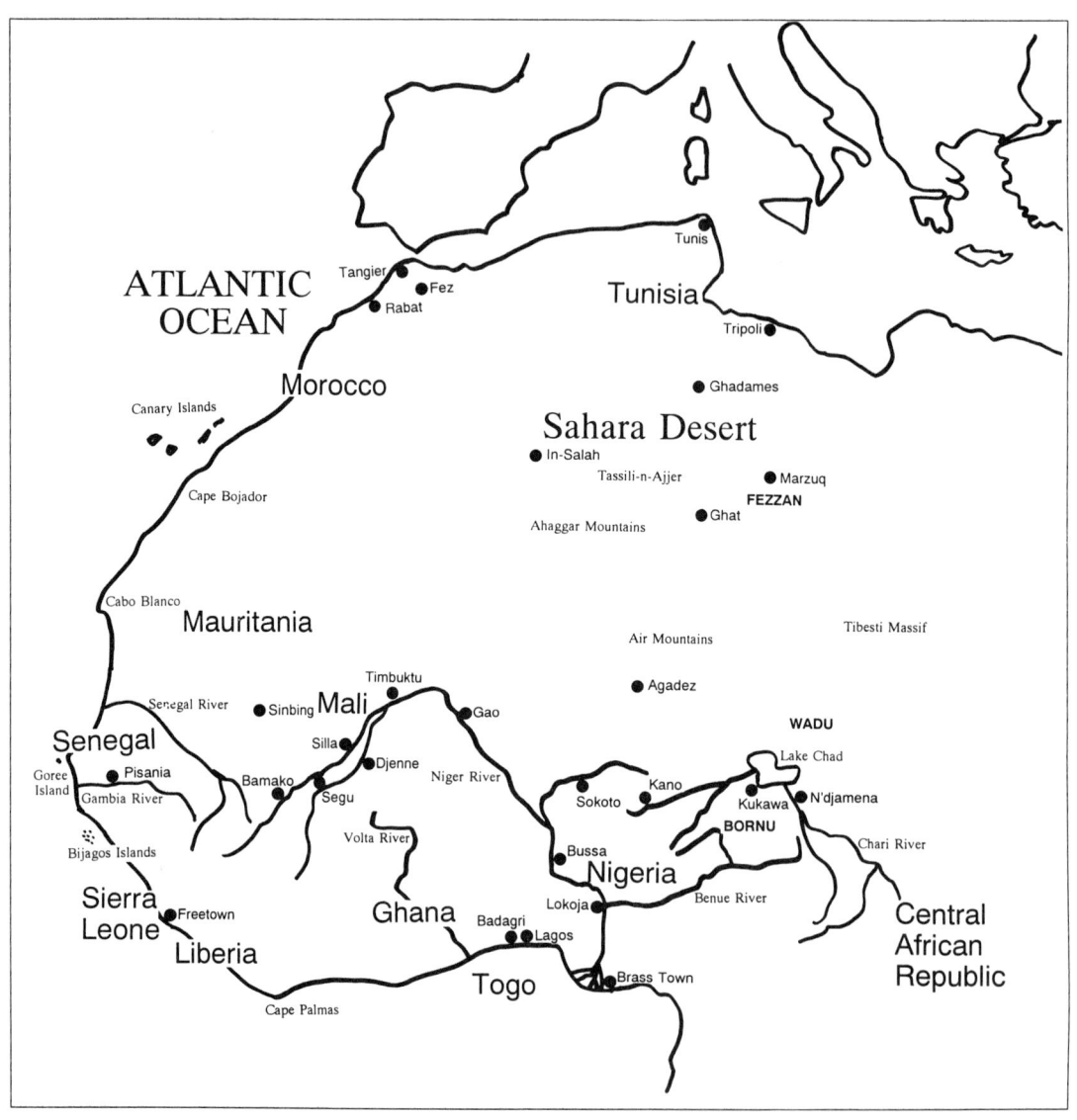

Africa and the Middle East—Northwest Africa.

Africa and the Middle East—The Middle East and Arabia.

Africa and the Middle East—Eastern Africa.

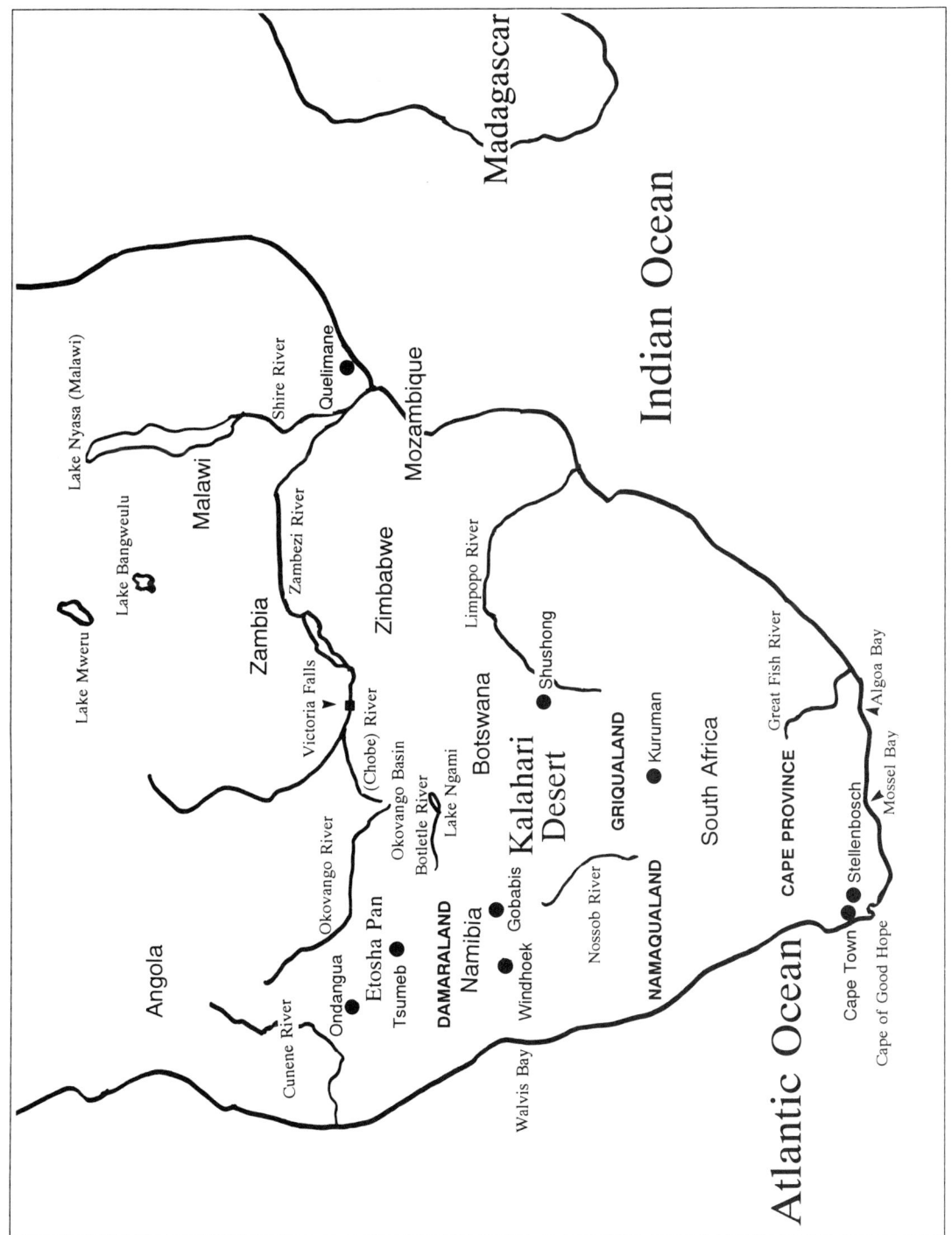

Africa and the Middle East—Southern Africa.

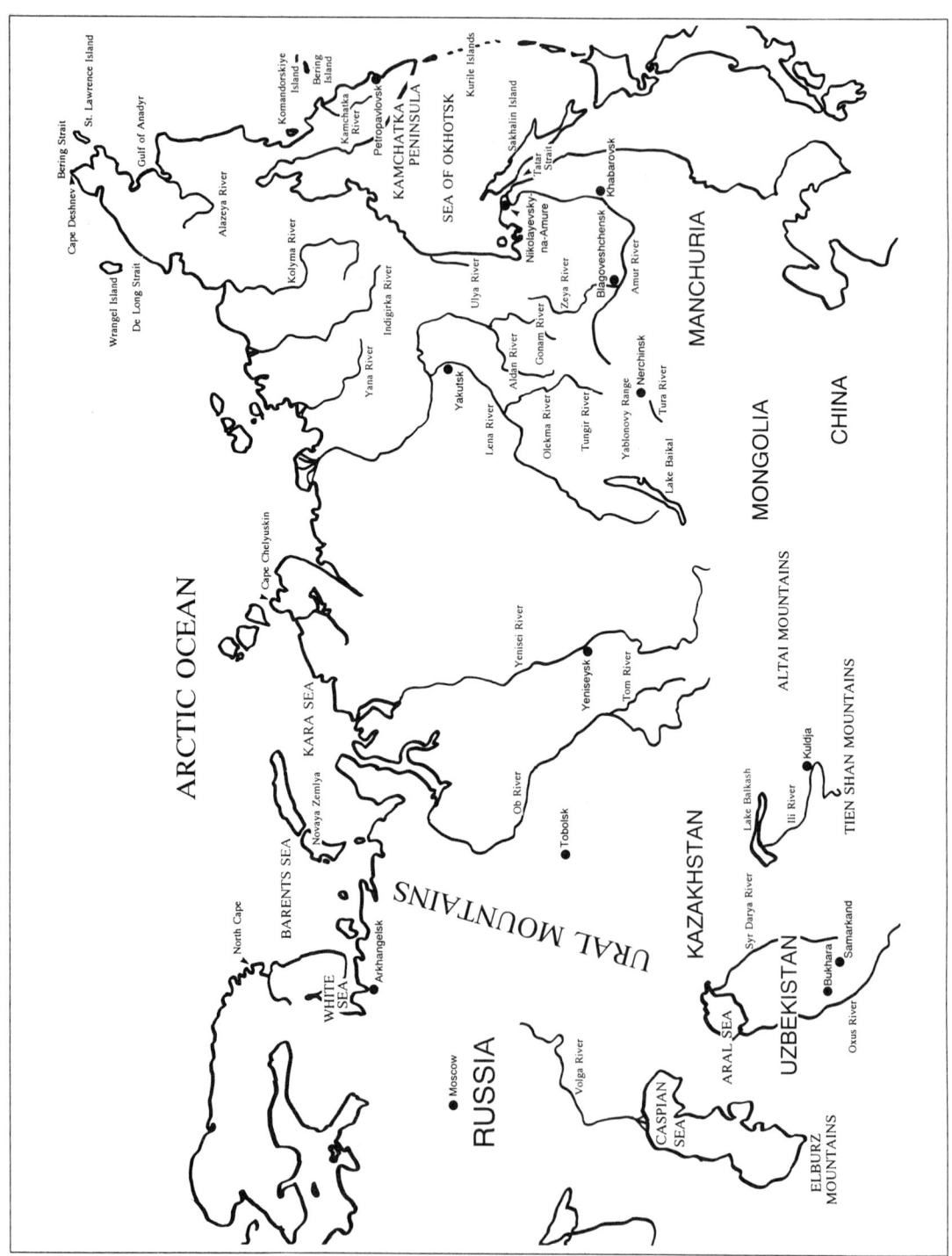

Asia–Siberia.

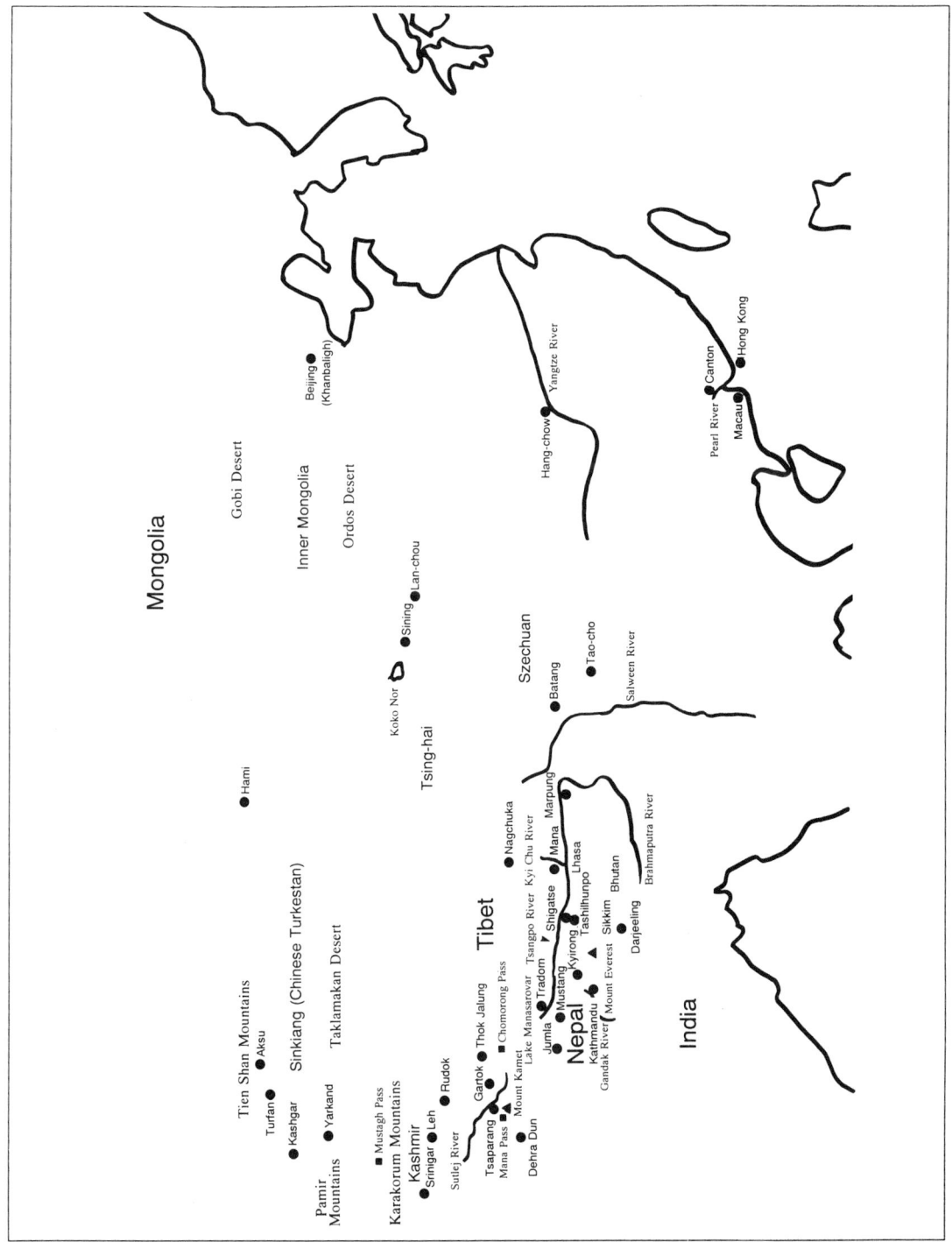

Asia–China and Tibet.

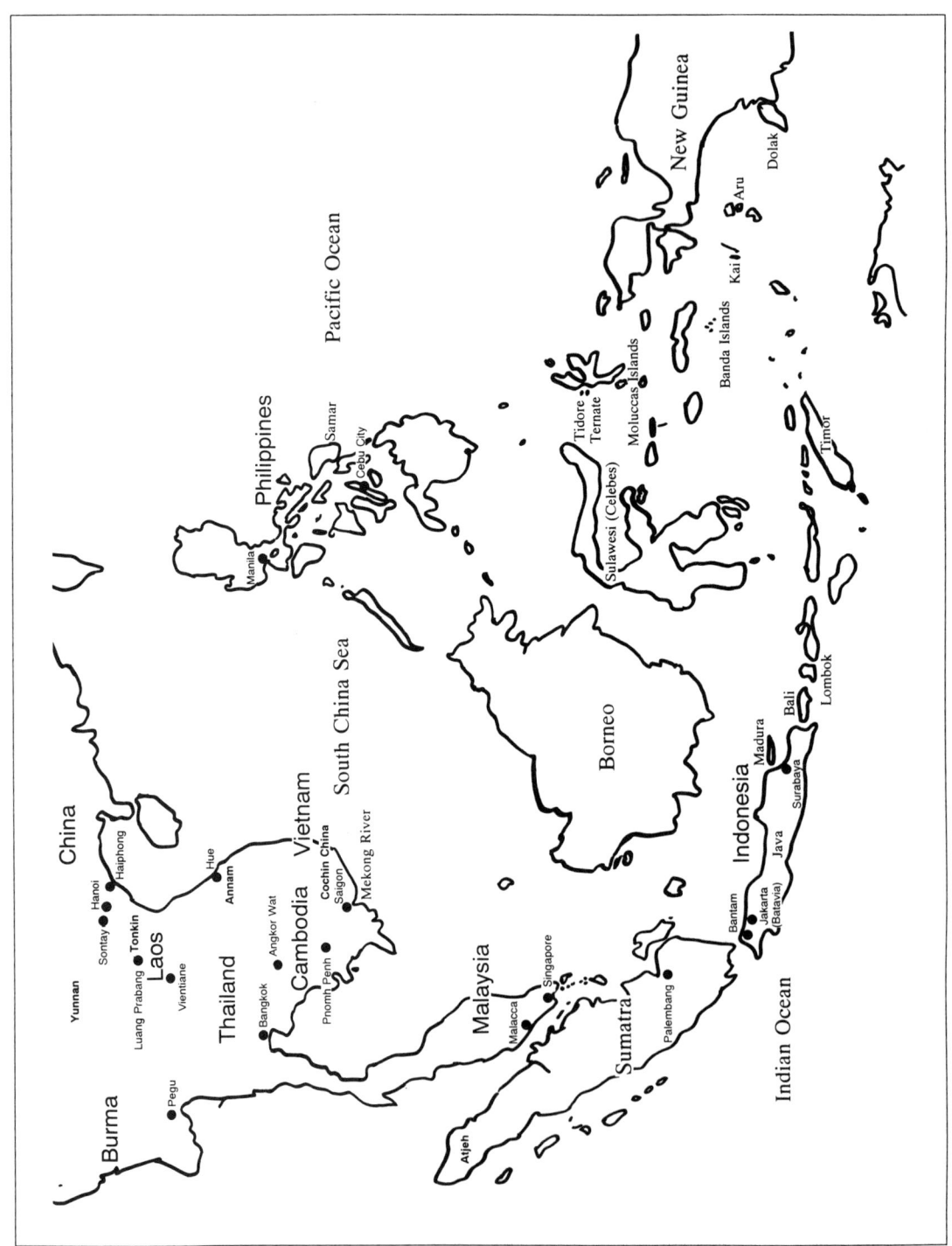

Asia—Southeast Asia.

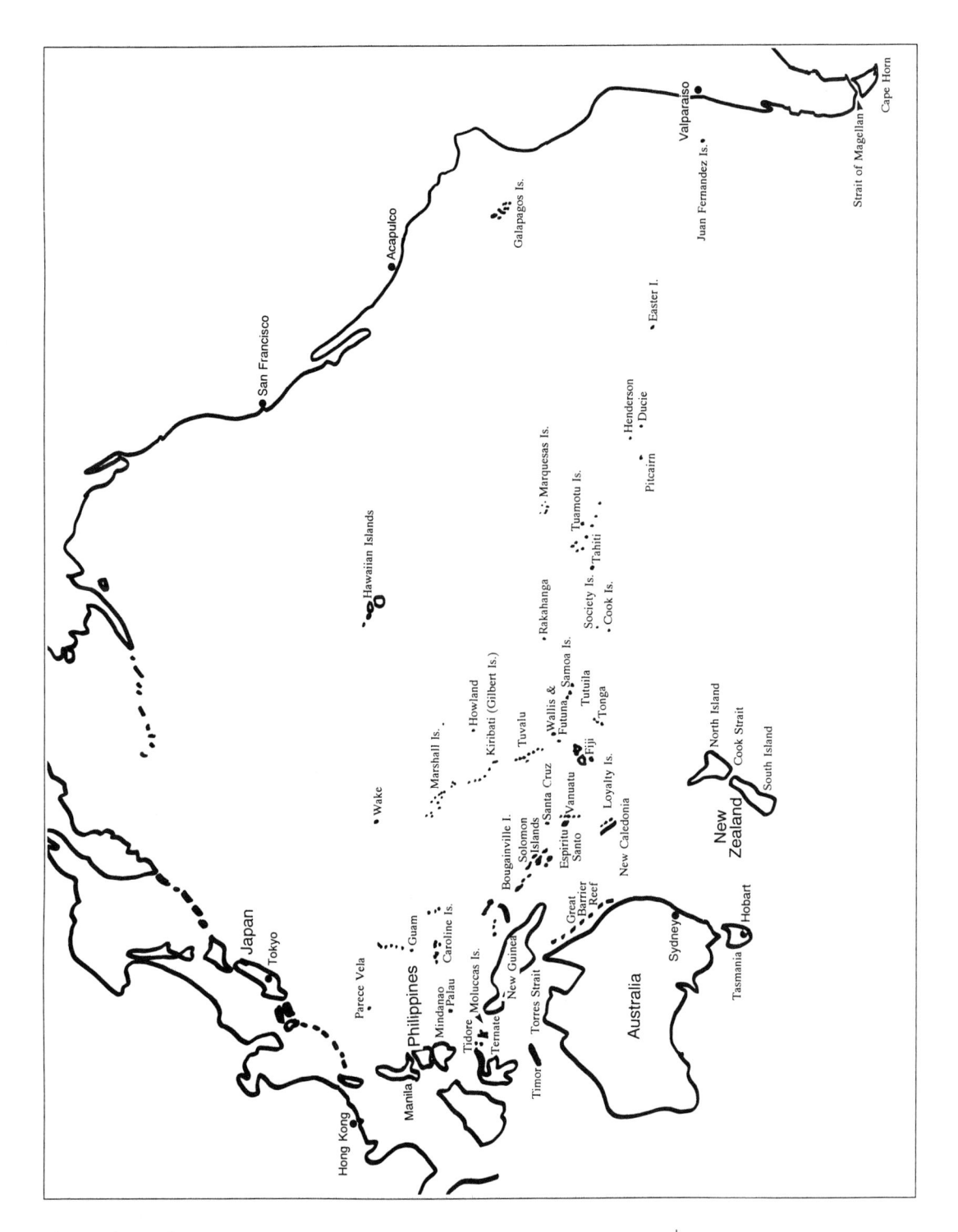

Pacific Ocean–Oceanea.

Pacific Ocean–Australia.

Arctic Region.

Antarctic Region.

EXPLORERS & DISCOVERERS

Delia Akeley

*Born December 5, 1875,
Beaver Dam, Wisconsin*

*Died 1970,
Florida*

The daughter of Irish immigrants, Akeley was born Delia Julia Denning on December 5, 1875, on a farm in Beaver Dam, Wisconsin. At the age of 13 she ran away from home to Milwaukee, where she was taken in by a barber. They were married the following year and divorced some time later. When Delia met Carl Akeley, he was a taxidermist who mounted wildlife exhibitions at the Milwaukee Public Museum. Carl had perfected a method of applying animal skin onto a mannequin to make animal displays more realistic. Having completely changed the science of taxidermy, he was appointed to the prestigious Field Museum of Natural History in Chicago. Delia married Carl on December 23, 1902, when she was 27. Two years later they traveled to Africa, where previously, in 1896, Carl had gone on an expedition for the museum.

Adventures in Africa

The Akeleys' destination was the Athi Plains in Kenya, famous for its wildlife, which was not far from Nairobi, the

An American who made several trips to Africa, Delia Akeley was one of the first Westerners to study the Pygmy tribes of Zaire. She was also the first woman known to have crossed the African continent.

country's capital. They stayed there for a year and a half collecting specimens. Delia quickly adjusted to life in the bush. For instance, she proved to be as proficient with a rifle as her husband, and she killed a bull elephant that is still on display at the Field Museum. After the Akeleys returned to the United States, their successes in Africa became well known, and they were invited by the American Museum of Natural History in New York to undertake another expedition in 1909.

They experienced some difficulties on the expedition. One of their main concerns was capturing animals and successfully preserving them for later study. Because the elephant population of Kenya was already being wiped out by hunters, it was especially difficult to find a bull elephant to take back to New York. They finally shot a large bull but were nearly charged by the wounded animal before a shot from Carl's rifle saved them. To make matters worse, Carl had become ill early in the trip, and the effects of his illness were still lingering.

After the close call with the bull elephant, the Akeleys moved their camp to higher ground, which was more comfortable for Carl and provided better safety. One evening while Delia was alone in the camp, two porters arrived to say that Carl had been injured by a charging elephant and was lying helpless several miles away. She set out immediately, traveling through the night to reach him. As morning dawned, however, the porters could not remember where they had left Carl. It was only by searching frantically and firing signals with her gun that Delia was able to find him. Although Carl had been seriously injured—he had several head injuries, and broken ribs were cutting into his lung—Delia was able to save him.

The Akeleys remained in camp for three months while Carl recovered. Delia took over the responsibilities of shooting game for food, managing the camp, and nursing her husband, who had in the meantime also come down with malaria. In 1911, after his recovery, they returned to New York. During Carl's recuperation Delia adopted a pet monkey that she took back with her. The monkey became the tyrant of their household, going into jealous rages whenever Delia paid attention to anyone else. Delia would later write a book titled *"J.T.": The Biography of an African Monkey* (1929).

Life on her own

Carl was able to resume his work, mounting exhibitions that can still be viewed today in the Akeley African Hall at the American Museum of Natural History. After World War I broke out, Delia went to Europe in 1918 to work in canteens for American servicemen. Five years later, in 1923, the Akeleys divorced; Carl remarried and then died on an expedition to Zaire in 1926. In the meantime, Delia had embarked on her greatest adventure, a commission from the Brooklyn Museum to travel to Africa to collect specimens. One newspaper headline announced, "Woman to Forget Marital Woe by Fighting African Jungle Beasts." Actually, her goal was to travel to the remote forests of the Ituri River, where she wanted to visit Pygmy tribes.

Akeley's party left New York in August 1924 bound for Mombasa, Kenya, and then moved into the interior via the Tana, Kenya's longest river. Ten weeks later they reached the post of San Kuri at the head of the Tana; from there they started out by camel across the Somali Desert but were forced to turn back by a Somali warrior insurrection. Diverted to the southwest, Akeley headed to Meru at the foot of Mount Kenya. The subsequent leg of Akeley's journey involved nearly every form of land transportation. She continued by truck to Nairobi, where she shipped her specimens back to Brooklyn. From Nairobi she headed northwest by train to Kisumu on Lake Victoria and then by boat across the lake to Jinja, Uganda. From there she traveled west by truck and bus to Lake Albert and even farther west by car to Zaire, which was then a colony known as the Belgian

The Pygmies of Africa

The Pygmies are dark-skinned people, averaging less than 59 inches in height, who inhabit the rain forests along the equator. They live in four major areas—Africa, Southeast Asia, New Guinea, and the Philippines. The African Pygmies, who numbered around 150,000 in the late twentieth century, are themselves divided into four subgroups; within these subgroups are several small bands, including the Mbuti, Aka, and Efe, who are located in the Ituri forest in northeastern Zaire, the area where Delia Akeley conducted her research.

The Pygmy tribes are nomadic hunter-gatherers who move around looking for food. Some anthropologists think the Pygmies existed before the region's agricultural peoples, who stay in one place and grow crops for food. Many Pygmy tribes conduct trade with agricultural peoples, exchanging forest products for such items as garden produce and tools. Most Pygmies no longer speak their own languages. The government has tried to force them to resettle and adopt the ways of agricultural peoples, but the Pygmies have resisted those efforts.

Congo. She crossed the Ituri River at the modern town of Nduye and headed for the post of Wamba.

Pioneering research on the Pygmies

At Wamba Akeley encountered members of a Pygmy tribe who took her to their lands in the tropical rain forest. Many of the Pygmy villages had never been visited by Europeans; in fact, only 50 years previously Georg Schweinfurth, a German botanist and Congo explorer, had confirmed their existence, which had been a source of myth for centuries. Akeley stayed with the Pygmy tribe for several weeks during the spring of 1925 before moving north to the town of Bafuka on the Bomokandi River to wait for supplies. Throughout her journey she had been keeping a detailed diary, but at this point her entries stop because she had become ill with fever. Upon her recovery Akeley traveled by bus to Kisangani on the Congo River and from there by riverboat southwest down the Congo to Kinshasa. On September 3, 1925, she arrived at Boma, a town located close to where the Congo feeds into the Atlantic Ocean. Having reached the Atlantic, she became the first woman known to have crossed the African continent.

Final voyage to Africa

Akeley's last trip to Africa was in November 1929. Bound for Zaire to conduct additional research on the Pygmy tribes, she traveled from Port Sudan on the Red Sea to Khartoum, where she took a steamer up the Nile River. She spent five months with the Pygmies, taking more than 1,500 photos and collecting numerous specimens of their material culture. On her return to the United States, the *New York Times* featured a full-page spread of her photographs. After this trip Akeley remained in the United States, writing and lecturing about her experiences in Africa. A collection of her photos, *Jungle Portraits,* was published by Macmillan in 1939. That same year she remarried. She later retired to Florida, where she died in 1970 at the age of 95.

Alexander the Great

*Born 356 B.C.,
Pella, Macedonia*

*Died June 1, 323 B.C.,
Babylon, present-day Iraq*

Alexander of Macedonia, better known as Alexander the Great, was one of the greatest military leaders of all time and one of the most charismatic figures in ancient history. He is credited with spreading Hellenism, or classical Greek ideals and values, throughout the civilized world. As a result of his conquests, he ruled over an immense empire, spanning more than 3,000 miles from the Balkan Peninsula to the Indus River (in present-day Pakistan). He died at the age of 33.

Conquests under his father's reign

Alexander was born in Pella, Macedonia, in 356 B.C. to the Macedonian king Philip II and his first wife, Olympias. Olympias had a strong influence on Alexander by introducing him to mysticism and art. Another important influence was Alexander's tutor, the Athenian philosopher Aristotle, who gave him a classical education.

Macedonia (or Macedon) was an ancient kingdom lying

Alexander the Great, king of the ancient country of Macedonia, led a great military expedition on which he defeated the Persian Empire and traveled as far east as India.

near the Aegean Sea on the Balkan Peninsula. Under Philip II the kingdom expanded to include the neighboring Greek city-states of Thrace, Chalcidice, Thessaly, and Epirus. By 338 B.C., with the battle of Chaeronea, Philip II had either conquered all the Greek city-states or forced them into an alliance. He was making plans to invade the Persian Empire when, in 336 B.C., he was assassinated at the wedding of his daughter to the king of one of his vassal states. According to some reports, Olympias (and possibly even Alexander) was involved in Philip's murder because he had neglected her for his other wives, but this story has not been proved.

Upon the death of Philip II, Alexander succeeded to the throne, though he was only 19 years old. The unhappy Greeks revolted, but Alexander quickly put them down, demonstrating early his genius as a military leader. He also subdued uprisings in Thrace and Illyria, two other countries on the Balkan Peninsula. When people in the Greek city of Thebes revolted on a false rumor that Alexander was dead, he moved in and destroyed everything but the temples and the house of Pindar, the famous Greek poet. Having subdued the whole of Greece and intent on carrying out his father's plan to conquer the Persians, Alexander headed east on a march that was to become one of the greatest military conquests in history.

Early battles with the Persians

In the spring of 334 B.C. Alexander's army crossed the Hellespont—a narrow strait between Europe and Turkey now called the Dardanelles—and stopped at the site of the ancient Greek city of Troy. Alexander met the Persians in battle for the first time on the Granicus River where it flows into the Sea of Marmara in Turkey. His forces smashed the opposing army, although Alexander himself narrowly missed being killed. Following this victory Alexander pressed on through Asia Minor. His army again overcame the Persians, this time at Miletus, the most important of the 12 Ionian cities that had been seized by Persia around 547 B.C. Alexander also took Halicarnassus, the birthplace of the historian **Herodotus** (see entry).

Alexander then moved into Syria. He was near present-day Iskenderun, now in southern Turkey, when he learned that the newly crowned King Darius III of Persia and his army were at Issus, a town just 20 miles to the north. Alexander attacked Darius's army at Issus, cutting them off as they retreated to the sea in an effort to escape. Alexander's men inflicted a crushing defeat that left an enormous number of Persians dead. Darius fled to safety.

Following this victory Alexander turned south to take the Mediterranean ports where the Persian fleet was based. After a siege of more than eight months, he conquered the Phoenician city of Tyre, located on an island off the coast of Lebanon. During the final battle in July 332 B.C., 8,000 Phoenicians were reportedly killed, and 30,000 were taken as slaves. Before the devastation had ended, Alexander received a peace offer from Darius. The terms were so favorable that Alexander's second in command, Parmenion, reportedly said that he would accept the offer if he were Alexander. "That," Alexander replied, "is what I should do were I Parmenion."

Pursuit of Darius

Alexander proceeded farther south, again claiming victory after a two-month-long battle at the fortress in Gaza, which housed a Persian garrison. Having taken Gaza, Alexander had now conquered all of Syria, so he then crossed over into Egypt. The Egyptians welcomed him as a liberator from the hated Persians; they also proclaimed him the son of Amon-Ra, the supreme Egyptian deity. Historians speculate this may be one reason Alexander considered himself divine. The following winter he founded the city of Alexandria on the site of the old Greek trading port of Naucratis. The largest of the 70 cities Alexander founded during the course of his conquest, Alexandria would become a lasting monument to his achievement. While in Egypt he visited the ancient oracle of Siwa. Although Alexander did not reveal the oracle's prophecy, his soldiers spread the rumor that Alexander was said to be destined to rule the world.

In the spring of 331 B.C. Alexander returned to Syria with an army of 400,000 foot soldiers and 7,000 cavalry. Crossing the Euphrates River into Mesopotamia, he once again met Darius, this time at the village of Gaugamela. Although his army was smaller than that of the Persians, Alexander's superior tactics won the field, and Darius was forced to flee once more. Pursuing Darius, he moved on to Babylon and then to Susa and Persepolis, where he burned the palaces and ransacked the city. Because of this victory, Alexander considered himself the conqueror of the Persians, although the Persian Empire would not disappear entirely for another three years.

Having penetrated this far into modern-day Iran, Alexander's army was now in territory that had not been mapped by the Greeks and was therefore virtually unknown to them. Still in pursuit of Darius, Alexander turned northwest to Ecbatana, or modern Hamadan, which he seized in 331 B.C. He moved on to Rhagae (modern Rhages), one of the great cities of antiquity, and then to Bactria, where he learned that Darius had been taken captive by Bessus, a cousin of Darius and the ruler of Bactria. Bessus executed Darius and declared himself king of Persia. In the meantime, Alexander had Darius body taken back to Persepolis to be buried in the royal tombs. Now that the king of Persia was dead, Alexander adopted the title Lord of Asia, the name given the ruler of the Persian Empire.

Growing despotism and cruelty

When Alexander learned that Bessus was also calling himself king and was leading a revolt in the eastern provinces of the empire, he led his army toward Bactria. Alexander's army crossed the Hindu Kush, a great mountain range, north of Kabul near the Khawak Pass in present-day Afghanistan, which lies more than 11,500 feet above sea level. Descending into Bactria, they discovered that Bessus had devastated the countryside and fled north over the Oxus River, now known as Amu Darya. By the time Alexander's men overtook him, he had already been deposed. Alexander had Bessus formally tried for the murder of Darius and then had his nose and ears cut off before sending him to Ecbatana to be publicly put to death by crucifixion.

By this time Alexander had become increasingly despotic, and his men were beginning to show dissatisfaction. He killed his own foster brother, Clitus, in a drunken brawl after Clitus insulted him. He antagonized his Greek and Macedonian followers by marrying a Bactrian princess, Roxana, and adopting Persian manners and dress. In 330 B.C. he learned of a conspiracy to murder him. Finding that the son of his general Parmenion was implicated, he not only had the son put to death but also executed Parmenion, who was innocent.

Alexander further alienated his soldiers by his treatment of the historian Callisthenes, a nephew of Aristotle, who had joined Alexander's expedition as official historian. At first Callisthenes portrayed Alexander as a godlike figure in his reports, but he became more and more critical of his leader's Persian garb and despotic behavior. Charging Callisthenes with being involved in the conspiracy against him, Alexander ordered his execution.

Campaign in India

After subjugating Bactria in 328 B.C., Alexander again crossed over the Hindu Kush and in 327 B.C. headed toward India. Sending half of his army ahead through the Khyber Pass with orders to build a boat bridge across the Indus River, Alexander fought his way to the river through the hills north of the pass. He and the forces who remained with him spent the winter fending off local hill tribes. His greatest accomplishment during this campaign was the scaling and taking of Mount Aornos (now called Pir-Sar), which was supposedly unconquerable, in 326 B.C. Following this victory, Alexander led his army to the banks of the Indus, where they rested until spring. Crossing the river, they marched for three days to the city of Taxila and then into India, where they were generally well received by the princes. As Alexander and his army continued to the Hydaspes River—the present-day Jhelum—they were met by the army of King Porus.

Alexander handily defeated Porus and his forces, thus conquering the Indus Valley. Yet this was to be Alexander's last great battle. As he pushed east to the Hyphasis River, now called the Beas, his army rebelled and refused to go any far-

The voyage of Nearchus

Nearchus's voyage provides an interesting story of exploration. He and his fleet left from the mouth of the Indus in late September 325 B.C. After being delayed for 24 days at the site of modern-day Karachi by unfavorable winds, they took another five days to sail to the mouth of the Hab River. While sailing on the Hab, three ships were capsized in a storm, but the crew members were saved. At the mouth of the Hingol River, Nearchus and his men were attacked by 600 native inhabitants. He wrote, "They were hairy over their heads as well as the rest of their persons, and had nails like wild beasts; at least they were said to use their nails like iron tools, and to kill fish by tearing with them, and to cut up soft wood with them."

Twenty days later, after traveling along the arid Makran coast, they encountered "savage" fish-eaters. When Nearchus saw a religious center for sun worshippers on an island in the Kalami River, he landed on the sacred island to prove that he would not be harmed by violating local taboos. At one point the expedition was running short of supplies, so they hunted wild goats on the shore.

When Nearchus and his party entered one port along their voyage, he remarked that the people paddled canoes rather than rowing the way the Greeks did. They were also surprised to see nearby great towers of water rising into the air. When they asked their guides what was happening, they were told they were watching a school of whales. At the port of Gwadar they were once again in need of supplies. Rather than bartering with the inhabitants, who seemed willing to trade, Nearchus attacked the town. After a stalemate he accepted the only food the townspeople had to offer—fishmeal.

When the fleet went inland along the Minab River, Nearchus met Alexander at the town of Golashkerd, and there was much rejoicing over the success of their adventure thus far. Resuming the voyage, the fleet was soon delayed for three weeks to make ship repairs after running aground on sandbanks. They finally reached the port of Hormuz on the Persian Gulf, and Nearchus rejoined Alexander in Susa. His report enabled the Greeks and Macedonians to see that the Persian Gulf led into the Indian Ocean and that it was possible to trade with India by that route.

ther. They were tired after years of fighting the long war, and they wanted to return to their families. Unable to persuade them to press on, Alexander sulked in his tent for two days before agreeing to lead the army back home. In determining the best route for the return trip to the Mediterranean, Alexander decided to test the classical theory that the Indus and the Nile were one river.

Alexander constructed a large fleet of boats for sending part of his army downstream on the Jhelum to the Indus delta. He divided the remainder of his forces into three groups that would make the journey by land. Departing down the river in November 326 B.C., Alexander engaged in constant warfare because the Indians would not provide supplies to his troops without a fight. According to one account, at the modern-day city of Multan Alexander climbed a ladder to lead an attack and was badly wounded. For several days, as he appeared to be near death, his men went berserk, destroying the city and killing its inhabitants. When Alexander recovered from his wounds, he continued the journey down the river, reaching the Indus delta in the summer of 325. He explored both arms of the river and proved it was not connected to the Nile.

Exploration of coastal areas

Before the expedition arrived at the Indian Ocean, Alexander sent Craterus, one of his senior officers, back to Persia with the largest part of the army. He instructed Nearchus, who commanded another part of the army, to wait until the monsoon season in October and then sail along the coast to the Persian Gulf, where he was to find a sea route back to the mouth of the Euphrates River in eastern Turkey. The object was to open a trade route from the Euphrates to the Indus.

Meanwhile, Alexander and the remainder of his forces would make their way on land along the unexplored Makran coast (now in Pakistan), where he intended to build supply depots for the ships. But the Taloi Mountains, which reach all the way to the coast, forced him to turn inland, thus leaving Nearchus and the fleet to find their own supplies on a desolate shore.

Death at banquet

Alexander had no alternative but to lead his party across

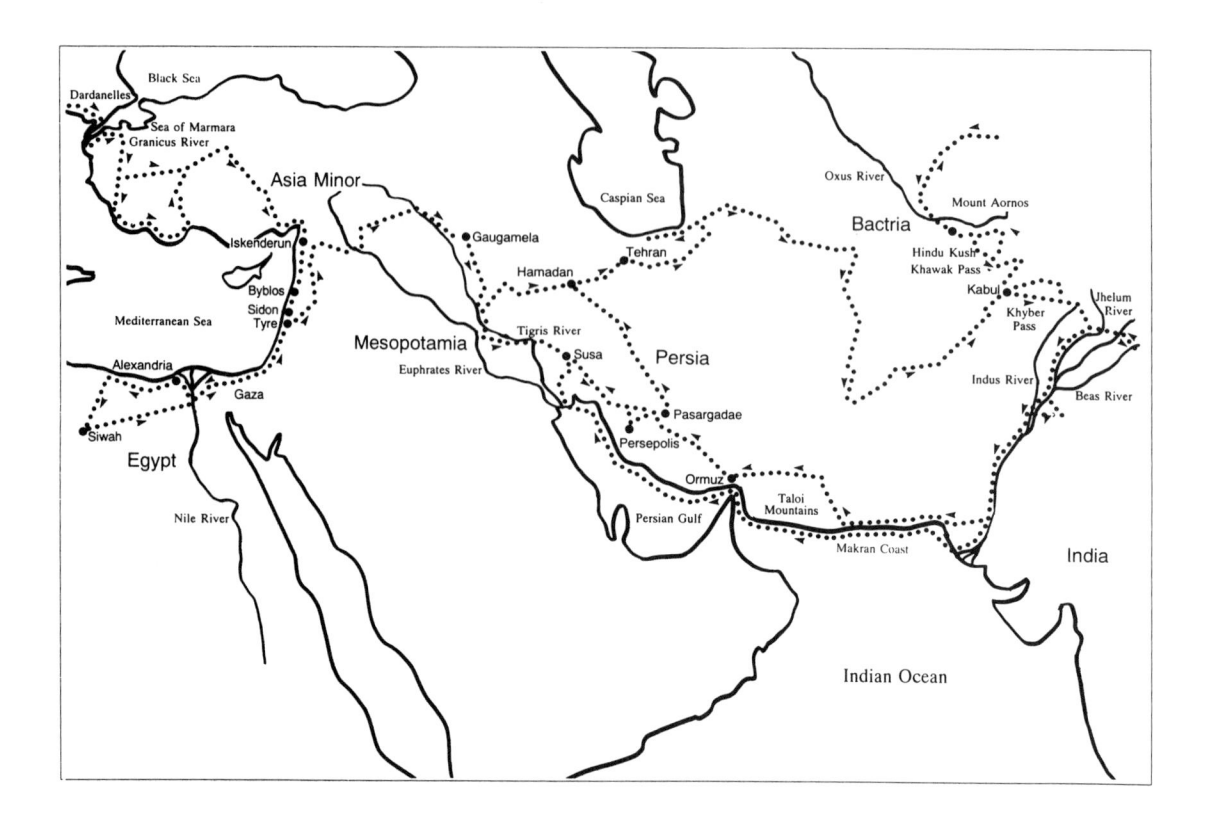

Leading an allied Greek army and viewing himself as the champion of Hellenism, Alexander the Great set out in 325 B.C. on what would become one of the greatest conquests in history.

a vast expanse of desert in Gedrosia, now part of Pakistan and Iran. This journey, which lasted through the months of August, September, and October in 325 B.C., was one of the most difficult of his campaign. Alexander marched his forces, which included women and children, at night in order to avoid the intense desert heat. They did not have enough food or water, and many people died before they reached Pura, the capital of Gedrosia. Alexander went to Kerman, a Persian province, to meet Craterus and his forces. It was another six months before Alexander and Nearchus met at the port of Hormuz on the Persian Gulf.

Alexander's army reached Susa in the spring of 324 B.C. By this time his men had become even more distressed by his having increasingly adopted the customs of an Asian despot. He had also taken another wife, and he had integrated Persians into his army. These measures so alarmed Greek and Macedonian veterans that they voiced their discontent. Alexander discharged them, and many set out for Europe. During this time, however, Alexander was planning future expeditions. He sent one of his officers, Heraclides, to explore the Caspian Sea to determine whether it was connected to the ocean that supposedly stretched across the world.

Alexander also planned to place Nearchus in command of a fleet that would sail around Arabia in search of a route between India and the Red Sea. Alexander apparently intended to conquer Arabia as well. These projects were abandoned, however, when Alexander became ill at a banquet on June 1, 323 B.C.; he died on June 13 at the age of 33. Most accounts list the cause of death as fever, although there has been speculation that he was poisoned. His only son, Alexander Aegus, was born to Roxana after his death.

Roald Amundsen

*Born 1872,
Borge, Norway
Died c. June 8, 1928,
The Atlantic Ocean*

The Norwegian explorer Roald Amundsen was the first person to sail the Northwest Passage, an Arctic sea route connecting the Atlantic and Pacific oceans. He was also the first person to travel to the South Pole and to reach both poles.

The son of a shipbuilder, Roald Amundsen was born in Borge, a town in Norway near Oslo. He was 14 when his father died. The following year he began reading about the Arctic explorations of **John Franklin** (see entry) and decided that he wanted to be an Arctic explorer himself. He prepared for exploration with hard physical exercise, including skiing, and he even kept his bedroom window open at night in cold weather. He also resolved to gain experience as a navigator. "I had been struck by one fatal weakness common to many of the preceding Arctic expeditions," he later wrote about this decision. "This was that the commanders of these expeditions had not always been ships' captains."

Amundsen's mother had wanted him to become a doctor, but after she died he had no one to oppose his desire to explore the Arctic. His first job was as a deckhand on a seal-hunting ship that spent five months in the Arctic Ocean north of Norway. On another occasion he bicycled across France and Spain to catch up with a ship bound for Florida. Returning to Europe, the ship stopped in Grimsby in northern England, where Amundsen spent all his money on a secondhand copy of a book of memoirs by Arctic voyagers.

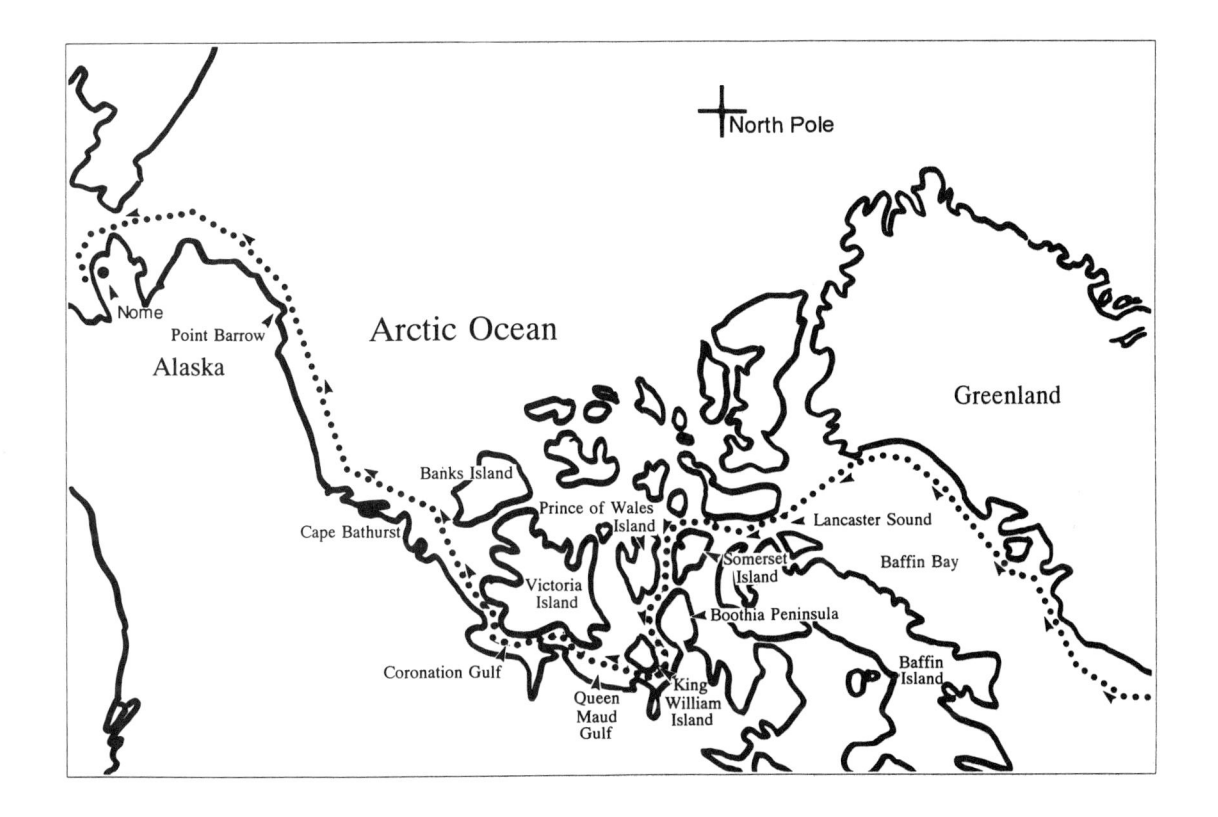

In 1897 Amundsen was chosen first mate on the *Belgica,* the ship carrying the first Belgian expedition under the command of Adrien de Gerlache. The *Belgica,* caught in the ice off Graham Land, was the first ship to winter in the Antarctic. Amundsen showed his ingenuity when the crew came down with scurvy, a disease caused by a lack of vitamin C. He dug in the snow around the ship for seal carcasses and then forced the men to eat the meat.

Voyage through the Northwest Passage

Amundsen secured his skipper's license when he returned to Norway in 1899. He immediately began making plans for his own expedition, and the famous Norwegian explorer **Fridtjof Nansen** (see entry) agreed to assist him. Amundsen's aim was to go to the North Magnetic Pole, which

In 1903-06 Amundsen closed the last unknown gap in the Northwest Passage, the sea route from the Atlantic Ocean to the Pacific Ocean.

had first been located by James Clark Ross, and then to try to sail through the Northwest Passage. The North Magnetic Pole, different from the North Pole, is the place on Earth toward which a compass points. In 1900 Amundsen spent a few months studying magnetism at the marine observatory in Hamburg, Germany. He returned to Norway and bought a small boat, the *Gjöa,* but because of the vessel's size—it had one mast and a 13-horsepower engine—it could accommodate only a crew of six. Amundsen's creditors, wanting to stop the voyage, sought to confiscate the boat, but Amundsen was able to escape, leaving from Oslo harbor at midnight on June 16, 1903, in the middle of a heavy rainstorm.

On August 22, 1903, the *Gjöa* reached Lancaster Sound, the entrance to the Northwest Passage, and sailed along the southern coast of Devon Island. The ship then sailed around Somerset Island and into Peel and Franklin straits, heading in the direction the compass indicated the North Magnetic Pole should be. From that point on the *Gjöa* was beset with near catastrophes. On August 31 the engine room caught fire, but the blaze was put out before spreading to the reserve oil tanks. The next day the *Gjöa* hit a reef, and it floated free only after some of the deck cargo was thrown overboard. In early September the ship almost sank in the first winter storm. The ship was then anchored in a small harbor, which Amundsen named Gjöa Haven, off the southern coast of King William Island.

Amundsen and his crew stayed two winters at Gjöa Haven. On land they built two buildings for magnetic observations, as well as an astronomical observatory, a supply shed, and a hut where two crew members would live. Soon the Norwegians were joined by a large band of the Netsilik tribe of Inuit, who built a camp nearby. Amundsen learned from the Inuit many techniques for survival in the Arctic, and he would put these to use in later years. During the spring and summer of 1904 Amundsen and the other explorers made trips to map the surrounding land and to locate the North Magnetic Pole. When Amundsen reached the spot where Ross had found the pole in 1831, he discovered it had moved 30 miles away. Amundsen's realization that the Magnetic Poles were not in fixed positions was the most important result of the expedition.

Amundsen trekked to the South Pole after Robert Edwin Peary and Matthew A. Henson reached the North Pole.

On August 12, 1905, the *Gjöa* left Gjöa Haven and sailed westward through Simpson Strait into Queen Maud Gulf, a large body of water that Amundsen named after the queen of Norway. The ship anchored in Cambridge Bay, which had been approached from the west by Captain Richard Collinson in 1852. By reaching the bay, Amundsen had closed the last unknown gap in the Northwest Passage; however, he had also shown the passage was narrow, shallow, and so full of reefs and hidden rocks that it would never be navigated by any but the smallest ships. On the other hand, the more open northern route through Parry Channel was so clogged with ice that only the largest and strongest icebreakers, such as the S.S. *Manhattan,* could make their way through it.

The *Gjöa* continued westward south of Victoria Island until it reached open water in an area later named Amundsen Gulf. On August 26 Amundsen met an American sailing vessel that traded in Arctic waters. The ship's captain greeted Amundsen by saying, "I am exceedingly pleased to be the first one to welcome you on getting through the North West Passage." The *Gjöa* then became trapped in ice near Herschel Island west of the Mackenzie River delta. During the winter of 1905-06 Amundsen traveled overland by dogsled to the nearest telegraph station—located at Eagle, Alaska, on the Yukon River—where he sent a message to Norway announcing his success. When he returned to his ship in March 1906, he found that one of the crew members had died from a ruptured appendix.

By August the ice had melted sufficiently for the *Gjöa* to continue its voyage, but the ship still struggled through two masses of ice off Point Barrow in order to reach Nome, Alaska, in early September 1906. The entire population of Nome turned out to welcome the explorers. The nephew of the Norwegian explorer Otto Sverdrup, who happened to be present, played the Norwegian national anthem as the ship pulled into the dock. Amundsen broke into tears.

Amundsen stayed with the ship until it reached Seattle, Washington; he then returned to Oslo. Amundsen received a hero's welcome in Norway and addressed several European geographical societies. He wrote *The Northwest Passage,* the first of six books chronicling his expeditions. The *Gjöa* was later taken to San Francisco, California, where it was put on exhibit at Golden Gate Park until 1973; it was subsequently returned to Oslo and installed in the national ship museum.

Race to the Pole

Following this success, Amundsen renewed his determination to be the first person to reach the North Pole. He thought he could test Nansen's theory that it would be possible to follow the Arctic currents and drift aboard a ship as far as the pole. Amundsen talked Nansen into lending him the *Fram,* the ship Nansen had specially constructed for his own attempt to reach the North Pole. In September 1909, while Amundsen was preparing for his expedition, news arrived that **Robert Edwin Peary, Matthew A. Henson** (see separate entries), and three Inuit companions had reached the North Pole by dogsled. Amundsen secretly resolved to change his goal to the South Pole, but he kept his decision to himself because he did not want to lose financial backing.

On August 9, 1910, the *Fram* left Oslo with the announced purpose of sailing through the South Atlantic to Cape Horn, then north through the Pacific to the Bering Strait, and finally into the Arctic Ocean. When on September 9, 1910, the *Fram* reached the island of Madeira, located off the northwestern coast of Africa, Amundsen told the crew about his real destination and sent telegrams revealing his change of plans to Nansen and King Haakon VII of Norway.

In the meantime, the British naval officer Robert Falcon Scott had left England on an expedition to the South Pole. When Scott arrived in Melbourne, Australia, he was surprised to receive this telegraph message: "Beg leave to inform you proceeding Antarctica. Amundsen." The race to the South Pole was on. Amundsen and his Norwegian crew, who were traveling in the swift-sailing *Fram,* had an advantage over the British. Consequently, Amundsen had already set up his base on the Bay of Whales at the edge of the Ross Ice Shelf when Scott arrived at McMurdo Sound, which was 60 miles farther from the Pole.

Amundsen's crew left camp on February 10, 1911, to set up its first supply depot at latitude 80°. On the return trip the dog teams achieved a record performance of 90 miles in two days. The other depot runs were not as successful, but Amundsen had all the depots in position in time for the onset of winter. An April blizzard allowed the Norwegians to construct a series of tunnels and rooms underneath a massive snowdrift, where they lived and worked until the spring thaw. As the thaw began at the end of August, Amundsen set out for the South Pole, but, because they had started too soon, he and his companions were overwhelmed by blizzards. They were forced to turn back, and Amundsen, reportedly for the only time in his exploring career, lost his nerve and outran his colleagues in retreating to the base.

The Amundsen entourage made another attempt to reach the South Pole on October 20, 1911. Helmer Hanssen, Oskar Wisting, Olav Bjaaland, and Sverre Hassel were out in front leading four sleds pulled by 52 dogs, and Amundsen followed behind on skis. Amundsen and Bjaaland, heeding the advice of the Inuit, were able to reduce the weight of their sleds by wearing warm but loose-fitting and lightweight fur garments. Their

British rivals, by contrast, wore wool clothes that got wet and froze. The Amundsen party reached the first supply depot in four days and rested there for two days, and they arrived at the last advance depot, just south of latitude 85°, on November 3.

From that base Amundsen and his four colleagues took advantage of the smooth snow by wearing skis and tying themselves to the sleds which the dogs then pulled. "And there I stood," wrote Amundsen, "until we reached 85°05' S—34 miles. Yes, that was a pleasant surprise. We had never dreamed of driving on skis to the Pole." On November 17 the party left the Ross Ice Shelf and started up Axel Heiberg Glacier (named by Amundsen after one of his sponsors) to cross the Transantarctic Mountains. The dog teams had difficulty climbing the steep glacier. Making the trek even more difficult were massive blocks of ice that forced the explorers to retrace their steps. At the top of the glacier they set up camp on a site they called Butcher Shop. At this point not as many dogs were needed to pull the sleds, which had become lighter as the party consumed the supplies, so some of the dogs were shot and either fed to the other dogs or eaten by the explorers. Amundsen stayed in his tent to avoid witnessing the killings.

On December 7, 1911, Amundsen surpassed the record, set by **Ernest Shackleton** (see entry), for the southernmost point reached on Earth. He and his party were confronted by yet another obstacle, however, when they had to cross the treacherous Devil's Ballroom—a double dome of ice over a vast crevasse. Although their sleds kept falling through the ice, they eventually reached the other side safely. As the men came within 15 miles of the South Pole on December 13, Amundsen mounted a Norwegian flag on the lead dogsled. He later wrote about the event, recalling that he felt like he did "as a little boy on the night before Christmas Eve—an intense expectation of what was going to happen."

The following day, at three o'clock on a sunny afternoon, the Norwegians raised their country's flag over the spot their calculations indicated was the South Pole. The jubilant explorers celebrated their achievement by dining on double rations. On December 17 they headed back north. This time they detoured most of Axel Heiberg Glacier and, following an uneventful trip, reached their base at 4:00 A.M., January 25, 1912. They had covered 1,860 miles in 99 days. At the end of January they sailed the *Fram* to Hobart in Australia. In the meantime, Scott's expedition had arrived at the Pole on the morning of January 17, 1912, and discovered the Norwegian flag, evidence that Amundsen's party had won the race. Scott and his four partners all died on their way back.

Flight to the North Pole

Following his return to Norway, Amundsen revived his goal of drifting to the North Pole. He designed and constructed a ship named the *Maud,* which he captained between 1918 and 1921 in an attempt to drift to the North Pole. His efforts failed. Instead, he ended up navigating the Northeast Passage along the northern coasts of Europe and Asia to Nome, Alaska. Amundsen was the second person in history to make this voyage; Nils A. E. Nordenskiöld in 1878-80 was the first.

Amundsen's disappointment over not reaching the North Pole by land led him to think he could make the trip by airplane. After a lecture in New York City, Amundsen met the American explorer and millionaire **Lincoln Ellsworth** (see entry), who offered to finance a flying expedition to the North Pole. Departing in Junkers and Curtiss aircraft in the spring of 1925, they made two unsuccessful attempts to go over the ice pack and land at the North Pole. Determined not to give up, they then outfitted two Dornier-Wal flying boats, which were designed to take off and land on water, with twin Rolls-Royce engines of 360 horsepower each.

Amundsen and Ellsworth flew from Spitsbergen, the largest island in the Arctic Ocean, on May 21, 1925. With half of its fuel gone, one of the planes developed engine trouble; the party was forced to land in open water at 87°43' N. When the ice rapidly crushed one of the planes, the stranded men modified the remaining plane so it could take off from the ice. They then improvised a makeshift runway, and on June 15 the plane took off, barely clearing the runway. The plane glided to a landing in open water off Spitsbergen, where the party was eventually rescued by a seal-hunting ship.

A successful trip to the North Pole was finally made by plane less than a year later, on May 9, 1926, by **Richard Evelyn Byrd** (see entry). On his return to Spitsbergen, Byrd met Amundsen, who was about to make another attempt, this time in an airship named the *Norge,* which had been designed by Umberto Nobile, an Italian engineer and pilot. The *Norge* was equipped with two 250-horsepower engines, carried seven tons of fuel, and could travel up to 50 miles per hour. At 8:55 A.M. on May 11, the airship left the ground. The temperature was -49°F in almost windless conditions.

At 1:15 P.M. the *Norge* was hovering over the North Pole, and the crew tossed Italian, Norwegian, and American flags onto the ground. After leaving the pole, the *Norge* ran into a number of difficulties: the propellers threw ice against the side of the airship and put a hole in the canvas, fog reduced visibility to almost zero, and the radio stopped working. The Amundsen party reached Point Barrow, Alaska, on May 14, having flown 3,400 miles from Europe to Alaska.

Amundsen's flight, which had crossed previously unknown territory, yielded important new information about the Arctic and made Amundsen the first man to travel to both poles. Nobile, however, was jealous of the recognition Amundsen received. Since he had designed and flown the *Norge,* Nobile claimed, he had not been given proper credit for the achievement. He subsequently solicited support from Benito Mussolini's Italian government to build another airship, the *Italia,* and to fly it over the North Pole.

On May 23, 1928, Nobile took the *Italia* on his second Arctic flight. No communication came from the *Italia* for six days. Then Amundsen received a telegram saying the *Italia* had been officially declared lost. In spite of Nobile's bitterness toward him, Amundsen said, "I am ready to go at once." Two search parties set out on June 8. One of them found the crashed *Italia,* whose survivors included Nobile. Not knowing about the discovery, Amundsen's party was already in a French seaplane heading for Spitsbergen. They never arrived at Spitsbergen, however, and some time later the wreckage of their plane was spotted from the air. Amundsen was 56 years old when he died.

Antonio de Andrade

*Born 1580,
Portugal*

*Died 1634,
Goa, India*

Following the first Portuguese expeditions to India in the early 1500s, the Roman Catholic church established several missions on the subcontinent and achieved some success in converting Indians to Christianity. The most successful missions were those founded by the Jesuit order. In 1615 the Jesuit missions were placed under the leadership of Father Antonio de Andrade, a native of Portugal. At the time rumors were circulating among the Jesuit missions that Christian communities existed in Tibet, north of the Himalayas. Andrade was determined to discover the truth.

Journey to Tibet

In March 1624 Andrade and a lay brother named Manuel Marques joined the entourage of the Mogul emperor Jahangir and traveled from the Indian capital at Agra more than 115 miles north to Delhi. In Delhi they adopted disguises and attached themselves to a caravan of Hindu pilgrims headed for

Antonio de Andrade, a Portuguese missionary, was the first European to travel over the Himalayas into Tibet.

Kashmir, a region in the far north of India. Crossing through the Himalayas, the two Jesuits reached the province of Garhwal, where they were discovered and forced to explain their presence. Andrade said that he was a Portuguese merchant on his way to Tibet to visit his sick brother. After a weeklong detention they were allowed to proceed.

Andrade and Marques traveled through the narrow paths of the Himalayas and several times crossed the headwaters of the Ganges River on "bridges formed by frozen snow." In May or early June 1624 they reached Badrinath, a holy Hindu shrine located high in the Himalayas. They were the first Europeans to reach Badrinath, and not for another 200 years would Europeans again visit the shrine.

At the town of Mana, lying on the Indian border with Tibet, they were stopped and forbidden to continue their journey. Marques stayed in the town to deal with the authorities, but Andrade went on his way. At the crest of the mountains, he was halted once again, and his guide returned to Mana. Andrade tried to continue alone, but heavy snowfall and extreme cold forced him to turn back and set up camp lower on the slopes. There Marques caught up with him, and, after waiting for better weather, the two men finally crossed through the Mana Pass into Tibet. They were the first Europeans in the country since the visit, 300 years before, of Odoric of Pordenone, the first Westerner to see the Tibetan capital of Lhasa and its Buddhist monasteries.

Missionary work in Tsaparang

In early August 1624 Andrade reached Tsaparang, the capital of a kingdom in the southwestern part of Tibet. He had decided he would return to India before the autumn snows began, but the king of Tsaparang liked him so much that Andrade was able to get permission to leave only by promising to return the following year. The king gave him a letter stating that the two Jesuits could count on his full protection and indicated his interest in learning about the Christian religion.

Andrade returned to India in November 1624 to write his report; he then headed back to Tsaparang, arriving there in

August 1625. He built a church in Tsaparang with money donated by the king. Three other Jesuits joined Andrade and his two companions to help in the mission's work. The king was baptized by Andrade in 1630, but the ceremony had been delayed because the king did not want to obey Andrade's command to give up his many mistresses.

Andrade left Tsaparang in 1630 to become the Jesuit superior in the main Portuguese base at Goa. Shortly after his departure the Buddhist subjects of the king of Tsaparang rebelled under the leadership of the king's brother, the chief lama, or spiritual leader. The king was taken prisoner, and many of the 400 converts to Christianity were enslaved. The church was destroyed. None of the missionaries were hurt, but they were forced to leave the country. The following year news of these developments reached Andrade in Goa, and he sent Francisco de Azevado, another Portuguese Jesuit missionary, to Tsaparang to find out what had happened.

Azevado achieved temporary success in convincing the Buddhists to let him rebuild the mission. Andrade was so encouraged by this that he sought permission to resign as head of the Jesuits in India and to return as a missionary to Tsaparang. His death in 1634, however, prevented him from fulfilling this wish.

Apollo

Began April 1957
Ended December 14, 1972

◀ Apollo 11 *on the launch pad at Cape Canaveral*

NASA's Apollo program consisted of 17 unmanned and manned space missions. Apollo astronauts made six successful lunar landings, the first in 1969, during which they walked on the Moon's surface to conduct scientific experiments and gather rock specimens.

The Soviet Union's successful launching on October 4, 1957, of the first **Sputnik** (see entry) artificial space satellite gave the United States incentive to revitalize its own dormant space program. The consequent competition between the United States and the Soviet Union, lasting for a decade, became known as the "space race." In fact, during that time the two countries together launched a total of 50 unmanned space probes in their efforts to be the first to explore the surface of the Moon.

The idea for a lunar landing program called *Apollo* has been credited to Abe Silverstein, director of Space Flight Development at the U.S. National Aeronautics and Space Administration (NASA). Silverstein also proposed using the name of the Greek god of the sun as the title of the space exploration program in July 1960. President John F. Kennedy provided the necessary political leadership when he addressed the U.S. Congress on May 25, 1961, and challenged the nation to land an American safely on the Moon before the end of the decade.

Development of the *Saturn V*

Once the United States was committed to reviving its space program, the first challenge was to design, develop, and test the spacecraft and related technology for spaceflight. Under the auspices of NASA, Dr. Wernher von Braun and his colleagues—who developed the V-2 rocket for Nazi Germany during World War II and afterward emigrated to the United States—developed the three-stage *Saturn V* rocket to launch the spacecraft. The *Saturn* worked in stages. The rocket's first two stages propelled the spacecraft out of Earth's gravity into space and then dropped off. The third stage put the spacecraft into Earth's orbit. The rocket was then refired to send the spacecraft at a speed of 25,000 miles an hour toward the Moon, with the third stage dropping off along the way.

The spacecraft itself consisted of the command module (similar to the cockpit of an airplane), where the astronauts were stationed; the service module, which contained the electrical power and fuel; and the lunar module, which, after entering the Moon's orbit, could separate from the rest of the spacecraft and carry the astronauts to the surface of the Moon. The lunar module, which stood 23 feet high and weighed 15 tons, rested first on spiderlike legs used for landing and then on a launch platform for departure from the Moon's surface. The lunar module lacked heat shields and operated only in the vacuum of space. After launching itself from the Moon's surface, the lunar module would go into lunar orbit and dock with the command module, which would then readjust its course to head back to Earth. The service module powered the spacecraft on the return trip, falling away prior to reentry into Earth's atmosphere.

Tragedy aboard *Apollo 1*

Disaster struck the program's first space mission, *Apollo 1*, raising serious questions about the feasibility of spaceflight. Three astronauts—Virgil I. "Gus" Grissom, Edward White, and Roger Chaffee—had entered *Apollo 1* at 1:00 P.M. on January 27, 1967, for a "plugs-out" test. The test continued routinely throughout the afternoon, but at 6:31 P.M. the technicians in the control room heard someone say, "There's a fire in here." It took five minutes to open the hatch. By that time the three astronauts were dead, having been suffocated within a matter of seconds by lethal fumes; their space suits had protected them from incineration.

The cause of the fire was determined to be a short circuit near Grissom's seat. The accident delayed the progress of the program as safety precautions were reviewed. The next *Apollo* missions were unmanned flights that tested the safety of the equipment.

Apollo 7

The first manned flight was *Apollo 7*, which took place on October 11-22, 1968, and was commanded by Walter "Wally" Schirra. Having previously flown on *Mercury 5* and *Gemini 6*, Schirra became the first American to make three flights in space. The crew also included Don Eisele and Walter Cunningham. The aim of the mission was to test the service module by firing its engines eight times during the 11 days in space. When *Apollo 7* landed in the Pacific Ocean off the coast of Baja California, it flipped over. There was no radio contact with the crew for 20 minutes. Fortunately for the astronauts and the future of the *Apollo* program, they all emerged unharmed.

Apollo 8

The *Apollo 8* mission, the first Moon flight, received considerable public attention because it took place during the Christmas season. *Apollo 8* was launched on December 21, 1968, from Cape Canaveral, with Frank Borman, James Lovell, and William Anders on board. As the astronauts entered lunar orbit on December 24, they moved to the far side of the Moon, where they were beyond voice contact with Earth. Starting at 7:00 P.M. on Christmas Eve, they broadcast live pictures from the Moon's surface; that night the crew members read the first ten verses of *Genesis* from the Bible. After making ten orbits around the Moon, the astronauts headed back to Earth on Christmas morning.

Apollo 9

The aim of the *Apollo 9* mission was to fire and recover the lunar module in space. James McDivitt, David R. Scott, and Russell Schweickart formed the crew, which was launched into space on March 3, 1969, from Cape Canaveral. Scott piloted the command module, and McDivitt, accompanied by Schweickart, commanded the lunar module. At first the lunar module did not reach its required speed. Schweickart, whose assignment was to test his space suit by walking in space, had vomited twice during the mission, so a space walk posed too great a danger. Instead, Schweickart stood in the doorway of the spacecraft to avoid becoming ill; Scott was in the open hatch. The two vehicles were separated for six hours and then reunited. This was a crucial test because no one knew how much "kick" would occur when the lunar module docked.

Apollo 10

The command module for the next mission, *Apollo 10,* was nicknamed "Charlie Brown," and the lunar module was dubbed "Snoopy," both after the Charles Schultz comic strip characters. The mission was a final test run before a landing on the Moon. The crew for *Apollo 10* included Thomas Stafford, John Young, and Eugene Cernan; the launch date was May 18, 1969, for an eight-day mission that would conclude on May 26, 1969. *Apollo 10* made 31 orbits around the Moon. The lunar module practiced flying close to the Moon's surface, coming within 50,000 feet, the distance a commercial jet flies over the surface of Earth. NASA concluded that a lunar landing was possible.

Apollo 11

It was on *Apollo 11* that men would travel from Earth to the Moon. **Neil Armstrong** (see entry) commanded the mission; Michael Collins and Edwin E. "Buzz" Aldrin, Jr., completed the crew. On July 16, 1969, the *Apollo 11* left the space station. The lunar module with Armstrong and Aldrin on board descended to the surface of the Moon on July 20 and stayed for 15 hours. Armstrong, the first to leave the spacecraft, was the first person to walk on the Moon. When Aldrin joined him, they mounted a television camera to broadcast pictures back to Earth, collected rock samples, and conducted scientific experiments. Armstrong planted an American flag and left a plaque to commemorate the visit.

Apollo 12

The success of the *Apollo 11* mission did not end the program. NASA officials had planned more missions to explore the Moon's surface. *Apollo 12* left on November 14, 1969, with Pete Conrad, Richard Gordon, and Alan Bean on board. President Richard M. Nixon watched the launch on television. Although lightning struck the rocket as it took off, there was no significant damage, and the mission proceeded. Targeted to land close to the site of the unmanned *Surveyor III*, launched in 1967, *Apollo 12* landed 535 feet away in the Ocean of Storms and 955 miles west of where *Apollo 11* had landed. Conrad and Bean took two moon walks—the first for 3 hours and 56 minutes and the second for 3 hours and 49 minutes. *Apollo 12* returned safely to Earth on November 24.

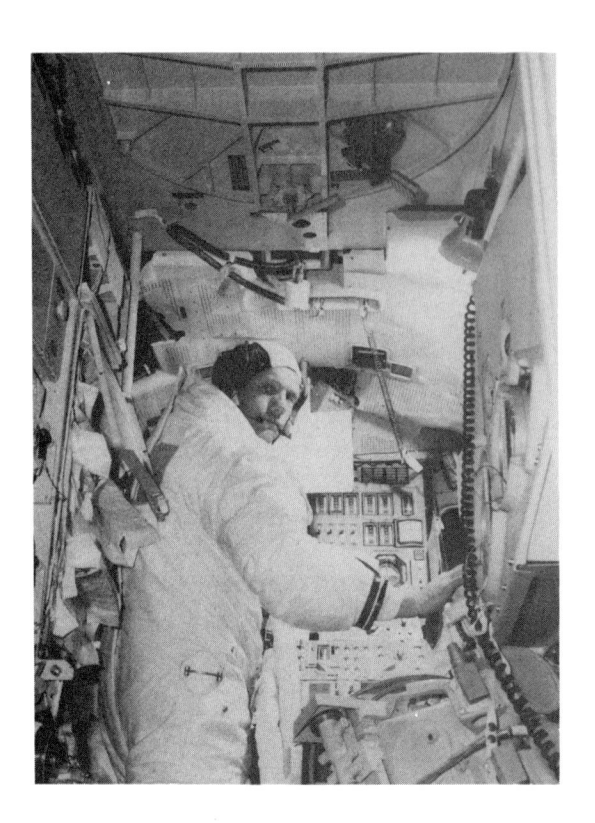

Neil Armstrong underwent extensive training for his job as commander of Apollo 11.

Apollo 13

Apollo 13 was the only aborted mission in the program. The spacecraft was launched at 1:13 P.M., April 11, 1970, with James Lovell, John Swigert, and Fred Haise on board. At 10:13 P.M. on April 13 an oxygen tank in the service module behind the crew exploded, eliminating oxygen, electricity, and water from the command module. The crew retreated to the cramped quarters of the lunar module, which was designed for a maximum of 45 hours of use; they were confined there for 90 hours. The interior temperature dropped to 38°F, and frost formed on the inside of the windows. The crew was able to make necessary course corrections to return to Earth, jettisoning the damaged service module prior to reentering Earth's atmosphere on April 17.

Apollo 14

The commander of *Apollo 14* was Alan Shepard, who earlier, in 1961, had become the first American to travel in space. His 1961 *Mercury* flight, lasting just 15 minutes, came one year before the first orbit of Earth by a U.S. spacecraft, manned by **John Glenn** (see entry). Shepard, however, developed an inner ear problem, which affected his balance and kept him grounded. He thus underwent a secret operation to correct this disability and was restored to flight status. Shepard was accompanied by Stuart Roosa and Edgar Mitchell on the launch, which took place on January 31, 1971. Shepard and Mitchell landed on the Moon at 4:18 A.M. on February 5, 1971. They made two moon walks in the Fra Mauro Highlands not far from the landing site of *Apollo 12*. Using a cartlike vehicle that they pulled behind them, the astronauts collected lunar soil and rocks. When they returned to Earth on February 9, NASA quarantined all the astronauts to determine if any viruses or other diseases had developed; this practice was stopped after *Apollo 14*.

Alan Shepard, the first person in space in 1961, commanded the Apollo 14 *mission in 1971.*

Apollo 15

The first mission to land in mountainous terrain, *Apollo 15* lifted off on July 26, 1971. Its crew consisted of David Scott, who flew with the *Apollo 9* mission, Alfred Worden, and James Irwin. Scott and Irwin landed in the Appenine Mountains, which are higher than any found on Earth and located about 465 miles north of the lunar equator. For the first time the astronauts were equipped with a powered vehicle, the

Lunar Rover, giving them greater mobility. They made three trips to collect geological specimens, remaining outside the lunar module for more than 18 hours. In an attempt to demonstrate Italian mathematician and astronomer Galileo's famous discovery—that objects will fall at the same speed regardless of their weight—the astronauts dropped a hammer and a falcon feather onto the Moon's surface. Accidentally stepping on the feather, Irwin lost it in moon dust and was not able to retrieve it. Among their successful discoveries was a moon rock, later dubbed the Genesis Rock, that was 4.1 billion years old.

Apollo 16

John Young, who had served on the *Apollo 10* crew, commanded *Apollo 16*. The other crew members were Thomas Mattingly and Charles Duke. The mission was launched on April 16, 1972, and landed on the Moon at an elevation of 25,688 feet in the Descartes Mountains. As the spacecraft touched down, Duke had an amusing experience. His microphone cord became entangled with the tube that supplied him with orange juice, squirting the inside of his helmet with sticky liquid. Traveling around in the Lunar Rover, Young and Duke covered 22.4 miles and set a lunar speed record of 11.2 miles per hour. The astronauts left the Lunar Rover behind, having attached a television camera to relay live pictures of the blast-off of the lunar module. They brought back 213 pounds of lunar rock and soil for analysis.

Apollo 17

The last *Apollo* mission to the Moon was *Apollo 17*, a 12-day trip that left Earth on December 7, 1972, and returned on December 19. The lunar module, with astronauts Eugene Cernan and Harrison Schmitt aboard, touched down in the Valley of Taurus-Littrow at 2:54 P.M. on December 11. With Ronald Evans remaining in the command module, the two lunar astronauts spent 75 hours on the surface of the Moon, remaining outside the module for 22 hours. Cernan, the last human to walk on the Moon, made a short speech before departure, saying that humans would return one day. Like Neil Armstrong, he also left a plaque to record the event. When the astronauts left the Moon at 5:50 P.M. on December 14, 1972, they were carrying 250 pounds of lunar material.

The *Apollo* program, fraught with danger and risk, concluded with the *Apollo 17* mission. Its astronauts had demonstrated heroism and technological brilliance, and the program brought to a close one of the most productive periods of exploration in U.S. history.

Neil Armstrong

*Born August 5, 1930,
Near Wapakoneta, Ohio*

> Neil Armstrong is an American astronaut who was the first human to walk on the surface of the Moon.

When Neil Armstrong walked on the surface of the Moon on July 20, 1969, he captured the attention of the world. A feat that had been thought impossible had been accomplished—and then televised into the homes of millions. The Moon, the Earth's single natural satellite located 240,000 miles away, was no longer just the subject of poetry or science fiction. And walking on it was no longer simply a dream. The effort to travel to the Moon grew out of a pledge made by President John F. Kennedy in the early 1960s to put an American on the Moon by the end of the decade. On July 20, 1969, the name of one individual, Neil Armstrong, became synonymous with human exploration of the Moon.

Early interest in flying

Born on a farm near Wapakoneta, Ohio, on August 5, 1930, Armstrong says his earliest memory was attending air races in Cleveland at age two. He took his first plane ride at age six in a Tin Goose and marveled at how small everything looked down below in his hometown. Now interested in flying, he turned to model airplane building to learn more about the mechanics of flight. He spent much time improving his models, which were more advanced than those of his playmates, and he even built a wind tunnel in the family basement, using a fan to test the durability of his models.

An adult neighbor owned a telescope and invited the children to study the planets and stars. Armstrong liked looking at the Moon best because of its proximity to Earth: he could see its details more clearly. Armstrong, who skipped first grade, was good in science and mathematics in school and enjoyed reading astronomy books. He also read biographies of Orville and Wilbur Wright, the brothers who made the first flight in an engine-powered airplane on December 17, 1903, at Kitty Hawk, North Carolina. The Wrights had grown up near Wapakoneta. Armstrong worked at odd jobs to save money for flying lessons, which cost $9 an hour, a considerable amount of money at that time. He started learning to fly at age 14 and earned his wings two years later, before he even had a driver's license. The day he soloed at 15 was the happiest day of his teen years.

War hero

Wondering how he could attend college, Armstrong learned that the United States Navy offered scholarships in return for naval service. He applied for and received a scholarship to Purdue University, a state university in Lafayette, Indiana, to study aeronautical engineering. Armstrong began at Purdue in the fall of 1947, but before his junior year, the navy ordered him to flight school in Pensacola, Florida. The Korean War began in 1950 and Armstrong's unit was sent there. He was the youngest pilot in his unit and would fly 78 combat missions from the aircraft carrier *Essex*. Armstrong earned the admiration of his fellow pilots when he flew his Panther jet back to safety after its wings had been damaged by a cable stretched across a North Korean valley. He was awarded three air medals.

After the Korean War Armstrong returned to Purdue and received his bachelor of science degree in 1955. While in college, Armstrong met Janet Shearon, who also loved flying; the couple married in January 1956. He took a job as a research pilot at the Lewis Flight Propulsion Laboratory in Cleveland. Next Armstrong was hired as a civilian research pilot flying experimental planes out of Edwards Air Force Base in California. The Armstrongs refurbished a cabin in the San Gabriel Mountains and started to raise their family. Ricky and Karen, who would die at three of a brain tumor, were born; Mark came later.

This period was the golden age of test piloting, when speed and altitude records were frequently set. Planes such as the *X-1* and *X-15*, half-rocket and half-airplane, could go 4,000 miles per hour (mph) and as high as 40 miles above the earth. The flights were a dangerous but necessary preparation for the next stage—space travel. Armstrong enjoyed the challenges and learned as much as he could about the airplanes themselves.

Astronaut training

The Soviet Union's launching, in 1957, of *Sputnik* satellites to study the earth's atmosphere sent shock waves through American society. The United States government responded by creating the National Aeronautics and Space Administration (NASA) in 1958, with all space research centers such as Edwards becoming part of this new endeavor. Positions in the astronaut training program were competitive, and Armstrong, being a civilian, did not think he would be selected. But in 1962, Armstrong was chosen to join NASA's second group of astronauts. He was the first civilian. He relocated his family to El Lago, Texas, next to the NASA Manned Spacecraft Center in Houston, to begin a two-year training program.

Armstrong made his first space flight on March 16, 1966, as commander of the *Gemini 8* mission, which he and crewman David R. Scott flew 105,000 miles to an orbiting spacecraft. Armstrong's job was to "dock" the nose of *Gemini 8* into the *Agena* target vehicle's docking collar; this docking of two orbiting spacecraft was an historic first. Half an hour after the linkup, however, the two vessels starting spinning out of control. Armstrong thought it was the *Agena* that was causing the problem and he disengaged. But then his spacecraft started spinning wildly—one revolution per second—and lost contact with ground control. The ground control crew thought the *Gemini 8* was lost in space. Then they heard Armstrong's voice. He had righted the errant spacecraft and earned himself a reputation as a brave, cool pilot.

Trip to the Moon

On January 9, 1969, Armstrong was named commander of the *Apollo 11* mission which was to be the first attempt to land humans on the Moon. The astronauts studied Moon maps and practiced walking in their space suits, which were tough enough to resist small meteoroids, in simulated Moon laboratories. Although risk could not be completely eliminated, every conceivable safety precaution was taken. On July 16, 1969, Armstrong and his pilots, Edwin E. "Buzz" Aldrin, Jr., and Michael Collins, blasted off from the John F. Kennedy Space Center at Cape Canaveral, propelled by a three-stage *Saturn* rocket that was 36 stories high. Aboard the spacecraft were small sections of the wing and propeller of the Wright brothers' airplane that had first flown from Kitty Hawk. Three days after launch, *Saturn* entered lunar orbit. On Sunday, July 20, Armstrong and Aldrin entered the lunar module *Eagle,* which was to separate from the command module *Columbia,* which Collins would captain. After about five hours of tests, the *Eagle* separated from *Columbia* and entered its own orbit. Armstrong's job was to fly the *Eagle* to the Moon's surface. After less than two hours in orbit Armstrong fired the engines which steered the landing craft to the surface of the Moon, 300 miles below, in a descent that took about 12 minutes.

The computer-guided landing was to be in the Sea of Tranquility. But when Armstrong looked out the window, he knew he would have to land the craft manually: the spot selected by scientists was in fact a large crater littered with huge boulders. Armstrong searched for a new landing site, finding one about four miles away. He landed the *Eagle* with just 30 seconds worth of fuel left. At 4:17 P.M. (EST) on July 20, 1969, Armstrong radioed to mission control in Florida: "Houston, Tranquility base here, the *Eagle* has landed."

First man on the Moon

Seven hours after touchdown, the two astronauts opened the *Eagle*'s hatch. Armstrong climbed down the nine-step ladder. At 10:56 P.M., he became the first human to reach the surface of the Moon. His words, "That's one small step for a man, one giant leap for mankind," were transmitted around the world. Aldrin joined him shortly thereafter. As Aldrin climbed down the ladder, he radioed to Armstrong, "Now I want to partially close the hatch, making sure not to lock it on my way out." Armstrong replied, "A good thought." The two astronauts quickly adjusted to the Moon's lighter gravity and found walking easy to do.

The moonwalkers began their work—performing scientific experiments, taking photographs, collecting moon rocks, setting up a television camera, and placing an American flag on the Moon's surface. They also set up a plaque telling about their achievement: "We came in peace for all mankind." All the while they were able to transmit live television pictures back to Earth. President Richard M. Nixon placed a telephone call to them from the White House. The Moon visit lasted 157 minutes.

Armstrong and Aldrin then returned to the *Eagle* and rested for eight hours. The astronauts fired the rocket boosters, launching the *Eagle* off the Moon's surface. The ascent rocket burned itself out seven minutes after putting the spacecraft in an orbit about 50 miles above the lunar surface. Within two hours after reaching orbit, the *Eagle* docked with the *Columbia*. During docking, the two space vehicles were not perfectly aligned and they started to spin, but the astronauts were able to use their thrusters to control the spin. The crew then unloaded its equipment and payload from the *Eagle* onto the *Columbia* and jettisoned the *Eagle*. The *Columbia* set off for Earth during its thirty-first orbit of the Moon. The return voyage took 60 hours.

Astronaut hero

The three men splashed down in the Pacific Ocean on July 24. Navy frogmen from the aircraft carrier *Hornet* picked them up. Although the possibility of germs existing on the Moon is remote to nonexistent, the spacemen were quarantined for 18 days while the ship traveled to Hawaii. From there the astronauts were flown to Houston, where they received a hero's welcome—the first of many to follow, including a ticker tape parade in New York City. The astronauts received the Medal of Freedom, America's highest civilian honor. Armstrong went on to address a joint session of the U.S. Congress on September 16, 1969. The astronauts toured 22 foreign countries, where each time they were greeted with appreciation and admiration. In Armstrong's hometown of Wapakoneta, the street where his parents lived was renamed after their son, as was the airport. A Neil Armstrong museum is also located in Wapakoneta.

Private life

Six more Moon landings would follow, but Armstrong did not make a return trip. Following the Moon voyage, Armstrong was appointed deputy associate administrator of NASA for aeronautics. He left the agency in 1971 to become professor of aerospace engineering at the University of Cincinnati, leaving the university in 1980. He resettled his family in Lebanon, Ohio, a small community north of Cincinnati, where he serves as board chairman of Cardwell International and sits on corporate boards of directors nationwide. In 1979 Armstrong founded his own computer systems company, and in 1986 was named vice-chairman of the presidential commission appointed to investigate the *Challenger* space shuttle disaster. Today, for pleasure, Armstrong flies a glider, a relaxing activity for a private, shy hero.

Vladimir Atlasov

*Born seventeenth century,
Veliki Ustyug, Russia*

*Died 1711,
Kamchatka, Russia*

Vladimir Atlasov, a Russian Cossack, explored the Kamchatka Peninsula and claimed it for Russia.

Vladimir Vasilyevich Atlasov, a Cossack peasant, was born in the town of Veliki Ustyug in northern Russia. As an officer and explorer in the Russian army, he helped expand Russia's territory by claiming the Kamchatka Peninsula on the Pacific Ocean. There he built forts and exacted tribute from the indigenous peoples. Atlasov encountered the Ainu, a people of Caucasian origin who were the original inhabitants of Japan. He also sighted the Kuril Islands, one of which is now named Atlasova Island.

Seventeenth-century Russia was a vast, sparsely populated country that looked eastward for trade and exploration. Its feudal government was controlled by the Great Russians, or Muscovites, who had expanded from Moscow into Siberia and across 5,000 miles of northern Asia. The Russian motive for seeking a northern route was economic. The area to the north was the source of the best furs. During that era Russian settlements and forts spread to the east, eventually reaching the Pacific Ocean.

Exploration of Kamchatka

In 1656, as part of this movement to the east, the Russians had built a fort on the Anadyr River, which flows into the Pacific Ocean at the far northern Bering Sea. In their trade with local tribes, they heard about a great peninsula to the south called Kamchatka. Atlasov was made manager of the Anadyr fort and charged with investigating Kamchatka as a possible area for expanding settlement and trade.

After sending one of his men, Luka Morozko, to the northern part of Kamchatka in 1696, Atlasov led a major expedition there in 1697. With a 120-man force that was made up of Russians and Yukagirs, who were indigenous to the area along the Anadyr, Atlasov started down the western side of the peninsula. Along the way he demanded tribute from the Koryaks, who lived in that part of Kamchatka. He then crossed the Kamchatka mountain range, which makes up the central peninsula, and headed down the Pacific side. In 1697, after proclaiming Russian annexation of Kamchatka, Atlasov erected a cross on the Krestovka River, a tributary of the Kamchatka River. By this time the Yukagirs in his expedition learned that their kinsmen had revolted against Russian rule, and as a result they rose up against Atlasov, killing three Russians and wounding Atlasov and fourteen others. Atlasov and the Russians were finally rescued by Morozko, who brought reinforcements.

Russian Cossacks

The Cossacks, who were peasant soldiers, originated in the fifteenth century in Ukraine, which was then a part of the Polish-Lithuanian state. Cossack companies were formed to defend Ukraine against the Tatars, who swept down from the north into east-central Asia and central Siberia to raid and pillage the country. Consisting mainly of Russians, Poles, and runaway serfs, the Cossack companies had by the sixteenth century formed communities along the Dnieper and Donn rivers in southern Russia. These self-governing communities were based on social and political equality for all their inhabitants.

The Cossacks participated in peasant revolts in the seventeenth and eighteenth centuries. By the late eighteenth century the Cossacks had become an elite class within the Russian military. Although the Soviet government abolished Cossack privileges and collectivized the villages in 1920, their traditions continued to survive. Cossack cavalry units have remained part of the Russian army.

Discovery of the Kamchadals and Ainu

Atlasov crossed and recrossed the peninsula until he discovered the Kamchatka River on the eastern side. Here he found numerous settlements of another people, the Kamchadals, whom he estimated to number 25,000. The Kamchadals did not use metal tools of any kind, but they did have some wooden lacquered instruments they had acquired from tribes to the south, who have since been identified as Japanese. On returning to camp, Atlasov found that his reindeer had been stolen by a party of Koryak marauders. He chased the thieves and fought a pitched battle that left 150 Koryaks dead.

As Atlasov continued south, he encountered the Ainu, a people of Caucasian origin who were the original inhabitants of Japan. They showed Atlasov a prisoner named Denbei, who fascinated the Russians because he was the first person from the Orient they had ever seen. Denbei, who historians now know was Japanese, spoke a different language and wrote a script that Atlasov called "Hindu." Atlasov sent Denbei as a gift to Czar Peter I in St. Petersburg, where Denbei lived until his death four years later.

Atlasov returned to Anadyr on July 2, 1699, after building a fort called Verkhne-Kamchatsk on the Kamchatka River. His superiors were so impressed with his efforts that he was sent to Moscow in 1701 to present his report in person. As a reward, he was made officer in charge of governing the new territory he had claimed for Russia. Atlasov made an error, however, when his returning party attacked and robbed a Russian merchant returning from China. For that offense he was thrown into prison.

Violent death

Other Cossacks attempted to control Kamchatka, but their methods were so cruel that the people revolted. Upon his release from prison in 1707, Atlasov was commissioned to restore order in the settlement. His methods were even more harsh, so much so that the Cossacks revolted and put him into prison at Verkhne-Kamchatsk. In February 1711 Atlasov escaped and sought refuge in another fort but was killed by a rebel band of Cossacks as he was sleeping.

Samuel White Baker

*Born June 8, 1821,
Gloucestershire, England*

*Died December 30, 1893,
Sanford Orleigh, Devon, England*

Florence Baker

*Born August 6, 1841,
Transylvania, Romania*

*Died 1916,
England*

Unlike other famous nineteenth-century explorers of Africa, Sir Samuel White Baker did not need sponsorship from the British government. He was independently wealthy and was able to finance expeditions from his own resources. After meeting his future wife, Florence, Baker traveled with her for years through the Nile River basin, where in 1864 they became the first Europeans to see Lake Albert. Soon afterward they also discovered nearby Murchison Falls, now called Kabalega (or Kabarega) Falls. In 1866 Baker was knighted by the British Crown, and in 1869 he was appointed governor of the Equatorial Nile Basin.

Baker was born in the county of Gloucestershire, England, on June 8, 1821. His father, a wealthy sugar merchant, owned estates in the Caribbean and on the island of Mauritius in the Indian Ocean. Baker was educated at home and then sent to Frankfurt, Germany, to complete his studies. An avid hunter, he took pride in the number of animals he killed. For a while he helped manage one of his father's estates on Mauri-

Sir Samuel Baker, an Englishman, and his future wife, Florence, explored the Nile River basin in Africa. They were the first Europeans to see Lake Albert.

tius, and in 1846 he took a brief trip to the island of Sri Lanka (also known as Ceylon). He was so impressed with Sri Lanka that he returned the following year with his first wife and 18 other settlers to found a farming colony in the Sri Lankan highlands.

The colony was a success, and Baker stayed in Sri Lanka for nine years, spending much of his time exploring the island and hunting. He wrote about his experiences in two books—*The Rifle and Hound in Ceylon,* published in 1854, and *Eight Years' Wanderings in Ceylon,* published in 1855. Baker was finally forced to return to England in 1855, however, because he and his wife were suffering from tropical diseases. His wife died from typhus shortly after their return.

Florence Baker

Visit to a slave auction

Three years later Baker agreed to accompany Duleep Singh—a young Indian maharaja, or Hindu prince, who was being educated in England—on a trip to Constantinople (now Istanbul), Turkey. Along the way, in 1860, they stopped at a port on the Danube River called Widdin (now Vidin, Bulgaria). At that time all of the Balkan Peninsula was ruled by the Ottoman Turks, and slavery still existed in the Ottoman Empire. Baker and Duleep Singh attended a slave auction in Widdin, where Baker bought a young ethnic German woman, whom he named Florence. She had been born in what is now the Romanian province of Transylvania in 1841 into a German family named Sass. When her family was killed in an uprising in 1848, she was adopted by an Armenian merchant named Finnian; he later put her on the auction block. From these facts Baker eventually concocted the tale that his future wife was the daughter of a wealthy German named Herr Finian von Saas.

Baker soon took a job with a British company that was building a railroad to Constanta, a Romanian port on the Black

Sea. He and Florence stayed in Constanta until the end of 1860. While they were in Romania, **John Hanning Speke** had returned to England from his expedition with **Richard Burton** (see separate entries) and reported the discovery of Lake Victoria in East Africa, which he believed was the source of the Nile River. In order to prove his theory, Speke had gone back to Africa in April 1860 with the Scottish army officer James Augustus Grant. Learning of Speke's presence in Africa, Baker decided to travel south on the Nile River, which flows north, and meet Speke and Grant as they emerged from the source of the Nile in the area that is now Uganda.

Expedition on the Nile

Departing from Cairo on April 15, 1861, Baker and Florence traveled on the Nile to present-day northern Sudan. Since Speke was not expected to emerge until 1863, they spent the time exploring the tributaries of the Nile that originated in the highlands of Ethiopia. They journeyed along the Atbara, Tekeze, Bahr-el-Salam, and Angareb rivers before continuing on the journey to Khartoum, which they reached on June 11, 1862. Khartoum, now the capital of Sudan, was the last outpost of Egyptian rule, as well as a major slave-trading center.

In Khartoum Baker met the British consul John Petherick, who had been officially delegated to proceed south and meet Speke and Grant. Petherick was slow in making his preparations, so Baker and Florence decided to travel ahead on their own. Unable to obtain official backing, Baker procured a flotilla of ships and recruited a small army, whose uniforms he designed and paid for. The party left Khartoum on December 18, 1862; the following February they reached Gondokoro, a slave emporium and the last outpost on the route from the north. Within a few days, on February 15, Speke and Grant arrived in the company of an Arab slaving expedition on February 15.

Speke had expected to be met by Petherick, but it was Baker who greeted him, shouting, "Hurrah for Old England!" When Petherick finally arrived on February 20, Speke charged that Petherick had been delayed because he was misusing funds that had been raised for Speke. On Speke's return to England, he had Petherick removed from office, thus ruining the reputation of an innocent man. Baker was disappointed to learn that Speke had, in fact, found the source of the Nile River; however, Speke told him about another large lake, Luta N'Zige, which was supposed to be connected to the Nile system but which remained unexplored.

Search for Luta N'Zige

Deciding to investigate this report, Baker started out with Florence and part of their original party in March 1863. In order to proceed, they were forced to attach themselves to a slave trader's caravan. In January 1864 they reached a Nyoro settlement in the kingdom of Bunyoro. They were met by a man they believed to be Chief Kamurasi. He was actually the king's younger brother, Mgambi; Kamurasi was afraid to meet Baker himself because he suspected a trap.

Baker requested porters and canoes to explore the lake, but the Nyoros agreed to assist him only if he helped them in their civil war against Kamurasi's brother Ruyonga, who was the pretender to the throne. Although Baker refused to be Kamurasi's ally, they managed to reach an agreement with an exchange of gifts and a promise that the Nyoros would provide porters and canoes. Mgambi did not reveal his true identity, however; still posing as Kamurasi, he told Baker to leave Florence behind in exchange for a Nyoro woman. Failing to recognize that the Nyoro custom was to present women to visitors as gifts, Baker then terrified Mgambi by threatening him with a gun.

Baker would later describe the incident: "Drawing my revolver quietly, I held it within two inches of his chest.... I explained to him that such insolence would entail bloodshed.... My wife made him a little speech in Arabic with a countenance almost as amiable as the head of Medusa." The Bakers left for Luta N'Zige without Nyoro guides and canoes. Along the way Florence was overcome by heat and went into a coma that lasted for several days; after she came out of the coma, she was subject to delirium for a time. Refusing to be delayed any longer, Baker had her tied to a litter and carried for the remainder of the journey.

In February they came upon the river Kafu, which was still in Bunyoro. In his report Baker noted the beauty of the countryside and the signs of "comparative civilization." Bunyoro villagers wore clothes, engaged in manufacturing, lived in huts, and ran blacksmith shops. They also had plentiful food, such as sweet potatoes, beans, sorghum, maize, and plantains.

Discovery of Lake Albert

Finally, on March 14, 1864, the Baker party reached Luta N'Zige. Baker described their first sight of the lake:

> The glory of our prize burst suddenly upon me! There, like a sea of quicksilver, lay far beneath the grand expanse of water—a boundless sea horizon on the south and south-west, glittering in the noonday sun; and on the west, at 50 or 60 miles distance, blue mountains rose from the bosom of the lake to a height of seven thousand feet above its level.

Identifying the lake as the second source of the Nile, Baker renamed it Lake Albert in honor of Queen Victoria's prince consort.

Baker and Florence obtained canoes and set out along the eastern shore of Lake Albert toward the site where the Nile enters the lake. On this trip they encountered storms and were bitten by mosquitoes; their canoe paddlers also deserted them. When they reached the kingdom of Bugungu, they found a river they had crossed on their trip through Bunyoro. Since the stream was sluggish, whereas the river had moved swiftly when they saw it earlier, Baker had to be assured by local people that it was the same river. Yet his guides refused to lead him downstream because they were afraid they would be attacked by hostile tribes on the return trip.

Arrival at Murchison Falls

Realizing they could not proceed alone, Baker decided to

investigate an unexplored part of the Victoria Nile River between the Karuma Falls and Lake Albert, which he had discussed with Speke before leaving Gondokoro. Although they would miss the boats they had arranged to meet in Gondokoro, the party began the journey up the Victoria Nile. Eighteen miles from Bugungu they came upon one of the world's greatest waterfalls. Baker gave a detailed account of the discovery:

> When the paddles ceased working we could distinctly hear the roar of water ... upon rounding the corner a magnificent sight burst suddenly upon us ... on either side of the river were beautifully wooded cliffs rising abruptly to a height of about three hundred feet; rocks were jutting out from the intensely green foliage ... roaring furiously through the rockbound pass [the river] plunged in one leap of about one hundred and twenty feet perpendicular into a dark abyss below.

Baker named it Murchison Falls in honor of the president of the Royal Geographical Society. (Even before he returned to England, he was rewarded for his discovery with the gold medal of the Royal Geographical Society.) Leaving their canoes, the party traveled east and reached an island in the river, where they spent the night. They found they could not go any farther; the other islands to the east, not far from the Karuma Falls, were controlled by Ruyonga, the brother of Kamurasi. Since a war was in progress, Baker and Florence could not find any porters for a safe journey through the area; they remained on the island for two months, living on finger millet and spinach. Kamurasi knew they were there, but he would not help them because they refused to be his allies against Ruyonga.

Involvement in tribal warfare

Baker finally managed to convince Kamurasi to meet with them. When he and Florence were escorted to the camp, they found that the "Kamurasi" they had previously met had actually been Mgambi. Baker was furious. He went to the meeting in a Highlander costume (the traditional Scottish kilt ensemble) in an attempt to intimidate Kamurasi, who responded by bowing at his feet. Baker pretended to believe Kamurasi was himself an impostor, saying he had been prepared to meet a great king and had found only a poor beggar. Kamurasi seemed to be amused, so the two men started a friendly conversation. Soon Kamurasi began asking for presents and renewing his demands for military aid in the war against Ruyonga. When Baker said he was in poor health—he had become ill with fever—and could not give Kamurasi what he wanted, the chief stormed out and cut off all food supplies.

At that point forces commanded by Ruyonga's ally, Mphuka (who was also his half brother), began advancing on the settlement. To ward them off, Baker raised the British flag, saying it was the emblem of the great "White Queen," who had a million soldiers with "fire sticks." After he had successfully chased the invaders away, Baker took his party to nearby Foweira, where they stayed while he recuperated. To cure his fever, he made potato whiskey in a still he had constructed. Kamurasi took a liking to the whiskey and made plans to manufacture it. Baker's party left Bunyoro in November 1864, arriving in Gondokoro the following February. They went on to Khartoum, then to Cairo, and from there back to England.

Upon their arrival in England in October 1865, Baker and Florence were secretly married in a formal ceremony so she could be introduced to his family and to English society. In 1866 Baker received a knighthood. They quietly spent the next few years at an estate they had acquired in Norfolk County.

Appointment as governor in Africa

In 1869 the Bakers were invited to accompany the Prince of Wales on a trip to Egypt. As a result of this trip, on April 1, 1869, the khedive, or ruler, of Egypt appointed Baker to a four-year term as governor of the Equatorial Nile Basin. At this time Egypt was nominally part of the Turkish Ottoman Empire but was, in fact, increasingly coming under the control of the British Empire. Baker's appointment was one of the first in which the two countries collaborated in order to found what was to become known as the Anglo-Egyptian Sudan.

Baker and Florence (by now known as Lady Baker) left Khartoum in January 1870 with an expedition of 1,600 men and 58 vessels. After experiencing difficulty navigating the White Nile, which was clogged with vegetation, they reached Gondokoro in April 1871. Baker took possession of Gondokoro in the name of Egypt in May. Realizing he had already served nearly two years of his contract and had not yet reached his destination, Baker headed south with his massive expeditionary force to the regions he had explored in 1863 and 1864. Because the Africans were not willing to be annexed to Egypt, he met hostility everywhere. One tribe that was particularly reluctant to accommodate Baker's troops was the Bari, who did not obey Baker's command to surrender their cattle to feed his men.

Baker had again violated the customs of the host country, this time by failing to recognize that cattle represented not only wealth but also social status for the Bari. When the Bari tried to explain their position, Baker used his firepower to seize the cattle by force. In the process, however, he alienated the people the khedive had sent him to befriend. Although Baker had the Bari cattle, he was still unable to feed all his men, and he sent 1,000 back to Khartoum. By now the mission was doomed. Baker knew he would not be able to cross the rapids of the Nile, nor could he make a second trip to Lake Albert. In January 1872 he moved south with a drastically reduced force of 200 men.

Renewed problems with tribal warfare

The Bakers' problems only increased as the party trekked through the Equatorial Basin. At Fatiko, a post north of the Victoria Nile and the border of Bunyoro, Baker was ambushed by the henchmen of an Arab slave trader named Abu Su'ud. He managed to drive them off with the help of the Acholi, the only friendly African tribe he had encountered. By the time he left Fatiko, however, his travel plans had collapsed; he subjected his men to forced marches even to reach Bunyoro.

When the Bakers arrived at Bunyoro in April, they learned that Kamurasi had died, and his son Kabberga had become king. Baker and Kabberga took an immediate dislike to one another. Baker's attempts to convince the Nyoro to swear allegiance to Egypt ended in a stalemate after three rounds of talks, for Kabberga would give in only if Baker would aid him in the civil war against Ruyonga. Baker further offended him by raising the Egyptian flag over Nyoro territory.

By May each side was prepared to use force against the other. After Kabberga tried to poison Baker's men and made surprise attacks on the explorer's party, Baker planned a secret retreat that involved setting fires to cover his movements. During a series of skirmishes that lasted two weeks, he lost several men, and many were wounded. They had nearly run out of ammunition before they were safely across the Nile.

When they reached the other side, Baker was greeted by Ruyonga, with whom he joined in blood brotherhood. Although Ruyonga wanted Baker to become his ally against Kabberga, Baker said he needed to return to Fatiko. Warning that Abu Su'ud, the slave trader, planned to attack Fatiko and eliminate the Europeans, Ruyonga gave Baker supplies for the journey. After his men easily defeated Abu Su'ud at Fatiko, Baker built a fort that became the southern outpost of the Egyptian empire.

Retirement in England

Upon returning to Gondokoro on April 1, 1873, Baker relinquished his command and left for Cairo. Following this retreat, Florence refused to allow her husband ever to return to the Sudan. But Baker kept abreast of Sudanese affairs and was largely responsible for the ill-fated tenure of General Charles "Chinese" Gordon as governor at Khartoum. Gordon's presence incited a religious uprising during which Gordon and all of his troops were killed by warriors of a popular Muslim leader known as the Mahdi.

Baker occupied the last 20 years of his life with traveling and big-game hunting. He shot elephants in Africa and Sri Lanka, took seven trips to India to shoot tigers, went deer stalking in Japan, and tried bear hunting in the Rocky Mountains of the United States. Baker died quietly at home on December 30, 1893. Florence lived until 1916.

Joseph Banks

*Born February 13, 1743,
London, England*

*Died June 19, 1820,
London, England*

Sir Joseph Banks, a British naturalist, sailed with James Cook on his first voyage around the world. Later, as president of the Royal Society, he sponsored explorations in Africa, Australia, and the Arctic.

Sir Joseph Banks initially became interested in exploration through his love of nature. An Oxford graduate born to wealth and power, he became a talented naturalist and had the vision and resources to pursue his many interests. He also promoted the exploration of Africa and Australia, as well as fostered England's ambitions to find the Northwest Passage. Banks founded the African Association, a society formed to find the source of the Niger River. Knighted in 1795, Banks was sometimes accused of being despotic by fellow scientists, but his herbarium, or collection of dried plant specimens, was considered the world's most important, and his collection of books on natural history and travel came to be housed in the British Museum.

Banks was born in London on February 13, 1743. His family lived on a large estate in the English county of Lincolnshire. When Banks was a 14-year-old student at Eton, a famous school in Buckinghamshire, he had an experience that would change his life. Walking back to Eton along a country lane after swimming in a nearby pond, he came upon such a profusion of flowers that he vowed to devote the rest of his life to the study of nature. Banks studied botany at Eton and then went on to Oxford University, but he soon discovered that the only professor of botany at Oxford did not give lectures. His desire to learn was so great that he traveled to Cambridge University, where he hired a professor to return with him to Oxford as a kind of private tutor.

Expedition around the World

Upon his father's death Banks inherited the family estate, as well as a great fortune. He graduated from Oxford in December 1763 at the age of 20. Already well known for his knowledge of natural science, Banks was in 1766 made a fellow of the Royal Society, the leading British institution for the study of science. Later that year he sailed on a Fisheries Protection ship called the *Niger* to visit Newfoundland and collect plant specimens. On his return to England he learned about the upcoming voyage of **James Cook** (see entry) to the South Pacific. The Royal Society endorsed his request to accompany the explorer as an onboard naturalist. Banks agreed to pay all the expenses for himself and his staff.

Cook's first expedition, on the *Endeavour,* left England in 1768. It first stopped in Brazil and then sailed to Tierra del Fuego at the tip of South America. While the ship was anchored in port, two of Banks's servants went ashore, drank heavily, and subsequently died of exposure. The *Endeavour* then went to Tahiti in the South Pacific, where Banks became one of the first Europeans to be tattooed by Polynesian artists; according to reports, he also had romantic attachments with Tahitian women. After leaving Tahiti the explorers went to New Zealand and Australia. On his return to England Banks brought back 1,000 new species of plants, 500 fish, 500 birds, and "insects innumerable." Lionized by English society, he was received by King George III; the two remained friends for the rest of the king's life. The great Swedish naturalist Carolus Linnaeus (Carl von Linné), who was the first person to classify plants and animals, was enthusiastic about Banks's success.

Following this highly successful voyage around the world, Cook was preparing to set out again in 1772. Banks was eager to join Cook on the voyage, but the two men clashed when cabins had to be built to accommodate Banks's personal party of 15 people, complete with two horn players. Recognizing that the ship could not sail with these obstructions, Cook ordered that the cabins be torn down. Banks was furious. He refused to reduce his party or to compromise his comfort. Eyewitnesses said that he stamped his feet in rage on the dock as Cook sailed away without him.

President of the Royal Society

In 1772 Banks led his own expedition to Iceland, where he stayed for six weeks. It was to be his last journey abroad. Six years later he was elected president of the Royal Society, probably the most prestigious scientific post in the world at that time. He was only 35 years old when he accepted this position, which enabled him to initiate a number of ambitious projects, among them the library for which he became famous. He supported several expeditions that collected plant specimens from around the world, which have since been placed on display at the Royal Botanic Gardens, better known as Kew Gardens. He also sent Captain William Bligh to Tahiti on the *Bounty* to collect seedlings of the breadfruit tree, which could then be grown in the West Indies to supply food for the slaves in the cane fields.

Banks's home became a meeting place for a free exchange of ideas, and under his tenure as president he cultivated exchanges with scientists from other countries and generally advanced the cause of science in England. His other great passion was exploration. As early as 1774 he interviewed James Bruce, a Scottish explorer who had just returned from Ethiopia after finding the source of the Blue Nile (a section of the longer Nile River in Africa). At a meeting of interested gentlemen in a London tavern on June 9, 1788, Banks proposed the concept of a society whose sole purpose would be to promote the exploration of Africa. The Africa Association was formed on the following day and set as its first goal the discovery of the headwaters of the Niger River.

Search for the Niger's source

Within a month John Ledyard, a 37-year-old American who had attended Dartmouth College for a time and had served with Cook, was on his way to Africa. Ledyard returned penniless and in rags. The Africa Association sent him out again, but he died in Cairo after drinking medication for a stomach ailment. Daniel Houghton, an Irish explorer, was then selected in July 1790, but he also failed to return. The next recruit, hired through a friend of Banks, was the luckless **Mungo Park** (see entry), a young Scotsman studying medicine at the University of Edinburgh, who had a desire to travel. Park's mission was also ill-fated. Although he managed to write a book about his first trip, he was killed by natives during his second expedition on the Niger River.

Thus far Banks had tried three approaches to the Niger: from Tripoli with Simon Lucas, from Cairo with Ledyard and Friedrich Hornemann, and from Gambia with Houghton and Park. Undeterred, he now decided on a fourth strategy, an approach from the south. In 1804 the association hired Henry Nicholls to start from one of the trading stations on the Gulf of Guinea and to head north to find the Niger. Nicholls never knew that he came very close to discovering the headwaters of the Niger River because he died of fever soon after arriving at the mouth of the Cross River, just east of the Niger Delta, on January 14, 1805. After the death of Nicholls the African Association became less active, sending out only two more explorers during the period between 1805 and 1831. Lacking resources and membership, the organization was absorbed by the newly founded Royal Geographical Society in 1831.

Lasting contributions

Banks turned his attention to Australia, where he was to have greater success. In 1801 he sponsored the voyage of **Matthew Flinders** (see entry) around Australia, paying for the necessary equipment out of his own pocket. Banks encouraged Gregory Blaxland to move to the new British colony in Australia, and Blaxland would later become the first person to find a way through the mountains west of Sydney. In 1817, following the Napoleonic Wars, Banks also became involved in renewed attempts by the British to find the elusive Northwest Passage—a sea route across the North American continent from the Atlantic Ocean to the Pacific Ocean. For years Banks corresponded with the whaling captain William Scoresby, who had written about his Arctic experiences and observations. Banks was also visited by a furloughed naval captain, **Edward Parry** (see entry), who advocated a concerted effort at northern explorations. This meeting led to the first of four voyages made by Parry and Sir James Ross, the Scottish explorer, to the Arctic. The Northwest Passage was not fully navigated, however, until almost 90 years later, when the feat was accomplished by a Norwegian, **Roald Amundsen** (see entry), in 1903-06.

As Banks grew older, he suffered from recurring attacks of gout, a disease of the metabolism involving painful inflammation of the joints. Because his movements became increasingly limited, he was confined to a wheelchair in 1804. He died on June 19, 1820, at the age of 77, having experienced a full life and an illustrious career.

Pedro João Baptista

Lived nineteenth century

Amaro José

Lived nineteenth century

Pedro João Baptista and Amaro José were *mestizo* (part African and part European) frontiersmen from Angola. In the early nineteenth century they were commissioned by Portugal to find a route across the African continent. Not only did they successfully complete this mission, which Portuguese explorers had attempted at least twice before, but Baptista kept a journal that was the only source of information about central Africa for many years.

Expedition leaders

When Baptista and José were appointed to head the expedition in 1802, Portugal had settlements on both coasts of Africa—Angola on the west and Mozambique on the east. The Portuguese had been in Africa since the sixteenth century, and they had long dreamed of signing trade agreements with the central African chiefs and establishing a trade route between the two settlements. Francisco José de Lacerda had tried to go

Pedro João Baptista and Amaro José made the first recorded trip between the western and eastern coasts of Africa. They were also the first persons known to have made the trip in both directions.

Pedro João Baptista
Amaro José

into central Africa in 1798, heading west from Tete, a large Portuguese trading center on the Zambezi River in interior Mozambique. The expedition failed because Lacerda died along the way, and the remaining members of his expedition returned to Tete.

Meanwhile, the captain general of Angola, Fernando de Noronha, made a similar search for a route through Africa from the west. He instructed Francisco Honorato da Costa, commandant of the frontier post of Kasanje, to send an expedition eastward to Tete. Honorato da Costa chose the Angolan frontiersmen Baptista and José—who were *pombeiros,* or traveling agents—to carry out this mission. Baptista, who had some formal education, decided to keep a journal of their expedition.

Captivity and insurrection

Baptista and José left Kasanje in November 1802. Eight days into the journey, just south of Kasanje, they came into the territory of a chief named Mawata Yamvo. Although Honorato da Costa had sent word that the two *pombeiros* were coming to look for the remains of the Lacerda expedition, the chief did not believe the story and took Baptista and José captive. Mawata Yamvo held them for two years. After their release in 1805, they set out again, eventually reaching the kingdom of Lovale, where they found guides who took them to the north around the Cassai River. After 39 days of travel, they arrived at the court at Muropue, the center of the Ovimbundu kingdom. They left there in the spring of 1806 led by guides and carrying the king's authorization to travel.

Baptista and José proceeded westward through Katanga (now in the country of Zaire) and into the large kingdom of Kazembe (in southeastern Zaire and northern Zambia). They were well received by the ruler of Kazembe, the Muata Kazembe. Baptista wrote about their visit in his journal, describing the chief's gorgeous costume and impressive retinue. He and José stayed in Kazembe for four years, longer than they had intended, partly because of a revolt against the Muata Kazembe's rule. African forces from Tete finally came to escort them out.

Arrival at Tete

They reached Tete in February 1811 after 57 days of travel. The day after their arrival Baptista delivered a letter from the Angolan governor to the local commandant, Gonçalo Pereira, who was one of Lacerda's former companions. Baptista and José wanted to return at once to Angola, but they were delayed because Pereira would not provide the goods they needed to trade their way back across Africa. While detained in Tete, Baptista recorded his observations about the town:

> The trade of the town of Tete consists in ivory and gold dust called money, which the traders from Mozambique, Senna and Quelimane came to buy with Indian stuffs. There is not a large trade carried on there in slaves, the price not being good enough to pay the traders. In former times they were worth more, but not at present.

Finally reaching an agreement with Pereira, Baptista and José left Tete in May 1811. Their trip back to Kasanje took three years. During that time they spent nine months with the Muata Kazembe. When they left Kazembe, they did not have the means to buy food for the rest of the journey. As a result, most of the slaves they had brought from Tete either starved to death or escaped on the return trip. According to Baptista, their party was forced to pitch camp by a river for two months "to fatten up the people who were lean and sick of hunger: the same was true of us."

First round-trip expedition across Africa

The successful completion of the expedition from Kasanje to Tete meant that Baptista and José were the first persons known to have crossed the African continent. More important, they had made the trip in both directions. The captain general at Luanda, Angola's capital, was so pleased that he ordered Baptista to deliver a report to the Portuguese court. Since it appears José had died somewhere along the route back from Tete, Baptista traveled alone to Rio de Janeiro in Brazil, where the court was then exiled because of the French occupation of Portugal.

An announced plan to send a yearly trading mission from Angola to Tete with Baptista at its head was never carried out. Baptista's journal was published in Portuguese in 1843. An English translation, sponsored by the Royal Geographical Society, appeared two years later. It was the only source of knowledge in Europe about central Africa until **David Livingstone** (see entry) started writing about his explorations in 1865.

Aleksandr Baranov

*Born 1746,
Kargopol, Russia
Died April 13, 1819,
Sunda Strait, near Java*

Aleksandr Andreyevich Baranov played an important role in Russia's control over the Alaska territory during the late eighteenth and early nineteenth centuries. His career was in the fur trade, though he initially studied to be an accountant and later opened a glass factory. When the failure of his Siberian fur-trading business threatened to ruin him, he accepted an offer to manage Russian trading posts in Alaska. At the height of his career, he controlled most of "Russian America."

The son of a poor itinerant merchant, Baranov was born in Kargopol, a village in northern Russia near the Finnish border. At the age of 15 Baranov ran away to Moscow, where he witnessed the coronation of the empress Catherine the Great. He then went to work for a German merchant, who taught him German and accounting. At some point he was also married. In 1780 he moved to Siberia to become a trader, sending his wife and daughter to stay in Kargopol. Using the capital he had saved from his trading, Baranov started a small glass fac-

Aleksandr Baranov, a Russian trader and administrator, was responsible for much of the early exploration of the Alaskan coast.

tory in Irkutsk, a city on the shores of Lake Baikal in southeastern Siberia.

In 1787 Gregory Shelekhov, the founder of Russian trading posts in Alaska, asked Baranov to take charge of his operations. Thinking he could do better on his own, Baranov refused Shelekhov's offer. From 1789 to 1790 he and his brother Peter traded for furs in the Chukchi Peninsula of far northeastern Siberia. They had collected a large quantity of furs when they were robbed by a party of Chukchis. Baranov went to the Siberian port of Okhotsk to seek help in recovering his valuable goods, but the local military governor refused to give him any assistance. Baranov was faced with catastrophe because he was heavily in debt, so his only option was to accept Shelekhov's offer.

First years in Alaska

Baranov left Okhotsk at the end of August 1790 and sailed to Unalaska, one of the Aleutian Islands off the southwestern coast of Alaska. When the ship wrecked a week later in a small port on Unalaska, Baranov and his crew were forced to spend the winter there. In the spring they constructed three whaleskin boats to sail to Kodiak Island, located off the coast of southern Alaska, which was the center of Russian trading operations. During the long sea passage Baranov became ill. When the ship arrived at Kodiak on July 8, 1791, Baranov was carried unconscious into the small Russian fort. By mid-August he had recovered and was traveling around the Russian settlement.

In the spring of 1792 Baranov moved the settlement to the other side of the island. The following summer he led an expedition to Prince William Sound on the southern coast of Alaska to look for a place to set up a new trading post. While he was there, Baranov met an English ship captain who told him about Spanish settlements in California and about Hawaii. The following summer he went to Cook Inlet—where the city of Anchorage, Alaska, was later established—and encountered the ships of British captain **George Vancouver** (see entry). Baranov and Vancouver did not actually talk to one another because Baranov did not want the English to learn too much information about the Russian operations.

In the summer of 1794 the chief of the tribe at Prince William Sound visited Baranov and offered his daughter in "marriage." Baranov, agreeing to the arrangement, gave her the Russian name Anna Grigorievna; they had two children.

Exploration of the Alaskan coast

In the summer of 1795 Baranov sent the *Phoenix,* a ship he had constructed the previous year from local materials, to Okhotsk with a load of furs. He himself made a brief expedition to Yakutat Bay on the southern coast of Alaska, where he built a Russian fort. He then headed south through the Alexander Archipelago. During his trip he discovered Sitka Island, which was later renamed Baranof Island in his honor.

For the next four years Baranov directed the affairs of the colony from Kodiak. In 1799 he traveled to Sitka, where he began the construction of a fort, New Archangel, which was completed on Easter Sunday 1800. Upon Baranov's return to Kodiak he encountered numerous problems. Native American tribes were refusing to trade because of Russian brutality. One of his local trading ships had also been wrecked, and the *Phoenix* had disappeared on its return from Okhotsk. By the end of the year the Aleuts of Kodiak, led by priests of the Russian Orthodox Church, were in full revolt. Baranov thereupon arrested all the priests on the island and had them imprisoned in a small hut. He spent the following years managing the affairs of the colonies to regain the trust of Native Americans.

In the spring of 1802 Baranov learned that he had been named governor of Russian America by Czar Alexander I. This news was quickly marred by word that the fort at Sitka had been attacked and destroyed by members of the Tlingit-Haida tribe. Baranov led an expedition to the fort in 1804 in the company of Yuri Lisiansky, who was making a trip around the world in the *Neva*. They recaptured the site and rebuilt Fort New Archangel, which Baranov then made the center of Russian America.

Expansion of Russian control

Baranov's goal was to establish Russian control down the western coast of North America as far as San Francisco. Beginning in 1804 he sent trading and exploring expeditions from New Archangel to California. In 1812 he sent his assistant, I. A. Kuskov, to found Fort Ross 50 miles north of San Francisco. He tried to work out a trading arrangement with John Jacob Astor's fur-trading company based in Astoria, Oregon, but the agreement fell apart during the War of 1812. In 1815 Baranov sent another assistant to Hawaii in order to take over the islands for Russia. The Russians annexed the island of Kauai but were driven out by King Kamehameha in 1817.

Because the Russians were losing too much money on Baranov's ambitious plans, he was relieved of his position in January 1818. Following his resignation, he attended the wedding of his Alaskan daughter, Irina, to a young Russian officer from a Ukrainian noble family. Baranov left Alaska in December 1818, sailing to Batavia (later renamed Djakarta), a city in the Dutch East Indies, where his ship docked for a month. It is said that Baranov stayed in his hotel room and drank. He contracted malaria and, on April 13, 1819, died on board the ship as it was passing through Sunda Strait west of Java.

Rabban Bar Sauma

*Born c. 1220,
Peking, China*

*Died c. 1294,
Baghdad, present-day Iraq*

Much is known about medieval travelers, such as Venetian **Marco Polo** (see entry), who journeyed from Europe to Asia, but there were also Asian travelers to Europe. For the most part, however, either no record was made of their trips or their accounts have remained undiscovered. One important exception was the journey of Rabban Bar Sauma, a Nestorian priest from Peking (now known as Beijing), China, who traveled to western France in the thirteenth century.

Bar Sauma was born around 1220 into a well-to-do Uighur family in Khanbalik, the capital of the Mongols, which later regained its Chinese name, Peking. At the age of 20 Bar Sauma became a monk and went to live in a cave, where he gained renown as a preacher. One of the people attracted by his preaching was a young monk named Mark. Sometime between 1275 and 1280 Bar Sauma and Mark set off to make a pilgrimage to Jerusalem. They were furnished with a letter of recommendation from the Nestorian bishop of Khanbalik and a travel permit from Kublai Khan.

Rabban Bar Sauma, a Nestorian Christian monk from Peking, made a pilgrimage to Persia and Iraq. He was also sent on a diplomatic mission to the rulers of western Europe.

Nestorians

The Nestorians—followers of Nestorius, an early patriarch, or bishop, of Constantinople—split off from the main branch of Christianity at the Council of Ephesus in 431. They became the most important Christian sect in what is now Iraq and Iran before this region was conquered by the Muslims in the seventh century. Starting in 635 missionaries were sent to sites throughout Asia, including an important Nestorian colony in China. This colony was later suppressed, but the religion continued to flourish among the Turkic-speaking Uighur tribes, who lived in the province of Sinkiang in western China. Following the conquest of Peking by the Mongols under Genghis Khan in 1215, the Nestorians returned to China and resumed their missionary work. Among the Mongols themselves were a number of influential Nestorians, including the mother of Kublai Khan, founder of the Mongol dynasty in China.

By the late twentieth century the Nestorian church—also called the Assyrian or East Syrian church—had approximately 175,000 members, some of whom lived in the United States. Nestorian churches are simple, with minimal ornamentation. An important part of the liturgy, conducted in the Syriac language, is "holy leaven," an altar bread believed to come directly from the dough used at the Last Supper. According to the Nestorians, Christ had two separate persons, one divine and the other human. They regard Nestorius as a saint but do not consider the Virgin Mary to be the mother of God. A large order of modern Nestorians, the Malabar Chaldean Catholics, has been recognized by the Roman Catholic church. The Nestorians and Chaldeans have a long history of persecution; during the twentieth century many were massacred by the Kurds and Turks in the Middle East.

Travels to Persia

Bar Sauma wrote an account of their journey, which provides valuable information about the religious and political situation in the countries they visited. They made their way through the Sinkiang Uighur region to central Asia, though with great difficulty, since at the time there was an armed rebellion against Kublai Khan's rule. Bar Sauma and Mark arrived at Khorasan, a region in eastern Persia (in present-day Iran), and made their way to Maragheh, a town in what is now Iranian Azerbaijan. There they were welcomed by the catholicos, the head of the Nestorian church and the patriarch of the East.

After visiting Baghdad, they were sent by the catholicos on a mission to the court of the Il-Khan, the Mongol ruler of Persia. The Il-Khan dynasty was the branch of the Mongol ruling family that descended from Genghis Khan's grandson Hulegu.

On their return they traveled by way of Christian Armenia. The catholicos then sent Bar Sauma and Mark back to China as his emissaries. In 1280 the catholicos named Mark a bishop and appointed him metropolitan, or head bishop, of part of northern China. When the catholicos died, the bishops chose Mark as his successor. Since most Nestorians were under Mongol rule, Mark's knowledge of the Mongol language and customs made him the prefect choice. Following the election, Bar Sauma traveled with Mark to Azerbaijan for Mark's confirmation by the Il-Khan Abaga.

Travels to Europe

In 1284 Abaga's son Arghūn took over the throne. Arghūn was friendly toward the Nestorians, and he was also ambitious. He wanted to drive the Muslims out of Syria and Palestine, so he tried to gain the help of the Christian Europeans. Arghūn sought the advice of the new catholicos, who recommended sending Bar Sauma to Europe to seek Christian support. According to Bar Sauma's writings, he left Iraq in 1287, heading north through Armenia to the Black Sea. He sailed from the Greek trading city Trebizond, located on the northern coast of Asia Minor, to Constantinople. There he met the Byzantine emperor Andronicus II and visited Hagia Sophia, an enormous cathedral.

Bar Sauma then set out for Naples across the Mediterranean Sea, a trip that took two months. While passing through Sicily he saw an eruption of Mount Etna. Since he arrived in Rome at a time when there was no reigning pope, he became involved in theological disputes with the cardinals at the Holy See. From Rome Bar Sauma went north to Thuzkan (modern-day Tuscany) and then to Ginuha (now called Genoa). Leaving northern Italy, he journeyed to Paris, where he had a meeting with King Philip IV. His next stop was Kasonia (now Gascony), a region in southwestern France, which was then ruled by the kings of England and known to Bar Sauma as Alanguitar. He met King Edward I of England in Bordeaux.

Bar Sauma had completed his mission for the Il-Khan by meeting the Christian kings and religious leaders in Europe. He set out on his return trip along the route he had taken from Persia. Stopping briefly in Rome in 1288, he received Communion on Palm Sunday from the newly elected Pope Nicholas IV. Upon his arrival in Persia, Bar Sauma reported to the Il-Khan that the Western powers were willing to unite with him against the Muslims. Although this alliance never took place, Bar Sauma's trip set the stage for diplomatic missions to the East from the West, including those of John of Monte Corvino and Galfridus of Langele.

Heinrich Barth

*Born 1821,
Hamburg, Germany
Died November 24, 1865,
Berlin, Germany*

Heinrich Barth, a German explorer, made a five-year expedition to Africa on behalf of the British government. He crossed the Sahara Desert to Lake Chad and went from there to Timbuktu. He completed his remarkable journey in spite of many dangers and the deaths of his companions, yet he never felt adequately recognized for his accomplishments.

Barth's father was a wealthy merchant in Hamburg, a port city in northern Germany. As a boy, Heinrich was sent to the best private schools, where he displayed exceptionally high intelligence; by the age of 11 he could read Latin and Greek and was studying Arabic on his own. Later at the University of Berlin he studied archaeology and geography, writing his thesis on the commercial history of the city of Corinth in ancient Greece.

Early travels in Africa and the Middle East

Following his graduation from college, Barth traveled for

Heinrich Barth, a German explorer in the service of the British government, made a five-year expedition to Africa, where he was the second European to visit Timbuktu.

three years in the eastern Mediterranean, going to North Africa, Egypt, Palestine, Asia Minor, and Greece. While he was in North Africa, he met a Hausa (black African Muslim) slave from the great city of Kano, now in northern Nigeria, who read his palm. The slave prophesied, "Please God, you shall go and visit Kano." Barth would indeed visit Kano within only a few years. On his return to Germany he became a lecturer at the University of Berlin. He was not an effective speaker, however, and his class was reportedly empty after the third lecture.

In 1849 the British government appointed James Richardson, an English explorer who had previously traveled to the Sahara, to lead an expedition along the caravan routes south from Tripoli, Libya, across the great desert. When Richardson announced that he wanted men with scientific knowledge to accompany him, Barth was recommended by Karl Ritter, the leading geographer of the day and a professor at the University of Berlin. A third member of the expedition was a young German geologist named Adolf Overweg.

Expedition to the Sahara Desert

Given the opportunity to participate in the expedition if he would pay his own expenses, Barth eagerly accepted the offer. On March 24, 1850, he and Overweg met Richardson in Tripoli, and the three men headed into the Sahara. They carried with them great quantities of supplies, equipment, and scientific instruments; they were also transporting a large wooden boat, as they planned to sail across Lake Chad in central Africa. Although the boat was cut into four sections to make it easier to carry, it was still a major encumbrance on the trip, so they hired a British sailor to manage the boat.

Unfortunately, the expedition was soon marred by religious discord. Richardson, who was a fervent Christian, and Barth, who had adopted the Muslim name Abd el Kerim, quickly came to dislike each other intensely. As a result, the party split up into two groups. Barth and Overweg rode ahead, while Richardson and the British sailor followed at a distance. The Germans and the English pitched separate camps at night.

When they reached the oasis of Marzuq, Libya, several weeks later, the sailor was sent back to Tripoli. The others waited in Marzuq for permission to continue to their next stop, Ghat, Libya.

On the way to Ghat, Barth had a brush with disaster. He decided to climb Mount Idinen alone, but, by the time he had reached the top of the mountain, he had drunk all of his water. While trying to find his way back to camp, he became lost. Desperate with thirst, Barth cut open a vein and drank his own blood before collapsing into semiconsciousness. He was eventually roused by the sound of a camel ridden by one of the expedition's guides, who had gone in search of him. The guide carried Barth back to camp, where he recovered and was well enough to travel the next day.

Important discoveries in the desert

From Ghat the expedition traveled over the Tassili-n-Ajjer Plateau in Algeria. Here Barth saw rock carvings of bulls and buffalo and guessed, correctly, that the Sahara had not always been a desert. After passing through the Air Mountains, Barth set out alone to visit the ancient city of Agadez, Niger, which had once been a major trading center in the Sahara. Barth reached the city on October 15, 1850. He attended the coronation of a new sultan and investigated the history of Agadez. Two weeks later he rejoined his companions at the oasis of Tintellust.

Joining a salt caravan that was heading south in early December, the men crossed the edge of the desert in January 1851. At that point they separated. Richardson headed for Zinder, Niger; Overweg went to Gobir, Niger; and Barth turned toward Kano. After a month of travel Barth reached Kano, noting that the city was a wealthy trading center that could one day serve as a commercial hub for a large part of Africa. He left Kano in early March and headed for Kukawa, Nigeria, on the western shore of Lake Chad, where the three explorers had agreed to meet in April.

As Barth entered the Muslim kingdom of Bornu near Lake Chad on March 24, he received bad news. A messenger informed him that Richardson had died of malaria in Kukawa and that Overweg, who was also suffering from the disease, would not arrive in Kukawa for two more months. Meanwhile, Barth himself had contracted malaria. After some time, however, he recovered; Overweg was also well by then and had joined Barth. They set out to explore Lake Chad in the boat they had brought from Tripoli. Barth also explored the territory to the south and east of the lake, thereby adding to Western knowledge of the rivers in the area.

Appointment as head of the expedition

The British government, having learned of the death of Richardson, appointed Barth in his place. Since Overweg was once again ill with malaria, Barth continued to explore alone. He had many adventures and terrifying experiences. At one point he was put in irons and held prisoner for four days until an African friend obtained his release. Another time he joined a slave caravan and saw 170 men massacred.

Barth returned to Kukawa in August 1852. Although Overweg was still sick, the following month they went on a hunting trip to Lake Chad. Barth was soon alone again, however. Overweg was soaked while retrieving a bird he had shot and the next day became delirious with fever. He died at the age of 29 on September 27, 1851. Following Overweg's death, Barth stayed for a year in Kukawa, making the town his base for several local expeditions before planning his next major journey, to Timbuktu (now often called Tombouctou) in Mali, West Africa.

Leaving Kukawa in November 1852, he traveled west. Several months later he arrived at the city of Katsina, Nigeria, and found a supply of sugar that had been sent to him by the British government. At the bottom of a box of sugar was $1,000. In March he reached Sokoto, Nigeria, where he was shown the house in which the Scottish explorer Hugh Clapperton had died 35 years earlier. In June 1853 Barth crossed the Niger River at the town of Say. From there he set off overland, disguising himself as a Tuareg, a Caucasian native of North Africa.

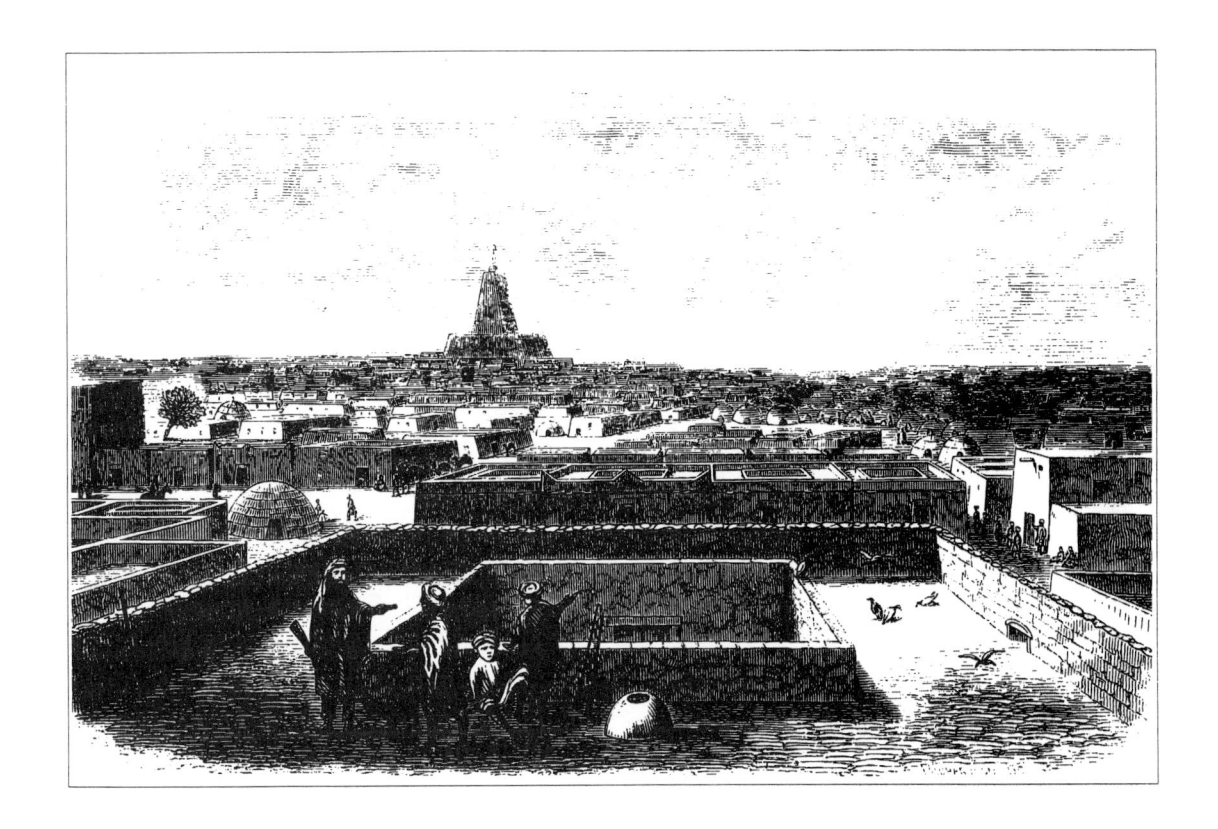

Journey to Timbuktu

Barth had estimated that it would take two years to travel to Timbuktu, but he made the trip in just ten months. He was the first European to visit the legendary city since **René Caillié** (see entry), who had been there 25 years earlier. Once again Barth found himself in danger. Accused of being a spy, he was detained in Timbuktu for seven months. He was reportedly saved several times by showing how his Colt revolver could fire six shots in a row. Barth was finally allowed to leave Timbuktu in May 1854.

On his way back to Kukawa, Barth heard that the British government had sent another German explorer, Dr. Edward Vogel, to look for him. The two men stumbled upon one another in December 1854 in the forest west of Kukawa. News of their encounter was relayed back to London with the message, "The rumour of Dr. Barth's death has most happily proved unfounded." Once back in Kukawa, Barth made plans

Barth was the second European to visit the legendary city of Timbuktu, where he was held prisoner on charges of being a spy.

to return to Europe. He left Kukawa in May 1855 and took the regular caravan trading route, east of his earlier path, to Tripoli, where he arrived in August. Taking a Turkish steamer to Malta, he reached London on September 16.

Recognition and honors

Upon his return to England Barth was received by the British foreign minister and was awarded the Order of Bath by Queen Victoria. He never felt his expedition was sufficiently recognized, however, as he believed other explorers of the time, such as **Richard Burton** and **David Livingstone** (see separate entries), received more recognition because they were British rather than German.

While in England Barth wrote several volumes documenting his expedition, and in 1857 he returned to Germany. His rejection for membership in the Berlin Academy of Sciences was a great disappointment to him. Later he was elected president of the Prussian Geographical Society, and in 1863 he was appointed professor of geography at the University of Berlin. These honors apparently did not make him any happier, and he spent the rest of his life as a recluse. At the age of 44 he died from a stomach perforation caused by ulcers he had developed during his travels in Africa.

Abu Abdallah Ibn Battutah

Born February 25, 1304,
Tangier, Morocco

Died 1369,
Fez, Morocco

Abu Abdallah Ibn Battutah, a Muslim legal scholar, was perhaps the most important traveler of the medieval period. In 30 years he journeyed 75,000 miles throughout Africa and Asia. He dictated a book about his travels that is still considered a reliable description of geographic locations during his time. Ibn Battutah was also an authority on the history and customs of Islam.

Ibn Battutah was born on February 25, 1304, in the city of Tangier, Morocco, into a family of Muslim legal scholars. A devout Muslim himself, he left his birthplace at the age of 22 (soon after finishing his studies) to make the *hajj*, the pilgrimage to Mecca and Medina that is required of Muslims who can afford it. "I set out alone, with neither companion to delight in nor caravan to accompany, my sole inspiration coming from an uncontrollable impulse and a desire long-cherished in my bosom to visit the holy places," he wrote in his memoirs.

Abu Abdallah Ibn Battutah, a native of Morocco, was one of the greatest travelers of the Middle Ages, eventually covering some 75,000 miles in Africa and Asia.

Pilgrimage to the Holy Land

On June 14, 1325, Ibn Battutah set out on his ten-month journey across North Africa, passing through present-day Algeria, Tunisia, and Libya before arriving in Alexandria, the main port of Egypt. There he saw the Pharos of Alexandria, a giant lighthouse in the harbor, which was one of the Seven Wonders of the Ancient World. He then traveled to the nearby retreat of a famous mystic. During his stay he dreamed he was riding on the wing of a giant bird that took him to Mecca and then eastward to a "dark and greenish" country. From there Ibn Battutah traveled up the Nile River via Aswan to Aidhab, a port on the Red Sea. He had planned to take a ship across the Red Sea to the Arabian port of Jeddah, but when he arrived, a rebellion was in progress. For this reason ships were not leaving the harbor, so he decided to return to Cairo and travel across the Sinai Peninsula to Jerusalem.

At the time of Ibn Battutah's visit, Jerusalem was a town of just 10,000 people, who subsisted by catering to pilgrims of the three great monotheistic religions—Judaism, Christianity, and Islam. After seeing the main sights of the Holy Land, Ibn Battutah departed for the ancient city of Damascus, where he arrived in August 1326. There he studied with some of the city's famous Islamic scholars and also married, apparently for the second time. In the course of his travels, Ibn Battutah would marry numerous women.

Journey with the pilgrim caravans

In September 1326 Ibn Battutah joined the main pilgrim caravan that was traveling south through Arabia on the Derb-el-Haj, the pilgrim road to Medina and Mecca. Fifty-five days later Ibn Battutah arrived in Medina, where he spent some time before going on to Mecca about 200 miles to the south. Ibn Battutah devotes only a short section in his journal to the performance of traditional rites practiced in both Medina and Mecca because the rituals were well known to his Muslim audience. Leaving Medina in mid-November, he headed for Iraq with a group of pilgrims who were returning to Baghdad.

During the next leg of his journey, Ibn Battutah visited other important Islamic sites. Leaving the caravan, he stopped at Najaf—a holy city for the Shi'ite sect of Islam—in southern Iraq. From there he went south to the port of Basra, which had once been a center of Islamic learning but had since declined. On a side trip to Persia (now Iran), he visited the cities of Shiraz and Isfahan. He later proceeded to Baghdad, which for a long time had been the center of the Islamic world. When Ibn Battutah saw the city, however, it was still in ruins after having been sacked by the Mongols in 1258. After visiting the walled city of Diyarbakir in what is now southeastern Turkey, he joined a caravan headed south for Mecca.

Ibn Battutah stayed in Mecca, studying Islamic law, from September 1327 until the fall of 1330. In order to finance his future travels, he became an itinerant *quadi,* or Muslim legal scholar. He traveled extensively throughout eastern Africa. When he passed through Zelia, a town in Somalia, he observed that it was "the dirtiest, most disagreeable, and most stinking town in the world." From eastern Africa Ibn Battutah sailed to Oman in Arabia and then in 1332 went back to Mecca for another pilgrimage. He wanted to go to India but decided to enter the country from the "back door"—that is, by way of Egypt, Turkey, and the Crimea, where he made one of his rare sojourns among Christians.

Land of the Mongols

From the Crimea Ibn Battutah headed inland through what is now southern Russia, entering the domains of the Mongol khan Öz Beg, also spelled Uzbek (whose name was later used to identify the people of Uzbekistan). At the request of one of the khan's wives, Ibn Battutah accompanied her back to her native city of Constantinople, where he met the Byzantine emperor Andronicus III. Ibn Battutah stayed in Constantinople for five weeks before returning to the khan's capital at New Sarai on the Volga River. New Sarai, now just an archaeological site, is not far from the Russian city of Volgograd, formerly Stalingrad.

By this time Ibn Battutah had become a wealthy man. Everywhere he went he was welcomed with lavish hospitality and valuable gifts, which in many cases included slaves and concubines. He had also accumulated an extensive entourage as he traveled across southern Russia to Khwarizm south of the Aral Sea. From there his party went by camel to Bukhara and Samarkand and stayed with the khan of Chagatae, another of the Mongol rulers of central Asia. Leaving Samarkand, they traveled through Persia and Afghanistan. When crossing the Hindu Kush Mountains, Ibn Battutah became the first person to record their name; he reached the Indus River in September 1335. From Multan, in present-day Pakistan, Ibn Battutah sent word to the court of the great Mughal emperor in Delhi of his impending arrival.

Years at the Mughal court

The Mughal emperor Muhammad Tughluq was noted for his capriciousness. Ibn Battutah wrote that "there was no day that the gate of the palace failed to witness alike the elevation of some subject to affluence and the torture and murder of some living soul." The emperor was, however, also a patron of scholars and Islamic learning, so Ibn Battutah remained at his court for seven years in the capacity of judge, earning a high salary. Spending lavishly, he fell into debt and was rescued by the emperor. But he soon fell out of favor with Tughluq when he visited a local mystic who had offended the emperor.

Ibn Battutah was put under house arrest for five months and was then called to the emperor's court, where he was named the head of a mission to travel, along with 15 returning Chinese emissaries, to the court of the last Mongol ruler of China. Unfortunately, the ship carrying the envoys and gifts was wrecked by a violent storm at Calicut, a city on the southern coast of India. Ibn Battutah was left destitute and also lost his child in the disaster. Afraid of returning to Tughluq, he sailed for the Maldive Islands in the Indian Ocean, 400 miles southwest of Sri Lanka, where he was befriended by Queen Khadija. He was given an official post, and he married and divorced six times in the eight months that he stayed there. He became involved in local politics but was forced to leave in August 1344 for Sri Lanka.

Voyages to China and Spain

In Sri Lanka Ibn Battutah visited Adam's Peak, a mountain with a large imprint on its summit, which Muslim legend says is the footprint made by Adam, the first man, as he took his first step on the earth after being cast out of heaven. Traveling up the coast of India, Ibn Battutah's ship was attacked by pirates, and he was once again left destitute. He eventually made it to Bengal and then sailed on board a Chinese ship to Sumatra. He was well received by the Muslim ruler of Samudra, on the northeastern coast of Sumatra, who gave him a boat and supplies to travel on to China. He left Sumatra in April 1346 and went to Ch'üan-chou, on the southeastern coast of China, and from there to Sin-Kalan, the Arabic name for Canton.

Ibn Battutah was impressed by Chinese civilization but deplored its "paganism." His itinerary in China is not clear, but he left Canton in the fall of 1346 and returned west by way of Sumatra, India, Arabia, Persia, and Damascus, where he saw the results of the great epidemic known as the Black Death. He made another pilgrimage to Mecca in November 1348 and then went back to Egypt. He took a boat along the North African coast and reached Fez, Morocco, on November 8, 1349. Ibn Battutah returned to his hometown of Tangier, where he learned that his mother had died a few months earlier. He was 45 years old and had been away for 24 years.

Soon after his return, Ibn Battutah went to the northern city of Ceuta (now part of Spain) and then joined a military expedition sent to defend the Muslim fortress of Gibraltar from a Christian army. Following the successful defense, he traveled in southern Spain, which was still a Muslim kingdom, and visited the cities of Malaga and Granada.

Visit to Timbuktu

In 1352 Ibn Battutah set out with a camel caravan that was headed south through the Atlas Mountains across the Sahara

Black Death

The bubonic plague, also known as the Black Death, swept across Europe and Asia during the fourteenth century. The Christian Crusaders, who caught the disease in Constantinople during a war against the "heathen" turks, spread the infection as they returned to their home countries in Europe; the epidemic lasted for 20 years. When Ibn Battutah visited Asia in 1346 the epidemic had been raging for 12 years; by 1354 it had killed 75 percent of the population on the two continents.

Carried by fleas from infected rats and other rodents, the disease spreads quickly, producing high fever, chills, extreme weakness, and delirium; the lungs can also become infected, with generally fatal results. The side effect from which bubonic plague gets its name is swollen lymph nodes, or buboes, that may discharge pus. The disease is called "Black Death" when hemorrhaged blood turns black and pervasive infection of the bloodstream causes death within three or four days.

The bubonic plague can be traced back to 430 B.C., when it struck Athens; during the third century A.D., the plague reportedly killed 5,000 people a day in Rome. The epidemic witnessed by Ibn Battutah was the most widespread occurrence of Black Death in history. The "great plague" of London, England, in 1665 also claimed many lives. Although quarantining, vaccination, and rodent control were introduced as preventive measures, the bubonic plague has continued into modern times. The disease still strikes in parts of Asia, where the mortality rate can be as high as 90 percent.

Desert. It took them 25 days to reach the salt mines of Terhazza in what is now Mali. From there he visited the trading center of Timbuktu and left one of the earliest written records of its growth, about 100 years before it reached the peak of its prosperity. On his return Ibn Battutah went eastward into what is now Niger and then turned north to the Ahaggar Mountains of southern Algeria. He arrived back in Fez in January 1354. It is estimated that in the course of his lifetime he had traveled at least 75,000 miles, not counting detours.

On Ibn Battutah's return to Morocco, the sultan provided him with a secretary named Ibn Juzayy, who helped him write down and edit the *Rihla,* the narrative of his travels. This project took about two years, and the book was published in December 1355. In this book Ibn Battutah proclaimed that, of all the lands that he had seen, his native Morocco was superior to all others. Ibn Battutah spent the rest of his life as a judge somewhere in the region of Fez, where he died in 1369 at the age of 64.

Jim Beckwourth

Born 1798,
Near Fredericksburg, Virginia

Died September 1867,
In the American West

Ambitious and restless, Jim Beckwourth was never able to settle down in one place for long. He lived as a trapper, trader, and pioneer among several groups of Native Americans and became a war chief of the Crow tribe. He discovered and promoted one of the main entry routes from the east into northern California during the California Gold Rush. A best-selling book on his adventurous life in the American West made him into a legend during his own lifetime.

Born a slave, Beckwourth was the son of Sir Jennings Beckwith, a descendant of a prominent Virginia family, and one of Beckwith's slaves, "Miss Kill," who herself was of mixed ancestry. He was given the name James Pierson Beckwith but was known as Jim. When Sir Beckwith moved to Missouri in 1806, he took Jim and Jim's mother with him. They settled on a large farm close to the meeting of the Missouri and Mississippi rivers and near the town of St. Charles. Jim's father sent him to school in St. Louis from 1810 until 1814, when the boy became an apprentice to a blacksmith in

Jim Beckwourth, an American fur trapper and trader, became a war chief of the Crow tribe and discovered one of the main entry routes from the east into northern California.

St. Charles. After a fight with the blacksmith, Jim returned to his father's farm. Although he was set free on his nineteenth birthday, he remained at home for a while longer. At some point he adopted the name "Beckwourth," his own version of the family name.

Journey to the American West

Beckwourth may have made an earlier trip west, but it is known definitely that he traveled to the West in 1824, when he joined a trapping and trading expedition led by William Henry Harrison, an American fur trader and explorer. Beckwourth's later account of the journey casts him in a favorable light and plays up his role in the expedition. His tendency to exaggerate has led many historians to question the truth of his accounts, but quite often his stories seem to have been based on actual events.

During one verified episode of the expedition, Beckwourth had a brush with death. Sent ahead to buy horses from the Pawnee tribe, he was unable to find the Pawnees. While trying to reach a trading post, he ran out of food. Had a band of Native Americans not helped him he would have starved to death. Throughout his life Beckwourth would continue to associate with many groups of Native Americans. In 1827 he married a woman from the Blackfoot tribe.

Once when he was unable to pay a debt, he took refuge among his friends in the Crow tribe, and during this period he married again. Beckwourth later claimed to have married eight women while staying with the Crow. Because he led a successful raiding party against another tribe, Beckwourth was made a chief of the Crow. In later years Beckwourth led the Crow in a great battle against their Blackfoot enemies. He boasted that all the Blackfoot were killed, while the Crow lost only 30 or 40 warriors.

Trapper, trader, and pioneer

Beckwourth trapped and sold furs to the American Fur Company of St. Louis until 1837, when he became a scout and mule driver for the U.S. Army. He joined the war against the Seminole tribe of Florida, and took part in the Battle of Okeechobee on December 25, 1837. Soon, however, he became bored with military life and returned to Missouri and the fur trade. Beckwourth then led a trading party west down the Santa Fe Trail to Taos, New Mexico, where he married a Mexican woman. In October 1842 he and his wife moved north to what is now Colorado. They opened a trading post next to the Arkansas River on a site that would eventually become the city of Pueblo.

In 1843 Beckwourth left Pueblo with a trading party of 15 and headed for California, which was then a part of Mexico. They arrived in Los Angeles in January 1844. When the local residents rebelled against the Mexican officials, Beckwourth joined their side in the "Battle" of Cahuenga, which took place in 1845.

Beckwourth continued to travel and work throughout the West. Leaving California for New Mexico, he traded along the Santa Fe Trail for several years. He was hired then by an official of the U.S. War Department to guide a party to Los Angeles and then north to Monterey, which at the time was the capital of California. At one point he even found himself leading a posse. He had taken a job as a courier to a ranch near the present-day city of Santa Maria, located north of Los Angeles. On his way to the ranch he discovered a massacred family, who had been living in the old Mission of San Miguel. Beckwourth joined the posse that successfully tracked down the murderers.

California Gold Rush

When gold was discovered in northern California, Beckwourth joined the California Gold Rush. He did not actively pan for gold but made his living among the prospectors by gambling and trading horses. One day in the spring of 1850 he was traveling in the remote mining areas of the Sierra Nevada, near present-day Lassen Volcanic National Park, and noticed what looked like a low pass just west of the California-Nevada border, about 30 miles north of Reno, Nevada. At the end of

April he led three men to the pass, which was subsequently named Beckwourth Pass. Realizing that it was an excellent passage into the gold mining region, Beckwourth and his companions spent the summer and fall of 1850 opening a road for prospecting miners.

During the spring of 1851 Beckwourth actively promoted his "New Emigrant Route," obtaining capital for development from the merchants of Marysville, California. In the summer of 1851 Beckwourth guided the first wagon train through the pass. When the wagon train arrived in Marysville that fall, there was so much celebration that the town almost burned down.

In the spring of 1852 Beckwourth decided to settle in the valley to the west of Beckwourth Pass, where he built a house and a hotel for travelers. The hotel soon became one of the main entry points for pioneers traveling through the pass to California.

Fame as a mountain man

Among the visitors to the hotel was a man named T.D. Bonner, who had previously met Beckwourth. Beckwourth reportedly dictated his life story to Bonner, who turned it into Beckwourth's "autobiography." Bonner took the manuscript to New York, where Harper and Brothers published it in 1856. Grandly titled *The Life and Adventures of James P. Beckwourth, Mountaineer, Scout, Pioneer, and Chief of the Crow Nation,* the book gave an account of tall tales and exciting adventures, making it a best-seller. Beckwourth was suddenly a celebrity.

Beckwourth lived on his ranch on the site of present-day Beckwourth, California, until late 1858. When he made a trip back east to Missouri, the St. Louis and Kansas City newspapers recorded the visit of the famous mountain man. Beckwourth later moved to Denver, Colorado, where he married once again and managed a general store.

Even toward the end Beckwourth's life was never routine. He had several scrapes with the law, including a charge of manslaughter, of which he was acquitted on the grounds of self-defense. He rejoined the U.S. Army as a scout and took part in several actions against the Cheyenne tribe. He was visiting a Crow village on a mission for the army when he died sometime in late 1867.

Gertrude Bell

Born July 14, 1868,
Washington Hall, Durham, England

Died July 11, 1926,
Baghdad, Iraq

Gertrude Bell, an English woman, was the best-known traveler in the Middle East and Arabia during the years before World War I.

Gertrude Bell traveled extensively in the Middle East at a time when few women had the opportunity to journey so far from home. She became a well-known figure in the Middle East and Arabia, wrote several books, and even founded a museum. Her thorough knowledge of the region's geography was of great importance to the British government during and after World War I.

Born in the county of Durham, England, on July 14, 1868, Gertrude Margaret Lowthian Bell was the daughter of a wealthy industrialist who owned an ironworks. After her mother died in childbirth two years later, Bell was raised by a stepmother. At the age of 16 Bell attended Queens College; she went on to Lady Margaret Hall, a women's college at Oxford University, where she graduated with high honors in history.

Early travels in the Middle East

In 1892 Bell traveled to the Middle East for the first time,

Lawrence of Arabia

T. E. Lawrence, a British soldier and scholar, became interested in the Middle East while he was a student at Jesus College of Oxford University. After participating in a British archaeological expedition in Mesopotamia in 1911, he stayed in the Middle East to learn Arabic and explore the area. He served briefly in the intelligence unit of the British Army in Egypt during World War I, then in 1916 he became active in the Arab revolt led by Faisal I against Turkish domination of Arabia. Lawrence became known for his battle strategy, which involved using small Arab forces to make quick assaults against the Turkish army. As a delegate to the Paris Peace Conference, he campaigned unsuccessfully for Arab independence; in 1921 and 1922 he continued to work for the Arab cause while he was the Middle East adviser to the British colonial office.

Having become "Lawrence of Arabia," a celebrity of almost legendary proportions, Lawrence apparently wanted anonymity, as in 1922 he enlisted in the Royal Air Force as a mechanic under an assumed name. After his true identity was discovered, he remained in the military in various capacities. In 1927 he legally changed his name to T. E. Shaw; around this time he also began publishing narratives on his experiences in Arabia. The most famous is *Seven Pillars of Wisdom,* which was privately released in 1926 and commercially republished a year later under the title *Revolt in the Desert.*

---

making a visit to an uncle who was the British ambassador to Tehran, Persia (now Iran). While in Tehran she met a young diplomat and wrote to her parents asking permission to marry him. They ordered her home, and the young man died nine months later. Bell wrote a book about her experiences titled *Persian Pictures, A Book of Travels,* which was published in 1894.

Five years later Bell went to Jerusalem, where she studied Arabic. She visited the Druze, a religious community in the mountains of southern Lebanon. She also toured Palmyra, the ruins of a Roman city in Jordan, which she poetically described as "a white skeleton of a town, standing knee-deep in the blown sand." Later she went mountain climbing in the Alps and made two trips around the world with her brother. In January 1905

Bell returned to the Middle East, traveling through Syria to Cilicia and Konya in Asia Minor (present-day Turkey). She traveled with Arab servants but without other Europeans. Sometimes she slept in tents, and at other times, when her family could provide her with introductions, she stayed in the homes of wealthy Europeans. Seeing ancient ruins during the trip increased her interest in archaeology. Bell's second book about her travels was published in 1907.

Archaeological expedition

In 1907 Bell returned to Turkey with the British archaeologist Sir William Ramsay to help excavate early Christian churches. She and Ramsay collaborated on a picture book of their discoveries. In 1909 she traveled through the valley of the Euphrates River to Baghdad, Iraq (until World War I a territory of Turkey), visiting Babylonian sites along the way.

During a trip to Karbala, the holy city of the Shi'ite Muslims, Bell was robbed of her money and her notebooks. The whole countryside turned out to try to find the thieves. The stolen items soon reappeared on a rock above her camp, but meanwhile Turkish soldiers had arrived. A nearby village was found to be deserted; the inhabitants had fled, fearing retribution. Bell blamed herself for causing difficulty for the local people. She returned to the area in 1911 to revisit the great castle at Kheidir, crossing the desert between Baghdad and Damascus, Syria. She then went back to England.

Diplomatic role during World War I

On her next trip Bell traveled to the city of Hail in the center of Arabia, an area that had rarely been visited by Westerners. There her money was taken from her, and she was virtually held prisoner. She finally managed to regain her freedom, but Arab hostility toward Westerners forced her to cut the trip short. Rather than continuing on to Riyadh, Arabia, as she had originally intended, she returned to Damascus in May

1914. Bell had gained unprecedented knowledge about the deserts and ruined cities of northern Arabia.

Bell's knowledge was soon to have great value. World War I broke out in Europe in August 1914, and three months later Turkey, which then ruled all of the Middle East, joined Germany in the fight against Great Britain. Bell was hired by the Arab Bureau in Cairo, Egypt, as a liaison officer. There she became friends with T. E. Lawrence, the famous "Lawrence of Arabia," who helped formulate the British strategy of encouraging the Arabs to revolt against the Turks. She is credited with the selection of Faisal I as the Arab king.

In 1916 Bell was sent to Basra, Iraq, as an assistant political officer, and in 1917 she was transferred to Baghdad. She was a key participant in the political negotiations that divided the Arab world into new countries and that established British political influence in the Middle East. She founded and directed the Iraq Museum in Baghdad, where she made her home until her death in 1926.

Fabian Gottlieb von Bellingshausen

Born 1778,
Ösel Island, Estonia

Died 1852,
Kronshlot, Russia

Fabian Gottlieb von Bellingshausen, an Estonian who served with the Russian navy, led an expedition that sailed around the continent of Antarctica. He was also one of the first persons to sight the Antarctic mainland.

Although Fabian Gottlieb von Bellingshausen made pioneering explorations of the waters around the Antarctic continent, the significance of his voyage was not appreciated during his lifetime. In 1820 he sighted the Antarctic mainland—perhaps the first person ever to do so—but more than a hundred years would pass before his name would be associated with the discovery of Antarctica.

Bellingshausen was born on Ösel Island in the Baltic Sea, which lies between Sweden and the countries of Estonia, Latvia, and Lithuania. His family belonged to the German gentry, who had long been prominent landholders and merchants in Estonia, which at that time was part of the Russian Empire. In the Russian language he was known as Faddey Faddeyevich Bellingshausen. As a young man, Bellingshausen attended the Russian Naval Academy at Kronshlot near St. Petersburg, Russia. He served as a junior officer on the ship that made the first Russian voyage around the world.

In the following years Bellingshausen carried out hydrographic surveys in the Black Sea.

Expedition to Antarctica

In May 1819 Bellingshausen was summoned to St. Petersburg, where he learned that Czar Alexander I had decided to send two ships to explore Antarctica. Bellingshausen was informed that he had been chosen to lead the expedition. In July, after hurried preparations in Kronshlot, he set sail as commander of a newly constructed ship, the *Vostok* (East); it was accompanied by a smaller and slower ship, the *Mirnyi* (Peaceful), commanded by Mikhail Lazarev.

Bellingshausen's voyage began with stops in Denmark and England, where he tried unsuccessfully to persuade the naturalist **Joseph Banks** (see entry) to join the expedition. The *Vostok* and the *Mirnyi* started the long journey south, stopping first at Rio de Janeiro, Brazil, and then heading toward the South Atlantic island of South Georgia.

An admirer of **James Cook** (see entry), the British sea captain and explorer, Bellingshausen kept Cook's works close at hand. Now Bellingshausen himself was sailing through a region Cook had begun exploring nearly 50 years earlier. He mapped the southern coast of South Georgia Island, completing the work that Cook had done along the northern coast in 1775. When Bellingshausen's ships crossed the Antarctic Circle on January 27, 1820, they were the first ships to have done so since Cook's voyage in 1773.

Sighting of the Antarctic mainland

The next day Bellingshausen sighted distant mountains in the area now called the Princess Martha Coast on the Antarctic mainland. The following three days he reported seeing ice cliffs and ice-covered mountains, not realizing they were part of a large continent. At almost exactly the same time as Bellingshausen's sightings, the British naval captain Edward Bransfield and the American seal-hunting captain Nathaniel Palmer also reported seeing mountains. It is not clear who actually saw the continent first.

On February 22 a severe storm forced Bellingshausen's ships to turn northward at about the longitude of Cape Town, South Africa. Sailing east to Australia, the *Vostok* arrived in Sydney Harbor on April 11; the *Mirnyi* trailed in eight days later. For several weeks the explorers stayed in the harbor to repair the ships and take on supplies.

Discovery of South Pacific islands

Bellingshausen set out during the southern winter, sailing among the islands of Polynesia and stopping at New Zealand along the way. When the ships passed through the Tuamotu Archipelago in the South Pacific, Bellingshausen became the first European to see some of the islands in that area. He also discovered and named the small, uninhabited island of Vostok. Returning through the central Pacific, where he fixed the location of many islands, he stopped again in Sydney in September 1820.

In November Bellingshausen left Australia and sailed back to the Antarctic. He spent a few days on isolated Macquarie Island south of the Australian continent, where he encountered several seal-hunting ships. He accurately forecast that the seal population would soon be destroyed.

Return to Antarctica

On January 21, 1821, Bellingshausen reached his farthest point south, 69.5°S, in the body of water now called the Bellingshausen Sea; the coast of this region of Antarctica is so heavily surrounded by ice that no ship has ever reached it. The following day Bellingshausen discovered an island and named it Peter I after the czar who had founded the Russian navy. A week later Bellingshausen sighted a group of mountains that he named Alexander I Land, which was actually an island connected by ice to the Antarctic Peninsula.

Sailing north to the South Shetland Islands, Bellingshausen met eight seal-hunting ships. The captain of one of them was Palmer, who came aboard the *Vostok* to visit Bellingshausen. According to an American account published

12 years later, Palmer told Bellingshausen that he had discovered the mainland of a continent. The Americans called it the Palmer Peninsula; actually it was the northern tip of the Antarctic Peninsula. Bellingshausen's account makes no mention of Palmer's claim. Bellingshausen's ships were now turning toward home. From the South Shetlands they sailed north, reaching Rio de Janeiro, Brazil, in March 1821 and arriving in Kronshlot on August 4, 1821.

Belated recognition

At the time of his return, Bellingshausen's discoveries were largely ignored. Although he submitted a report on his expedition, publication was delayed for several years. Meanwhile, Bellingshausen returned to active duty in the Russian navy with the rank of rear admiral and fought in the Russo-Turkish War of 1828-29. In 1831 he was promoted to admiral and in 1839 was made military governor of Kronshlot, where he served until his death in 1852.

The Russian Empire never sent another expedition to Antarctica. The Soviet Union, which replaced the Russian Empire after World War I, did not become actively involved in Antarctic affairs until much later, starting with the International Geophysical Year in 1957. It was then that the Soviets put forward the claim that Bellingshausen had been the first person to see the continent of Antarctica.

International Geophysical Year

Beginning in July 1957 scientists from 67 nations combined their efforts in an international study of the solar-terrestrial environment. This program, known as the International Geophysical Year (IGY), was the most important worldwide scientific project to that date. The IGY continued through December 1958 during a period of maximum sunspot activity.

The IGY produced significant discoveries in several fields: Earth satellites found the Van Allen radiation belts that are responsible for northern and southern polar auras; oceanographic studies produced new information about the ocean floor and deep ocean currents; and scientists developed more effective gravity measurements for mineral exploration. As a result of the IGY, Antarctica was designated a nonmilitary region reserved for international scientific study, such as the collection of meteorological data.

Benjamin of Tudela

Born early twelfth century,
Tudela, Spain

Died after 1173,
Tudela, Spain

Benjamin of Tudela, a medieval Jewish rabbi, traveled from Spain to the Middle East to report on the status of Jewish communities.

Benjamin of Tudela, a Jewish rabbi, was born in Tudela, a town on the Ebro River in northern Spain. He is best known for his journal *Massa'ot,* or *The Itinerary of Benjamin of Tudela,* which describes a 13-year journey from the Mediterranean to the frontiers of China. Benjamin's account discusses both commercial opportunities and the conditions under which Jewish people lived in the twelfth century. Although containing some errors, the journal remains a valuable record.

Persecution of Jews in the Middle Ages

The Jewish people of western Europe were persecuted throughout the Middle Ages and were sometimes forced to leave their homes and countries. This was partially because of the prejudice of Christians, who labeled the Jews "the murderers of Christ," and also because of jealousy. Many Jewish businessmen had become wealthy by lending money and trading in foreign goods. The sizable Jewish population living on the Iberian Peninsula, or Spain, had achieved a high level of prosperity, but they were subjected to intense discrimination; indeed, they were expelled in 1492.

Foreseeing this possibility, the Jewish people in Spain began thinking about suitable places of refuge as early as the twelfth century. Among them was Benjamin, who set out on a journey to report on the status of Jewish communities throughout the Mediterranean and the Middle East, potential places of refuge if the Jews were forced to leave Spain.

Journey through Europe

Benjamin started his travels around the year 1159 from the port city of Barcelona. He went north into France to the cities of Montpelier and Marseilles, where he noted the presence of large Jewish settlements. He noticed the beginning of the Albigensian heresy that led to warfare in the south of France; the Inquisition was initiated in 1233 to stop the spread of this strict Christian cult, whose members did not eat meat, believed that Jesus only seemed to have a human body, and followed their own preachers instead of the Catholic clergy. From Marseilles Benjamin took a ship to Genoa and Pisa in Italy. He noticed hardly any Jewish people in these cities but found several in prominent positions in Rome.

Benjamin journeyed south through Naples, Italy, and then to Sicily, an island at the tip of the Italian peninsula. Sicily at the time was ruled by the Normans from northern France, whose ancestors had come from Scandinavia. Moving on to Greece, Benjamin found a thriving Jewish colony in the ancient city of Thebes. The rabbis in Thebes were the most learned in the world, and Jewish businessmen engaged in the silk-working industries.

Visit to the Byzantine Empire

In December 1161 Benjamin reached the city of Constantinople, now Istanbul, in Turkey, which was the glittering capital of the Byzantine Empire. In Constantinople he viewed the festivities surrounding the marriage of Emperor Manuel Com-

The Crusades

For nearly 200 years, from the eleventh through the thirteenth centuries, European Christians waged war against the Muslims in an attempt to recover the Holy Land. After the Muslims had taken Jerusalem in the seventh century, they allowed Christians to continue their pilgrimages to the city; during the eleventh century, however, the Muslims began persecuting the Christians and they desecrated the Holy Sepulcher, the church built on the supposed site of Jesus' tomb. The Crusades began at the Council of Clermont (1095) when Pope Urban II called on all Christians to go to war for the Sepulcher. The Crusaders took their name from the Spanish word *cruzada*, meaning "marked with the cross."

There were nine Crusades altogether. The First Crusade ended in victory for the Christians when they conquered Jerusalem in 1099, but the Muslims won the city back during the Third Crusade, in 1187. At the end of the Fourth Crusade (1202-04) the Christians seized Constantinople (present-day Istanbul, Turkey), only to be defeated later at Cairo. In 1212 a French peasant boy named Stephen of Cloyes led thousands of children to the Holy Land on the Children's Crusade, which was intended to regain the victory the adult Crusaders had lost. This venture ended in disaster when the children were sold into slavery. Later a group of German children went to Italy on a similar mission, but most of them died of hunger and disease.

The Christians continued to have bad luck, and not long after the Ninth Crusade (1271-72), which ended in a truce with the Muslims, it was clear that the Crusaders had not won their holy war. In a final battle (1291) the Christians were defeated by the Turks at Acre in present-day Israel. The Christians conducted no further Crusades in the Holy Land, but they continued to fight heretics and heathens in their midst, especially in eastern Europe, until the late sixteenth century.

---

nenus. Benjamin described the magnificent church of Hagia Sophia, the largest in the world, and the bustle of numerous nationalities trading at the port. In spite of the city's size and wealth, Benjamin found discrimination against Jewish people in Constantinople. They were segregated in a distant suburb, forbidden to ride horses (except the imperial physician), and often attacked and ridiculed.

From Constantinople Benjamin voyaged through the islands of the Aegean to Cyprus. There he was shocked to find a heretical Jewish sect that did not even observe the Sabbath.

Arrival in the Middle East

Sometime in the year 1163 Benjamin reached the great

city of Antioch in Syria, an important military, commercial, and cultural center. Antioch had been retaken from the Arabs by the Crusaders in 1098 and was ruled by a French prince. Traveling south through Lebanon, Benjamin reported on the Assassins, a nonorthodox Muslim sect that specialized in the murder of its enemies. Benjamin entered the Holy Land, and in Jerusalem he saw many nationalities, including about 200 Jewish people. In Hebron he found the remnants of the Samaritans, a sect mentioned in the Bible.

Benjamin proceeded to Damascus, Syria, home to some 3,000 Jews, where he was overwhelmed by the beauty of the city's chief mosque. From Damascus Benjamin visited the ruins of Baalbeck in what is now Lebanon. From northern Syria he crossed over into Mesopotamia, which is considered to be the cradle of civilization. He eventually reached Baghdad, now in Iraq, which was then the capital of the caliph, or leader, of all Islam and probably the largest city in the world at that time. Benjamin reported on the high status of Jews in Baghdad and noted the respect enjoyed by the Jewish leader, "the Prince of the Captivity." The year of Benjamin's visit is estimated to have been 1164, almost a full century before Baghdad was destroyed by invading Mongols.

Return to Spain

After traveling to the ruins of the old city of Babylon, Benjamin proceeded into western Persia as far north as the Caspian Sea. Along the way he found numerous Jewish settlements. He then turned west and reached Egypt sometime during the year 1171, describing in his journal Alexandria and the Greek monasteries of the Sinai Desert. From the port of Damietta he journeyed to Messina in Sicily and then made his way back to Spain.

Benjamin reached his hometown of Tudela in 1173, having completed an epic 13-year journey. He then began writing *Massa'ot*. More than a narrative of his travels, this journal provides a firsthand account of the life of Jewish people throughout Europe and Asia in the twelfth century.

Hiram Bingham

*Born November 19, 1875,
Honolulu, Hawaii*

*Died June 6, 1956,
Washington, D.C.*

Hiram Bingham, an American archaeologist, located the famous Inca ruins of Machu Picchu and other important sites of the Inca civilization in Peru.

American archaeologist Hiram Bingham led a number of expeditions to Peru in the early twentieth century. There, in the Andes Mountains, he discovered important ruins of the once great Inca civilization. Most famous were Machu Picchu, the ruins of a large fortress city, and Espiritu Pampa, considered by many to be the remains of Vitcos, the "lost" Inca capital. Bingham's pioneering research also laid a solid foundation for subsequent exploration of the region.

Bingham was born in Honolulu, Hawaii, on November 19, 1875, the son of retired missionaries from an old Hawaii family. After his graduation from Yale University, he returned to Hawaii for a short time. He then decided to pursue an academic career, receiving an M.A. degree from the University of California at Berkeley and a doctorate in Latin American history from Yale.

Early trips to South America

In 1905, at the age of 30, Bingham made his first trip to

South America. He retraced the route of Simon Bolívar, a Venezuelan who led South American struggles for independence. This journey took him from Caracas, Venezuela, to Bogotá, Colombia. In 1908 and 1909 he made a second trip to South America, this time following the old Spanish trade route from Buenos Aires, Argentina, to Lima, Peru.

While in Peru Bingham visited Choqquequirau, a ruined city left by the Incas, who ruled Peru before the Spanish conquest of their empire in the sixteenth century. Choqquequirau was once thought to have been the last refuge of the Inca rulers after they were defeated by Spanish explorer **Francisco Pizarro** (see entry). This theory was discarded, however, and the location of the "lost city of the Incas," which some called Vitcos, remained a mystery. Visiting Choqquequirau aroused Bingham's interest in the legendary capital.

Search for the "lost city"

In 1911 Bingham returned to Peru to try to find the lost city. He also set himself the goal of climbing Peru's Nevado Coropuna in the Andes Mountains, a feat no one had ever accomplished, to see whether it was higher than Mount Aconcagua, another Andean peak, in Chile. He arrived in Arequipa, Peru, in June, a winter month in Peru and elsewhere in the Southern Hemisphere. Deciding it would not be wise to try to climb the mountain until the weather improved, Bingham turned his attention to finding the lost Inca city of Vitcos.

According to legend, the last Inca ruler, Manco II, had established his capital, Vitcos, in the Vilcabamba range. When Bingham was in Peru, it was possible to hear a variety of stories about the location of the ruins, but the best opinions seemed to point to somewhere in the valleys of the Vilcabamba and Urubamba rivers in central Peru.

Discovery of Machu Picchu

In July Bingham left Cuzco, in southeastern Peru, with a mule train. He traveled through the terraces of the valley of Yucay and past the gardens of Ollantaitambo. At Salapunco in the Urubamba Valley he saw the ruins of a small fortress of pre-European origin. One night, as Bingham camped near the Urubamba River, he met Melchor Arteaga, who lived in a neighboring hut and who came out to meet Bingham and find out what he was doing. As it turned out, Arteaga had important information for Bingham. He mentioned some nearby ruins called Machu Picchu, and Bingham persuaded Arteaga to take him there.

The next morning they set out. Crossing the rapids of the Urubamba River on a rickety bridge, they climbed a rough path through the forest. They ate lunch in the hut of some local people who lived by farming on the ancient Inca terraces. It took the two men an hour and 20 minutes to climb to the top of row upon row of terraces—almost 1,000 feet high in all. Above the terraces they walked through a forest and came upon a vast complex of houses made from granite and constructed with precise stonework. Bingham also saw a three-sided temple that rivaled any other yet found in Peru. Previously unknown outside Peru, Machu Picchu would soon be the most famous of all the Inca ruins.

Bingham did not stay long at Machu Picchu. According to legend, Vitcos was marked by a white boulder over a spring of water, and he had found no boulder. Concluding that Machu Picchu was not Vitcos and still absorbed by the idea of finding the lost capital, Bingham moved on. At Huadquina he learned of "important ruins" a few days' journey down the Urubamba River; however, they turned out to be merely the ruins of a small Inca storehouse.

Discovery of other Inca ruins

Bingham traveled up the Vilcabamba River to the village of Lucma, where he consulted Evaristo Morovejo, an official of the village. Morovejo's brother was said to have found some ruins while hunting for buried treasure in 1884. Morovejo took Bingham to the small village of Puquiura, three miles from Lucma, where they discovered only the ruins of a Spanish mill. On a hill above the village, however, were more ruins. Here Bingham found the remains of an Inca fortress containing 14 rectangular buildings, including a long palace with 15 doors on one side.

The next day Morovejo pointed out a white boulder and, some distance away, a spring. Bingham followed the stream until he came to an open space, where he saw what he had been looking for. A gigantic white boulder, with Inca carvings on its side, stood overlooking a pool, and nearby were the ruins of an Inca temple. Bingham was convinced this was the city of Vitcos.

Bingham's discoveries continued. From the "Vitcos" site he traveled into the jungle lowlands, reaching a remote sugar plantation on August 15, 1911. The plantation owner took him on a two-day trip into the forest to a spot called Espiritu Pampa (Plain of the Spirits). Here they found more Inca ruins, which, though Bingham did not realize it at the time, were the remains of a large town. Since his guides and porters were impatient, he was not able to stay long at the site.

After so many important discoveries within the space of a few weeks, Bingham's climb up Nevado Coropuna was anticlimactic. He made the climb with a Peruvian guide, a British naturalist, an American astronomer, and an American mountaineer, H. L. Tucker. Only Bingham, Tucker, and the guide went all the way to the peak, which they reached from a base camp at 17,300 feet. Although they were not frostbitten, the men suffered from soroche, an illness caused by lack of oxygen. Upon reaching the summit, they found that the mountain had three peaks; only by chance had they climbed the highest one. After making calculations, Bingham was disappointed to find that Coropuna was not as high as Aconcagua. Still, he thought he had conquered the second-highest mountain in the Andes. Coropuna was later found to be only the nineteenth-highest peak in the Andes.

Final expeditions to Peru

Bingham led expeditions back to the Vilcabamba region in 1912 and 1915 to clear the ruins, overgrown with vegetation, he had discovered and to make further explorations and scientific studies in the area. During these trips he uncovered many small Inca ruins in the hills near Machu Picchu. He also found traces of Inca roads and buildings at various places along the mountain range.

As a result of his investigations, Bingham became more and more convinced that Machu Picchu was the lost city of Vitcos. He supported this view for the rest of his life. More recent expeditions and interpretations, however, tend to support the theory that the ruins Bingham discovered at Espiritu Pampa are the city of Vitcos. Although the Inca capital has still not been identified with certainty, Bingham's work was the vital first step for ongoing archaeological study.

Bingham's career as an explorer in South America ended with the 1915 expedition. He spent most of the rest of his life as a writer, corporate board member, and politician. For the state of Connecticut he served as lieutenant governor, governor, and senator. He was also appointed by President Harry S. Truman to the Civil Service Commission, a position he held from 1951 to 1953. But his role in the discovery of the now famous archaeological ruins of Peru must be considered his most important accomplishment. The exploration of these sites made an enormous contribution to knowledge of the history of the Incas.

Isabella Bird

*Born October 15, 1831,
Yorkshire, England*

*Died October 7, 1904,
Edinburgh, Scotland*

A lifelong traveler, Isabella Bird journeyed through various countries in North America, the Middle East, and Asia during the nineteenth century. Her adventurous life often presented moments of great danger, but she responded to those with remarkable fortitude. Bird wrote about her experiences in several books, bringing her considerable fame in Great Britain, her native country.

Isabella Lucy Bird was born in the English county of Yorkshire on October 15, 1831. Her father was an Anglican clergyman, and her mother was the daughter of a clergyman. Bird was physically small and frail, and she suffered from ailments throughout her childhood. In 1850, when she was 19, a tumor was removed from her spine. Because the operation was only partially successful, she suffered from insomnia and depression.

Adventure in North America and Hawaii

Bird's doctor recommended that she travel to divert her

Isabella Bird, a nineteenth-century English traveler and writer, made a remarkable series of journeys through North America, the Middle East, and Asia.

attention from her poor health. In 1854 her father gave her £100, telling her she was free to do whatever she wanted with the money. Bird chose to travel to North America and stayed for several months in eastern Canada and the United States. On her return she used the letters she had written to her sister, Henrietta, as the basis for her first book, *The Englishwoman in America*.

When Bird's father died in 1858, she moved with her mother and sister to Edinburgh, Scotland. During the following years Bird took several short trips, including three to North America and one to the Mediterranean. The turning point in her life came in 1872, however. She was on a ship that was headed for New Zealand when she decided to get off at Hawaii. She stayed six months. During that time she learned how to ride a horse astride, which ended the backaches she had suffered from riding sidesaddle. She also climbed to the top of Hawaii's volcanic peaks. Later she wrote about her pleasure in "visiting remote regions which are known to few even of the residents, living among the natives, and otherwise seeing Hawaiian life in all its phases." Bird recorded her impressions of her visit in *Six Months in the Sandwich Islands*, which was published in 1875.

Leaving Hawaii, Bird went to the West Coast of the United States. From San Francisco she traveled alone on horseback to Lake Tahoe, located on the California border with Nevada, and then to the Rocky Mountains and Colorado. During this extensive trip she had many adventures; for example, she rode alone through a blizzard with her eyes frozen shut, spent several months snowed in with two young men in a cabin, and was wooed by a lonely outlaw. All these tales she told in *A Lady's Life in the Rocky Mountains*, published in 1879. This book, along with her volume about Hawaii, made Bird famous in Britain.

Travels through Asia

Bird's next trip was to Japan, where she hired a young Japanese man to be her translator. They traveled together to

Hokkaido, the northernmost part of the country, where she stayed among members of the Ainu tribe, the original, non-Japanese inhabitants of the islands. Her experiences formed the basis for her book *Unbeaten Tracks in Japan,* which was published in 1880. Bird continued her travels throughout Asia, visiting Hong Kong, Canton, Saigon, and Singapore. From Singapore she journeyed to the Malayan Peninsula, where she stayed for five weeks visiting the Malay states.

Soon after Bird's return to Edinburgh, her sister Henrietta died from typhoid. In 1881 Bird married John Bishop, the doctor who had taken care of Henrietta. They had a happy marriage, but Bishop died only five years later. Following her husband's death, Bird made a trip to India. While there she established the Henrietta Bird Hospital in Amritsar and the John Bishop Memorial Hospital in Srinigar. Traveling to Kashmir and Ladakh, areas of northern India on the border with Tibet, Bird continued her daring excursions. During the trip her horse lost its footing and drowned while crossing a river. Bird suffered two broken ribs in the accident.

Journey to Persia

Bird returned to Simla in northern India, where she met a British army major, Herbert Sawyer, who was on his way to Persia (now Iran). She and Sawyer traveled together through the desert in midwinter, arriving in Tehran in a state of extreme exhaustion. After leaving Sawyer at his new duty station, Bird set out alone and spent the next six months traveling at the head of her own caravan through northern Persia, Kurdistan, and Turkey.

On her return to England, Bird spoke out against the atrocities that were being committed against the Armenians under the Ottoman sultan Abd al-Hamid II, who had ordered their extermination. Bird met with William Gladstone, the British prime minister, and addressed a parliamentary committee on the subject. Having by this time become a celebrity in her native land, Bird was made a fellow of the Royal Scottish Geographical Society; she also became the first female member of the Royal Geographical Society.

Return to Asia

In 1894 Bird traveled to Yokohama in Japan and from there into Korea. She spent several months in that country before being forced to leave at the outbreak of the Sino-Japanese War, which would lead to the Japanese occupation of Korea. From Korea she went to Mukden in Manchuria and photographed Chinese soldiers headed for the front; she then managed to regain entry into Korea, where she witnessed the devastation of the war.

In 1896 Bird went from Korea to the Yangtze River in China, sailing by boat up the river as far as she could go and then traveling overland into the province of Szechwan. In Szechwan she was attacked by a mob. Calling her a "foreign devil," they trapped her in the top floor of a house, which they set on fire. She was rescued at the last minute by a detachment of soldiers. Later in her trip she was again attacked. Refusing to be intimidated, however, she traveled through the mountains bordering Tibet before returning home in 1897.

Bird based her last book, *The Yangtze River and Beyond,* on her experiences in China. This unusual and daring traveler continued to explore the world until the end of her life. She made her first trip to Africa when she was 70 years old and traveled to Morocco in 1901. Upon her return to Edinburgh she became ill, dying shortly thereafter.

Anne Blunt

Born 1837

Died December 15, 1917,
Near Cairo, Egypt

Wilfrid Scawen Blunt

Born August 17, 1840,
Petworth House, Sussex, England

Died September 10, 1922,
Newbuildings, Sussex, England

During their travels in Arabia, Lady Anne Blunt and Sir Wilfrid Scawen Blunt became surprisingly integrated into the Bedouin culture. They adopted many Arab ways, including political views that were not acceptable to most English people during the late nineteenth century. Both wrote about their travels, and Wilfrid became well known as an English poet.

Lady Anne Isabella Noel was a granddaughter of Lord Byron, the famous English poet. Born into a noble family, she spent most of her childhood on the Continent, where she learned to speak several languages. She was also an accomplished artist and violinist. She owned two violins made by Antonio Stradivari, the famous seventeenth-century Italian violin maker, and she practiced five hours every day.

Wilfrid Scawen Blunt, also from a wealthy family, was born in the English county of Sussex. His father died when Wilfrid was only two years old, and he spent an unhappy childhood traveling with his mother and attending boarding

Lady Anne and Sir Wilfrid Blunt, an English couple, visited the Bedouin tribes of Iraq and central Arabia. Anne was the first European woman to travel in Arabia.

schools. At the age of 18 he joined the British Foreign Service. For the next 12 years he served in various posts in Europe and South America.

Marriage and travel

Anne and Wilfrid met in Florence, Italy, and they were married in London on June 8, 1869. Three years later Wilfrid inherited his father's title and estates. In 1873 Anne gave birth to a daughter, their only child. The Blunts saw their new wealth as an opportunity to travel. The Middle East and North Africa were the areas that most interested them. In 1873 they made a trip to Constantinople (now the city of Istanbul) in Turkey, as well as to Asia Minor. The following year they went to Algeria in North Africa and journeyed into the Sahara Desert. In 1875-76 they returned to North Africa in order to visit Egypt.

Both of the Blunts had a desire to see Arabia, now known as the Arabian Peninsula, which lies in southwestern Asia. Thus, they chose it as their next destination. Leaving England in November 1877, they landed at Alexandretta at the eastern end of the Mediterranean Sea. From there they traveled to Aleppo in northern Syria, where they called on the British consul, who was Anne's distant relative. During their monthlong stay in the city, the Blunts discussed their plans with the consul. He encouraged them to visit the Bedouin tribes of the Tigris and Euphrates river valleys in the northern part of Arabia.

Life among the Bedouins

Little was known about the Bedouins in the outside world. The Blunts were intrigued by the idea of visiting these nomadic people and learning more about their way of life. After assembling a small caravan, the Blunts set out across the Syrian Desert in January 1878. They soon encountered resistance from the Turks, who had sovereignty over the area at the time. Almost immediately they were detained in the town of Deyr by Turkish officials, who suspected the Blunts were spies. After being freed a week later, they traveled on to Baghdad (now in Iraq).

Heading north, they began to travel from one Bedouin encampment to another. The Blunts had adopted Arab dress and rode on Arabian stallions, which they found more comfortable than camels. In mid-March they reached the camp of Faris, a powerful sheikh, or leader, of the Shammar tribe. Faris liked the Blunts very much and adopted Wilfrid as his "blood brother" during an impressive ceremony.

The Blunts' next stop was the ruins of Palmyra, an ancient city on the northern edge of the Syrian Desert. They met the son of a local sheikh, Muhammad ibn Aruk, who served as their guide to Palmyra. He then led them south to the camp of the Anazeh tribe and to the enormous tent city of the Rowallah tribe, which contained 20,000 tents and 150,000 camels.

On the last night of the Blunts' trip, Muhammad and Wilfrid became blood brothers, and the sheikh's son offered to take them on a trip into central Arabia the following year. Heading home, the Blunts passed through Damascus, Syria, where they were shocked at the manners of a group of visiting English tourists. They decided they liked the ways of the desert better. The Blunts took six Arabian horses back to England with them. With these mares they started a breeding farm for racehorses that was to become world famous.

> ### Bedouins
> The Bedouins live in nomadic tribal communities headed by sheikhs, although all members are considered equal; each tribe, or family group, is granted a section of land for maintaining their livelihood. Bedouins are primarily sheep and camel breeders, avoiding agricultural work, which does not accommodate their mobile way of life. Bedouins are noted for their hospitality, as well as for their code of swift justice, whereby punishment is immediately administered for a crime. Devout followers of Islam, the Bedouins now comprise about 10 percent of the population in the Middle East. During the twentieth century settlement policies have forced the Bedouins to become less nomadic.

Return to Arabia

Remembering Muhammad's offer to take them into central Arabia, the Blunts returned to Damascus in November 1878. They journeyed to the Najd, the central region of the Arabian Peninsula, where they were met by Muhammad. The three travelers took the Islamic pilgrimage route south toward Mecca. At one point they were surrounded by a Bedouin raiding party but were left unharmed because of Muhammad's presence.

The first large town the Blunts reached was Jauf, located on the northern edge of the Nafud Desert. South of Jauf they met distant relatives of Muhammad, and Wilfrid led the negotiations to arrange a marriage for the young man. With the city of Hail as their destination, the Blunts then crossed the red sands of the Nafud Desert, a journey that took 12 days.

Their visit to Hail was fascinating. They were received by the emir, and Anne was invited to visit the harem. Later she wrote about the boring life of the women in the harem. One evening at a banquet the Blunts were shown a telephone. Since this curious invention was only three years old, the Blunts had never seen one before. They also rode in the desert on the emir's horses, which were the most famous in Arabia. Wilfrid spent time studying the traditional methods of Arab government, which he was to write about on his return.

Hardship in the desert

The Blunts left Hail with a party of Persians who were returning to Iran after having made the pilgrimage to Mecca. When their caravan ran out of food along the way, they all traveled the last 170 miles in six days with nothing to eat. The Blunts finally reached Baghdad a month later in the middle of a heavy rainstorm. Their hardships were not over. Although Anne now wanted to return to England, Wilfrid had agreed to proceed on to India, where he was to make a report about the possibility of building a railroad from the Tigris River to the Persian Gulf.

The trip to India was a disaster because Wilfrid nearly died of dysentery. Anne wrote in a letter, "Wilfrid will never want to go on any hard journey again, I will swear to that!" She later described their journey as "disagreeable, difficult, dangerous and all but disastrous ... disappointing and disheartening." They finally reached the Persian Gulf port of Būshehr on April 25, 1879, after enduring a difficult 2,000 miles.

The Blunts were probably the first Europeans in modern times to travel all the way from the Mediterranean to the Persian Gulf. When they arrived at the door of the British consul, the guards refused to allow them in because they could not believe these two vagabonds were really English. Before returning to England the Blunts traveled on to India to complete their mission.

Final years

Back home the Blunts began to lose many former friends. Their travels had given them new political views, many of which were not popular with the ruling class in England. For instance, Wilfrid advocated Arabian nationalism because he was unhappy about the wave of Western imperialism engulfing western Asia. He ran for a seat in Parliament but was not elected. His anticolonial feelings were so strong that he was shunned by former associates. He was even jailed for a short time in 1888 for advocating the right of the Irish to rule themselves.

These two unusual people continued to be influenced by their experiences in Arabia until the end of their lives. In 1882 the Blunts returned to Egypt and bought a large estate called Sheykh Obeyd outside Cairo. It sat in the desert near the dramatic pyramids of Egypt. After they were separated, the estate became Anne's principal residence, and she generally spoke Arabic rather than English. Anne spent her final years in Egypt and died in 1917 at Sheykh Obeyd. Wilfrid died in England five years later. When he was buried on the grounds of his estate in England, his funeral was conducted in the manner of the Bedouin burial ceremony.

Sidi Mubarak Bombay

*Born c. 1820,
Malawi, Africa*

*Died October 12, 1885,
Zanzibar, Africa*

Sidi Mubarak Bombay, a freed African slave, served as a leader of caravans for European explorers in Africa.

Sidi Mubarak Bombay, a former African slave, was an unsung hero of African exploration. As leaders of caravans, Bombay and men like him were indispensable to the various parties of Europeans who explored Africa during the nineteenth century. They made the expeditions possible by hiring and training porters and guides, bartering for food with native tribes along the way, nursing the Europeans back to health when they became ill, and generally providing an efficient support system. Bombay was awarded a silver medal by the Royal Geographical Society in recognition of his outstanding service on an expedition led by the British explorer **John Hanning Speke** (see entry).

Sidi Mubarak was a member of the East African Yao tribe, whose homeland is around Lake Nyasa. At the age of 12 he was captured by Swahili traders and transported to the island of Zanzibar. After he was sold to an Arab merchant, he was taken to the city of Bombay, India. Upon the merchant's death Sidi Mubarak was freed and took the name of his adopted home, Bombay. Returning to Zanzibar, Bombay became a soldier in the army of the sultan of Zanzibar, who controlled a large part of the African mainland. He was posted to the small garrison of Chokwe, about seven miles from the coast.

Contributions to the Burton and Speke expedition

On February 8, 1857, the British explorers **Richard Burton** and John Hanning Speke arrived in Chokwe following a visit to the German missionary **Johannes Rebmann** (see separate entries) in Mombasa, an island off the coast of Kenya. Burton and Speke were recruiting porters and soldiers for an expedition into the interior of Africa to look for the source of the Nile. They paid the commander of the garrison at Chokwe for the services of six soldiers—among them Bombay—a guide, and five slaves. After making a short expedition into the interior, the two Englishmen were so impressed with Bombay's abilities that they hired him for a longer period. Speke in particular liked Bombay because they could converse in Hindi, a language Speke had learned when he was a commander in the British army in India.

The expedition departed on June 16, 1857. From the start Bombay proved to be the most loyal of all the Africans and Asians in the crew; he and his "brother" Mabruki sometimes carried Speke and Burton when they were too ill to walk. The party reached the Arab trading center of Tabora (now in Tanzania) on November 7, 1857. They stayed there several weeks to recover. When the party left, Bombay did not follow immediately, but he caught up with the expedition when they reached Lake Tanganyika on February 13, 1858. Because both Burton and Speke were almost blind, it was Bombay who first sighted the immense lake.

Once again the expedition returned to Tabora to recuperate. Burton stayed there while Speke and Bombay continued to search for a large lake they had heard about in the north. In August 1858 they reached Lake Ukerewe, which Speke renamed Victoria in honor of the British queen. Speke correctly assumed that Lake Victoria was the source of the great Nile River. When they returned to Tabora, Burton did not believe Speke; he felt there had been a misunderstanding resulting from Bombay's faulty translation of the Swahili language. On the return trip to Zanzibar, Bombay cared for Speke, who had become ill with fever. Burton and Speke sailed for England on March 22, 1858.

Second trip with Speke

In 1860 the Royal Geographical Society sent Speke, accompanied by the Scottish explorer James Augustus Grant, back to Africa to verify Speke's claim. Bombay, who in the meantime had obtained a job with the British consul in Zanzibar, was at the dock to meet the two men. They hired him immediately. Bombay's presence proved to be invaluable. Speke freely acknowledged that they could not have made the expedition without Bombay's help. Leaving in September and arriving on January 23, 1861, they traveled the 500 miles to Tabora in 71 days, an average of slightly more than 7 miles a day.

Speke found the laborers Bombay had hired much more efficient than the slaves and soldiers he had contracted. When they encountered a local war on the next leg of the trip, Bombay successfully negotiated their passage with the king of Karagwe and then with the king of Buganda. Following an argument with Speke, Bombay quit the expedition for a while, but he was later persuaded to come back. The party reached the site where the Nile flows out of Lake Victoria on July 21, 1862, conclusively proving Speke's theory. When the group was blocked from going forward by King Kamurasi of Bunyoro, Bombay again saved the day with his skillful negotiations. On February 15, 1863, they arrived in the town of Gondokoro in present-day southern Sudan, where they were met by British explorers **Samuel White Baker** and his future wife, **Florence** (see combined entry).

By the time the Speke party triumphantly entered Cairo, "Speke's Faithful," the 18 survivors from the original group that Bombay had hired three years earlier, had their photograph taken together and were treated as heroes. Speke parted with his "Faithful" in July. They were each given an extra year's wage and a $10.00 bonus to take home with them. Speke later praised Bombay as "the life and success of the expedition." It was because of the success of this trip that Bombay was awarded his silver medal from the Royal Geographical Society. Each of the other "Faithful" received a bronze medal.

Problems on the Stanley expedition

Bombay's next encounter with a European explorer was not without difficulty on both sides. The explorer, **Henry Morton Stanley,** had arrived in Zanzibar to begin a search for **David Livingstone** (see separate entries), who had been missing and was presumed dead. Stanley hired Bombay to outfit the expedition and oversee 12 soldiers; the party left the coast in March 1871. An argument between Stanley and Bombay in May led to Bombay's temporary demotion.

They reached Tabora in June and stayed until late July because Bombay was unwilling to leave sooner. Soon after they departed from Tabora, Bombay found himself having to protect Stanley as the party blundered into a war between Africans and Arabs. Forced to return to Tabora, they set out again on a different route. In October there was a mutiny among the crew when Stanley refused to allow the men an additional day of rest. Blaming Bombay for the troubles, Stanley had him put in chains for a short time before releasing him and restoring his command.

When the expedition reached Ujiji on the shores of Lake Tanganyika on November 10, 1871, they were met by David Susi, who led them to Livingstone. Stanley's first words to Livingstone have gone down in history. A famous example of British restraint, Stanley's greeting reportedly was, "Dr. Livingstone, I presume?" Livingstone, Stanley, and their African helpers set off across Lake Tanganyika, with Bombay serving as a canoe rower. On the return trip Bombay was put in charge of one of the groups of men. It took them six weeks to get to Tabora, and they reached Zanzibar on May 7, 1872. A pleased Stanley paid Bombay a generous bonus for his work.

Voyage across Africa with Cameron

Experiencing ill health, Livingstone set out on his last expedition. For months he was out of touch with civilization. Verney Lovett Cameron, who was charged with bringing Livingstone out of Africa, hired Bombay to be his caravan leader. The expedition had already reached Tabora when **James Chuma** (see entry), Livingstone's servant, arrived with the news that Livingstone had died on May 1, 1873. Cameron continued on, hoping to explore Lake Tanganyika and find its outlet. With Bombay in command of one of the two canoes, their journey began on March 13, 1875. Cameron became ill and probably owed his life to Bombay, who took care of him. After finding that the Lukuga River was the lake's only outlet, they returned to Ujiji in May. During the trip Bombay had traveled almost all the way around Lake Tanganyika.

In August, when Cameron decided to cross the lake in an effort to find the Congo River, they were met by the infamous slave trader Tippu Tib. The expedition successfully crossed the African continent, arriving at the coast of the Atlantic Ocean three months later. Of the 54 members who reached the Atlantic, 49 of them had been recruited by Bombay in Zanzibar. In Luanda Cameron bought a schooner and sent Bombay and the rest of his crew home; they sailed south around the Cape of Good Horn and then north to Zanzibar.

Retirement in Zanzibar

Bombay was then asked by the Reverend W. Salter Price to lead a caravan to Uganda with the purpose of opening a mission there. Bombay made a preliminary trip, but when he was informed that the Royal Geographical Society had offered him a life pension, he decided to retire. He died in Zanzibar on October 12, 1885, having spent a lifetime working with the superstars of African exploration. His intelligence, character, and resourcefulness had earned their respect and admiration.

Daniel Boone

*Born 1734,
Near Reading, Pennsylvania*

*Died September 26, 1820,
St. Charles, Missouri*

During his adventurous life as a hunter, explorer, and pioneer, Daniel Boone weathered a series of setbacks and misfortunes that would have discouraged others. But his perseverance enabled him to contribute greatly to the exploration of the North American wilderness.

Early life

Boone was born near Reading, Pennsylvania, the son of Squire and Sarah Morgan Boone. When he was 15, his family moved to the Yadkin Valley in western North Carolina. As a young man, he fought briefly in the French and Indian War, serving as a wagon driver in General Edward Braddock's expedition against Fort Duquesne in Pittsburgh. When Braddock's army was defeated on July 9, 1755, Boone escaped on one of the wagon horses.

Returning to North Carolina, Boone married Rebecca Bryan. They built a log cabin and began farming, but a raid by

Daniel Boone, an American frontiersman, founded Boonesboro, Kentucky, the first American settlement west of the Appalachian Mountains.

Native Americans drove them from their home. Boone was able to find work as a wagoner for a tobacco plantation in Virginia. He later joined a group of volunteers fighting the Cherokee tribe in Tennessee. The defeat of the Cherokees allowed the Boone family to return to their farm in North Carolina. In the following years Boone began to spend more time hunting and trapping. After a trip to Florida in 1765, he tried to convince his wife to move to Pensacola, then the capital of the new British colony of West Florida, but she refused.

Expeditions to Kentucky

While serving in the war, Boone had met a hunter named John Finley, who told him about Kentucky, the land west of Virginia on the far slope of the Appalachians. Boone made his first trip to eastern Kentucky in the winter of 1767-68. Soon after Finley showed up at Boone's farm, and the two planned another expedition.

Boone, Finley, and two other men left the Yadkin Valley in May 1769 with provisions supplied by Judge Richard Henderson, a land speculator in North Carolina. Traveling up the Watauga River valley and over the mountains, Boone's party then descended into the valley of the south fork of the Holston River in what is now northeastern Tennessee. Crossing the Clinch and Powell rivers, they reached the Cumberland Gap, a pass in the Appalachian Mountains, where they went into Kentucky. At Station Camp Creek, in present-day Estill County, they split into two groups.

The winter of 1769-70 was very cold and difficult. In December Boone and a companion were captured by a Shawnee raiding party; they were able to escape after a week but lost most of their supplies and ammunition. Luckily they were soon reunited with Boone's brother, Squire, and the fourth member of the party. But later one of the men went out hunting alone and was not seen again. Another returned home, leaving Boone and his brother alone.

In the spring of 1770 Boone's brother returned to North Carolina to get more ammunition. Boone traveled alone through the Kentucky and Licking river valleys and explored the Ohio River down to the area around present-day Louisville. When his brother returned, Boone spent the summer hunting along the Kentucky River, and the next winter he trapped furs in the Green and Cumberland valleys. In March 1771 they headed back to North Carolina with a large number of furs. Near the Cumberland Gap the brothers met a band of Cherokee tribesmen, who took their horses, supplies, and furs. The Boones returned on foot to the Yadkin Valley with nothing to show for the two years they had spent in Kentucky.

Boone told his neighbors about the fertile lands of Kentucky and in 1773 convinced a group of settlers to accompany him back over the mountains. They were attacked at the Cumberland Gap in October 1773 by Native Americans, who killed Boone's 16-year-old son, James, and five others. Against Boone's advice the rest of the party returned to North Carolina. After spending the winter in an abandoned cabin in the Clinch River valley, Boone and his family crossed over the mountains again and returned home.

Clearing the Wilderness Road

Meanwhile, Judge Henderson remained convinced that Kentucky offered great opportunities for land speculation. Although he did not have a charter, he organized the Transylvania Company to purchase land from Native Americans. He hired Boone to negotiate a purchase from the Cherokee tribe, which resulted in the Watauga Treaty. In March 1775 Henderson sent Boone with a party of 28 others to mark a trail across Cherokee territory into Kentucky as far as the Kentucky River. This was the beginning of what became known as the Wilderness Road. That spring Boone began building a fort on the Kentucky River, which later became Boonesboro (in present-day Madison County).

Henderson tried to organize a separate government for his Kentucky settlements, but the Continental Congress, which was then meeting in Philadelphia, disapproved. George Rogers Clark, a frontiersman and Revolutionary War leader, arrived to annex Kentucky as part of Virginia. Boone was appointed a justice and captain of the local militia. He spent the following years guiding parties of settlers to the new territory.

Capture by the Shawnee

In February 1778 Boone was again captured by Shawnee warriors. He was first taken to Detroit, a British outpost, and then moved to a camp at Chillicothe, Ohio. According to some accounts, Boone was adopted by his captors and promised to persuade the new settlers to surrender. He escaped four months later, however, making his way back to Boonesboro just in time to prepare for an attack by Shawnee warriors aided by British forces. The settlers spent the summer strengthening their defenses. The attack came in September, but, after extensive fighting and repeated efforts at negotiation, the British and Shawnee finally retreated.

At the time Boone arrived in Boonesboro, he learned his wife had returned to North Carolina, as she assumed he was dead. After the defeat of the Shawnee, Boone returned to North Carolina to find his wife and bring her back to Kentucky. In October 1779 he also brought back with him a new party of settlers, who included Abraham Lincoln's grandmother and grandfather. Upon arriving in Kentucky, however, they learned their deeds were not valid because the government had not accepted Henderson's claims to Kentucky. In order to rectify the situation, Boone had to deliver $20,000 to Richmond, the capital of Virginia, to purchase new land warrants. Not long after his journey had begun, however, Boone was robbed of the entire amount.

Election to legislature

Boone was elected to the Virginia legislature in 1781. The American Revolution was still being fought, and the legislature was meeting in Charlottesville, Virginia. In June 1781 the town was raided by British cavalry, and Boone and two other legislators were captured and held briefly. Before his election Boone had moved his family home to a place farther west called Boone's Station. When he returned from Charlottesville to his remote farm, he was attacked by a group of

Native Americans. During the skirmish his brother Edward was killed. Boone's son Israel was also killed while defending an outpost named Bryan's Station, located near present-day Lexington, Kentucky. These attacks led to a major campaign against the Native Americans, which eventually ended the threat to the Kentucky settlements.

In spite of holding many local offices, Boone had never been careful to register his own land claims. As a result, his rights to land were increasingly challenged, and he eventually lost all of the land he had settled up to this point. In the spring of 1786 Boone and his wife moved to Maysville, Kentucky, on the Ohio River, where they ran a tavern and a store for travelers coming down the river. Two years later they moved near the junction of the Kanawha and Ohio rivers, now in West Virginia. In 1791 Boone was chosen to represent his county in the first Virginia legislature formed after the adoption of the U.S. Constitution. During this time his wife kept the family store, and Boone also hunted and trapped in the Kanawha Valley.

Final years

Boone's son Daniel Morgan Boone founded in 1796 a settlement called Femme Osage, then in Spanish territory. The area, now in the state of Missouri, is near the town of St. Charles north of the Missouri River. A few years later Boone and his wife joined their son. Boone was appointed a magistrate in the Spanish administration and served until the territory was taken over by the Americans in 1804. Although his title to Missouri lands was contested, it was finally confirmed by an Act of Congress in 1814.

In 1810 Boone traveled back to Kentucky to pay off his debts, an act that reportedly gave him enormous satisfaction but also left him with only 50 cents in his pocket. After the death of his wife in 1813, he went to live with his son Nathan. Boone died at the age of 85, having made a remarkable contribution to the settlement of the American frontier.

Louis-Antoine de Bougainville

*Born November 11, 1729,
Paris, France*

*Died August 31, 1811,
Paris, France*

> Louis-Antoine de Bougainville, a French naval officer, commanded the first French expedition to sail around the world.

Louis-Antoine de Bougainville, a French naval officer, led an expedition around the world in the late 1760s. It was the first time that a French ship had circumnavigated the globe, and on the voyage was also the first woman ever to sail around the world. Bougainville sighted many Pacific islands and, with the aid of new instruments, was able to pinpoint their locations for the first time. He carried out a secret assignment to obtain spice-plant seedlings for the French, who wanted to break the Dutch monopoly in the spice trade. *Bougainvillea*, a genus of shrubs, vines, and small trees, was named after him.

Establishment of a new French colony

When the French and Indian War ended in 1763, France had lost all of its possessions in North America and India to the British. As a result, the French turned to other parts of the world to start a new empire. A nobleman and military officer, Bougainville had served in the war in North America as secretary to General Montcalm, the French commander in chief. A loyal officer of the king of France, Bougainville offered to lead an expedition to establish a new French colony.

Bougainville was soon given an assignment. In 1765 he sailed with a group of colonists to the Falkland Islands in the South Atlantic, which the French called the Malouines after the French port of Saint-Malo. At the same time, Spain had established colonies on the nearby mainland of South America where Argentina is today. The French had been living on the islands for only a year when King Charles III of Spain claimed the Malouines. Since Spain was France's most important ally, the French king, Louis XV, turned Bougainville's colony over to Spain. The Spanish changed the islands' name slightly, calling them the Malvinas.

Disputes over the ownership of the islands continued. At the same time that Bougainville was establishing the French colony, the British captain John Byron was in the westernmost islands, which he claimed for England. The British claim would be disputed by Argentina, an antagonism that almost two hundred years later led to the Falklands War of 1982. Since the French colonists now needed to be removed, Bougainville returned to the Falklands in 1766. Reaching a settlement in April 1767, he transported the colonists to the seaport of Rio de Janeiro, Brazil; from there they took other ships back to France.

Voyage to circumnavigate the globe

After the departure of the colonists, Bougainville turned to other business, as he had received orders to sail around the world. This was to be the first time that a French ship circumnavigated the globe. Aboard ship was a young astronomer named Pierre Antoine Verón, who was able to use new instruments to calculate for the first time the correct longitude of the places they visited, an important scientific advancement. Although Bougainville did not realize it, also aboard his ship was a woman, who, in fact, would become the first woman ever to sail around the world.

Bougainville commanded two ships, the *Boudeuse* and

the *Etoile*. They left Brazil in November 1767, sailing through the Strait of Magellan into the Pacific Ocean on January 26, 1768. Their first stop was supposed to be the Juan Fernandez Islands, but the wind blew the ships off course, so Bougainville headed instead to the Tuamotu Islands. After passing several small islands where it was not possible to anchor, they finally reached the larger, mountainous island of Tahiti, which turned out to be a pleasant resting place for the crew.

Stopover at Tahiti

Bougainville and his men were the second group of Europeans ever to reach Tahiti, the British captain **Samuel Wallis** (see combined Philip Carteret-Samuel Wallis entry) having been there the previous year. Bougainville, however, landed his ships on another side of the island on April 4, 1768. He and his crew stayed only two weeks, but his reports echoed those of Wallis; the Europeans thought the island was paradise on Earth. In general, the Frenchmen and the Tahitians got along well, and Bougainville was entertained by the local chief. When he left, Bougainville took with him the chief's brother, who said he wanted to see France. The Tahitian did reach France, but it is not known if he ever returned to Tahiti.

While in Tahiti Bougainville was also to discover something new about one of his crew members. Before the ships left France, an officer had hired a young man named Bare, who was looking for a job as a servant on the expedition. When the crew came on shore in Tahiti, the Tahitians recognized what the French had not—Bare was not a man. Bare confessed, revealing that she was an orphan who had first disguised herself as a boy to get employment as a valet. Later, when she learned about Bougainville's expedition to sail around the world, she decided to continue the disguise in order to have an adventure that otherwise would have been impossible for a woman at the time.

Search for the great southern continent

While sailing west from Tahiti to Samoa, Bougainville made an important decision. Previously navigators had sailed northwest from this area in order to get around the northern part of New Guinea. Bougainville decided to sail directly west to see if he could find Terras Australis, the great continent that many geographers thought existed in the Southern Hemisphere. As a result of his westward path, he sailed directly into the middle of the islands of Vanuatu, which had not been seen by Europeans since their discovery by Pedro Fernandez de Quiros in 1605. Bougainville was able to confirm what Quiros had found and record accurately the location of the islands.

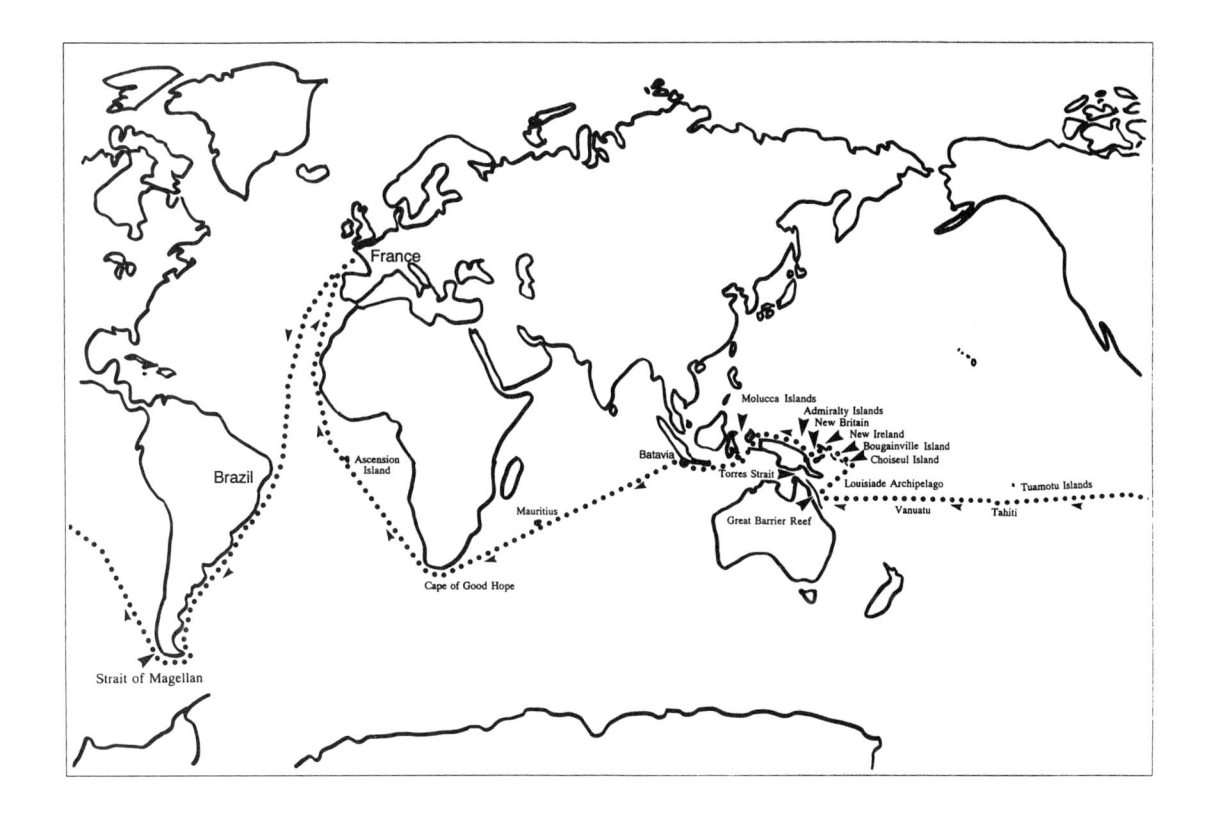

Bougainville did not know whether these islands were part of the great southern continent he sought. There is, in fact, a vast stretch of sea between Vanuatu and the Australian continent, but Bougainville continued to sail west. On the night of June 4, 1768, he almost wrecked his ship on the Great Barrier Reef, which lies off the shore of northern Australia. Unfortunately, Bougainville could not see the vast continent behind the reef. He tried for several days to sail north around it but finally gave up and turned back east.

If Bougainville had continued north from the Great Barrier Reef, he would have come upon the Torres Strait; he would therefore possibly have confirmed the existence of the continent that was later discovered and named Australia.

If Bougainville had continued north, he would have come upon the Torres Strait, which separates Australia from New Guinea. This strait had been discovered by the Spanish navigator Luis Vaez de Torres in 1606. Because news of his discovery had never been published, it was thought that New Guinea and Australia were all part of the same landmass. Had Bougainville reached the Torres Strait, he would have confirmed the existence of the separate continent that was later to be discovered and named Australia.

Arrival at the Solomons

Once Bougainville turned east, he entered a maze of small islands and coral reefs that he named the Louisiade Archipelago. This part of the voyage was nerve-racking for the French captain and his crew because the boats seemed to be constantly in danger of running aground. They finally emerged from this dangerous area on June 20, 1768, and headed east to the Solomon Islands.

The Solomons had been discovered by the Spanish explorer Alvaro de Mendaña in 1567, but his map locations had been so inexact that Europeans had not been able to find them since that time. Some navigators even doubted the existence of the islands, but the Solomons had been stumbled upon by the English captain **Philip Carteret** (see entry) just a few months before Bougainville's arrival. Ironically, neither Carteret nor Bougainville realized he had rediscovered the Solomons. Bougainville did, however, give many of these islands their present-day names. The largest of the Solomons he named Bougainville Island.

Bougainville headed north through the Solomons to the large island of New Britain, where he landed his ships on July 7, 1768, to obtain fresh water and provisions. By an amazing coincidence, he had landed next to the same cove where Carteret had rested in September of the previous year. One of Bougainville's men found a plaque that the English sailors had nailed to a tree. While the French were on the island of New Britain, an important scientific advancement was made. The astronomer Verón observed a solar eclipse and was able to use the information to calculate for the first time the width of the Pacific Ocean.

Secret mission in the Moluccas

The *Boudeuse* and *Etoile* sailed north and west along the coast of New Ireland, the Admiralty Islands, and New Guinea until they reached a Dutch settlement in the Moluccas Islands (or Spice Islands) in September. While in the Moluccas, Bougainville carried out a secret mission—to collect specimens of clove and nutmeg plants. He would take the seedlings to the French colony of Mauritius in the Indian Ocean, where they could be cultivated. In this way the French hoped to destroy the Dutch monopoly in the spice trade.

From the Moluccas the French ships sailed to Batavia (now Djakarta), the capital of the Dutch East Indies, on the island of Java, which they reached on September 28. From there Bougainville headed toward the island of Mauritius. He stayed there for several months so his men could recover from scurvy, a disease caused by a lack of vitamin C and that commonly afflicted sailors on long sea journeys. Many also needed to recover from a fever they had caught in the East Indies.

Now on the last leg of the journey, Bougainville's ships sailed around the Cape of Good Hope at the southern tip of Africa. Bougainville met Carteret at Ascension Island off the western coast of Africa and then sailed on to France, arriving at the French harbor of Saint-Malo on March 16, 1769. Only seven lives were lost among his crew, a record for that time.

Final years in France

After arriving in France Bougainville wrote a two-volume account of his trip around the world. This work, which was published in 1772, influenced other French writers, such as the philosophers Jean-Jacques Rousseau and Denis Diderot. Bougainville continued to serve his country. He fought in the French navy during the American Revolution, a war in which France was allied with the newly formed United States. He was made a field marshal in the French army in 1780.

Bougainville retired during the years of the French Revolution to write scientific papers. After the French emperor Napoleon Bonaparte came to power, he became a senator and a count of the empire. He was eventually awarded the Legion of Honor, the highest French decoration. Bougainville died in Paris in 1811.

Louise Arner Boyd

*Born September 16, 1887,
San Rafael, California*

*Died September 14, 1972,
San Francisco, California*

Louise Arner Boyd, an heiress turned Arctic explorer, delighted in living two totally different lives. In San Francisco she was a wealthy socialite. There she entertained lavishly and behaved properly at a time when appearances were all important to a woman's social standing. In her second life, as an explorer of Greenland, she became a seasoned professional. Often the only woman present on an expedition, she was tough and demanding, enduring with courage the hardships of the Arctic. Leading seven expeditions to this beautiful but dangerous area of the world, Boyd became an acknowledged authority on the eastern shores of Greenland.

Boyd was born on September 16, 1887, at Maple Lawn, an estate in San Rafael, California, now a San Francisco suburb. Her great-grandfather had purchased Maple Lawn 20 years after arriving in California from New York. Boyd's grandfather had made a fortune in the gold rush, and her father made a great deal of money in other ventures and as president of the Boyd Investment Company. Boyd was taught by gov-

Louise Arner Boyd, an American explorer, financed and led several expeditions to the Arctic. She became an expert on the fjords and glaciers of the eastern coast of Greenland.

ernesses and attended private schools; she never went to college and became a debutante in 1906.

Early trips to the Arctic

Boyd's two brothers had been sickly from birth and died as teenagers. Her mother and father died in 1919 and 1920, respectively. Finding herself the sole heir to the family fortune at the age of 33, Boyd assumed the presidency of her father's investment firm. After making the conventional grand tour of Europe with a friend, Boyd decided in 1924 to travel to the Spitsbergen Islands in a remote area between the coasts of Norway and Greenland. Cruising along these shores in a small chartered boat, Boyd was stunned with their majesty and beauty. Making a decision that would change her life forever, she vowed to return.

In 1926 Boyd gathered a small group of friends for a polar bear hunting excursion to Franz Josef Land, a place so close to the Arctic that it was only infrequently visited by seal and walrus hunters. Boyd's party sailed on the M.S. *Hobby,* a boat that had been used by Arctic explorers **Roald Amundsen** and **Lincoln Ellsworth** (see separate entries). Having become seriously interested in documenting this largely unknown land, Boyd returned from her trip with thousands of feet of film and more than 700 photographs.

In 1928 Boyd chartered the *Hobby* again; the ship was fully provisioned and ready to sail when Amundsen was reported missing in a search for Umberto Nobile, an Italian pilot and explorer. Immediately putting the *Hobby* at the disposal of the Norwegian government, Boyd joined in the rescue effort. They searched for four months. Although Nobile was rescued by another search team, Amundsen was never found. Boyd made a complete photographic record of every aspect of the search—for example, the ships and planes involved and the terrain covered—and King Haakon VII of Norway rewarded her efforts with the medal of St. Olaf.

Scientific discoveries

Influenced by the scientists and explorers she had met on

the Amundsen search, Boyd carefully prepared for her next voyage to the Arctic. She chose the sturdy vessel *Veslekari,* an oak-ribbed, 125-foot veteran of the northern seas, and embarked in 1931 with six friends. The party sailed inside a number of astonishing fjords, which were guarded by treacherous ice fields that shifted without warning. Boyd painstakingly photographed the expedition using the best equipment available, and her photographs helped reveal errors made in previous mapmaking. The inner reaches of one Arctic inlet, the Ice Fjord, were named "Miss Boyd Land" in her honor.

Having received recognition for her discoveries, Boyd was able to take several scientists on her next trip on the *Veslekari* in 1933. Boyd herself was the leader and official photographer. When the botanist fell ill soon after the party set sail, Boyd took over his tasks as well. This expedition included a four-week exploration of completely uninhabited land. Carrying equipment and provisions on their backs and crossing slippery glaciers, fields of boulders, and icy streams, the scientists achieved their goal of reaching the Jaette Glacier. After returning to the ship, they barely made it out of the fjords before winter set in, and the *Veslekari* had to navigate through fierce gales and floating ice floes. The findings of this trip were documented in a book titled *The Fiord Region of East Greenland,* published by the American Geographical Society, featuring 300 of Boyd's black-and-white photographs.

> ## Fjords
>
> A fjord is a narrow sea inlet along the coastline of a glacial region. Fjords are located in such places as Alaska, Antarctica, Greenland, New Zealand, Norway, British Columbia, Scotland, and even southern Chile. Norway in particular is noted for its beautiful fjords. Formed by glaciers, fjords resemble steep canyons, and their extremely high, perpendicular walls may be covered with brilliant-white ice formations. Nearby streams sometimes tumble over the walls, creating spectacular waterfalls. Usually shallow at the mouth, fjords become quite deep farther inland; for instance, the Sogne Fjord in Norway is 4,078 feet deep and 127 miles long.

Appointment as naval consultant

In 1934 Boyd was named a delegate to the International Geographical Congress. Although the expedition she undertook in 1937 was turned back by an early winter, she achieved a real breakthrough in 1938. She landed her ship on the eastern shore of Greenland at a point farther north than any ship had ever ventured. Upon her return Boyd was awarded the Cullum Geographical Medal by the American Geographical Society, becoming only the second woman to receive the award.

This was to be her last expedition to the Arctic, as the world apprehensively watched the German invasion of Scandinavia. Boyd was asked to delay publishing the book she had been working on and instead led a government-sponsored expedition that examined magnetic and radio phenomena in the Arctic. Soon the United States was involved in World War II, and her intimate knowledge of the Arctic waters became invaluable to the U.S. Navy. Boyd was appointed special consultant to the Military Intelligence Division. Her book, *The Coast of Northeast Greenland,* was published after the war in 1948.

Final years

Boyd continued to travel and never relinquished her role as a leader in San Francisco society. In 1955, at the age of 66, she chartered a plane and flew over the North Pole, fulfilling a lifelong dream. For a while she retained her apartment on fashionable Nob Hill in San Francisco, but she was eventually forced to give up her estate. Boyd died in a nursing home on September 14, 1972, just short of her eighty-fifth birthday. Her large fortune having dissipated, she existed at the end of her life through the kindness of friends.

Boyd's achievements were acknowledged and highly publicized during her lifetime. Although she had never attended college, she received three honorary degrees, countless medals, and memberships in the most distinguished scientific societies in the world. This recognition is all the more meaningful because at the beginning of her career Boyd was ridiculed for being a woman and a socialite who lacked scientific credentials.

Pierre Savorgnan de Brazza

*Born January 25, 1852,
Rome, Italy*

*Died September 14, 1905,
Dakar, Senegal*

B y the late 1800s the European powers were scrambling to divide the huge continent of Africa among themselves. The rivalry among explorers and countries was intense, and there were inevitably losers and winners. Brazza may be considered a winner. Largely through his efforts his adopted country, France, claimed a significant portion of the Congo. But Brazza would come to fight against the ruthless exploitation of the African population that occurred as these new territories were opened to commercial development.

Pierre-Paul-François-Camille Savorgnan de Brazza was born in Rome on January 25, 1852, the descendant of an aristocratic family. His father was an Italian nobleman who was prominent in nationalist and cultural circles. From the time he was a boy, Brazza was interested in a career at sea. Italy did not have a navy of its own, so Brazza received permission to continue his studies at the naval academy in France. Having become intensely loyal to France, he received his French citizenship in 1874. After serving in the French navy during the

Pierre Savorgnan de Brazza, an Italian nobleman in the service of France, explored along the Ogooüe and Congo rivers in West Africa, where he founded a French colony.

Franco-Prussian War, Brazza was assigned to the South Atlantic fleet and visited the western coast of Africa between 1882 and 1884. Although a previous French expedition had unsuccessfully tried to penetrate the interior of Gabon, Brazza believed that it could be done. If the Ogooúe River connected with the Lualaba River, he would have access to the upper Congo, which the English explorer **David Livingstone** (see entry) had recently discovered.

Voyage to the Congo

The French ministry approved his proposals, and Brazza set off from Bordeaux in August 1875. He was only 23 years old. He stopped at a trading post called Lambaréné, a place that later became famous as the site of Dr. Albert Schweitzer's hospital. He sailed up the Ogooúe only to find that it did not connect with the Lualaba. He then traveled overland to the Alima River, a tributary of the Congo, but was unable to follow it because of hostile tribes. Brazza never knew how close he had come until, shortly after he had returned to France, he learned that **Henry Morton Stanley** (see entry) had successfully navigated the Congo River.

Brazza's expedition had made him a hero in France, and he was approached by an agent of King Leopold of Belgium to help him claim further possessions in the Congo. Brazza, ever loyal to France, instead warned the French government of Leopold's intentions. The French government, now determined to claim part of the Congo, immediately approved an expedition with Brazza in charge. The purpose was to outmaneuver Stanley, who at this time was working for Leopold. Brazza's specific goal was to gain possession of the territory in the region of Stanley Pool, a large natural lake on the lower Congo.

Establishment of French control in the Congo

Brazza left France on his second expedition on December 27, 1879, with a small force of 11 Senegalese sailors. He rapidly worked his way up the Ogooúe and then crossed the watershed to a river, called the Olumo by local tribes, that turned out to be the Congo. Along the way Brazza asked the local chiefs to acknowledge French sovereignty. He signed a treaty with one of the most powerful chiefs, Makoko, on September 10, 1880. This accord gave France part of the right bank of the Congo and the adjacent territory. Brazza then went to the village of N'Tamo and set up a post under his Senegalese sergeant; the post would eventually grow into the city of Brazzaville, now the capital of the Congo.

From the new post Brazza traveled down the Congo and actually met Stanley at the village of Vivi near the mouth of the river on November 7, 1880. Brazza had won the race for France; when Stanley finally reached Stanley Pool, he found that the French had firmly established their authority on the west bank of the river. Brazza continued along the coast back to Libreville in Gabon, establishing supply posts and reinforcing France's claim to the territory. In 1881, however, Brazza was abruptly recalled to France. Trying to gain diplomatically what Stanley had lost, King Leopold had convinced the French government to give all of the Congo to Belgium.

Back in France, Brazza immediately started a campaign to convince the French government and the public of the potential value of colonies along the Congo. When Brazza and Stanley exchanged insults during a dinner in Paris organized to honor Stanley, the imagination of the French people was aroused. The vacillating French government finally confirmed the treaty with Makoko in December 1882.

Appointment as colonial governor

Brazza left on his third expedition with a large force to clearly establish French occupation of the Congo. Meanwhile, the great powers of Europe met in Berlin in November 1884 to divide up the African continent. As a result of Brazza's activities, what is now Gabon, Congo, and the Central African Republic were awarded to France. King Leopold was given the Congo Free State, now Zaire, as his personal territory.

In 1886 Brazza was appointed governor of the new French colony, where he served for a number of years. He personally supervised and coordinated numerous expeditions that solidified French claims between the Congo River and Lake Chad, thus containing German penetration from Cameroon. During that time he tried to develop the colony without violating the rights of the Africans. Brazza, however, was hindered in his efforts by the French government, which refused to invest the money that would have allowed for orderly growth and commerce. Brazza also opposed the issuing of large land grants to private firms, a policy that was pursued by Leopold in the adjoining territory. Leopold's holdings were ruled by private interests that made immense fortunes by exploiting the African labor force. Brazza was relieved of his position in 1898 as a result of flimsy charges made by **Jean-Baptiste Marchand** (see entry), a French explorer who had been sent to Africa the previous year to control the headwaters of the White Nile River.

Brazza's investigation into European brutality

Following Brazza's departure the French adopted Leopold's policy of granting concessions to large commercial companies to see if the Congo could be developed by private interests. In 1904 the situation in both the Congo Free State and the French Congo became an international scandal when enterprising journalists and public servants, such as Edmund Morel and Roger Casement, revealed that Africans were being brutalized and murdered for profit. The French government called Brazza out of retirement to investigate.

Brazza arrived in Libreville on April 29, 1905. He traveled in the colony for more than four months, encountering general hostility and deliberate noncooperation by the colonial civil service. He wrote a report attacking the conditions he found in the area. Saddened and ill with dysentery, Brazza left for France but died on the way in Dakar, Senegal (then part of French West Africa), on September 14, 1905. The French Parliament voted to suppress Brazza's report because it was considered too damaging to the prestige of France. Had he lived longer, Brazza might have seen at least some of those abuses eliminated.

Hermenegildo de Brito Capelo

*Born 1841,
Portugal*

*Died 1917,
Lisbon, Portugal*

Roberto Ivens

*Born 1850,
Portugal*

*Died January 28, 1898,
Off the coast of Africa*

The European powers long held trading posts along the coasts of Africa, but only in the second half of the nineteenth century did they begin to move inland, conquering African tribes and dividing the continent into separate colonies. Portugal had been an early participant in what came to be called the "Scramble for Africa," having already claimed Angola on the western coast and Mozambique on the eastern coast. The Portuguese plan was to unite these two colonies and thus control a broad band of territory across the middle of Africa.

In 1884 two Portuguese naval officers, Hermenegildo de Brito Capelo and Roberto Ivens, left on a hazardous journey across Africa to find an overland passage between the two colonies. The arduous trip took more than a year, and, having succeeded, they were honored by a reception with King Luis of Portugal. Capelo went on to an illustrious career serving the Crown, and Ivens remained a captain in the navy.

Hermenegildo de Brito Capelo and Roberto Ivens, two Portuguese naval officers, were sent on an expedition across the African continent from Angola to Mozambique.

Exploratory mission to Angola

Prior to the main expedition the Portuguese government requested that Capelo accompany an army major, Alexandre Alberto da Rocha de Serpa Pinto, on an exploratory mission to the interior of Angola. Capelo was an excellent choice, as he had already served in Angola and Mozambique. Capelo suggested that Roberto Ivens be included on the expedition. Ivens was a young naval lieutenant and former colleague of Capelo.

Arriving in Luanda, the capital of Angola, on September 1, 1877, the expedition got off to a rocky start. Because their goals had not been clearly defined, they received little cooperation from the Portuguese governor and had difficulty recruiting African porters and guides. After meeting the explorer **Henry Morton Stanley** (see entry) and learning of his success in navigating the Congo River, the three Portuguese officers decided to concentrate their efforts farther south. This proved to be a good decision.

They set out for the port of Benguela, south of Luanda, and then moved inland. An incident on the Bié Plateau, however, soon changed the makeup of the expedition. When Serpa Pinto left the party to try to find more African porters, Capelo and Ivens went on ahead. By this time Serpa Pinto had become ill, and he was angry with Capelo and Ivens because he believed they had deserted him. The three men reunited at the small outpost of Belmonte, but Serpa Pinto decided to leave the party permanently.

Capelo and Ivens traveled north from Bié and spent two years exploring the region around the town of Malange, as well as the upper parts of the Kwango River. They made extensive scientific observations and were the first Europeans to explore systematically northeastern Angola. This expedition, which ended in 1880, secured their reputations. Capelo and Ivens addressed the Society of Geography in Lisbon, Portugal, and the Royal Geographical Society in London, England. The books about their experiences were translated into English and published in 1886 and 1888.

Journey across the African continent

In 1883 Capelo and Ivens undertook a more important mission that would lay the groundwork for Portugal's future in Africa. They were asked to travel across Africa from Angola to Mozambique, establishing a link between the two colonies. A similar trip, the first across Africa, had been made by two Angolan mestizos, **Pedro João Baptista** and **Amaro José** (see combined entry), for Portugal early in the century. At that time, however, Portugal was not interested in follow-up expeditions.

Beginning their journey on January 6, 1884, Capelo and Ivens traveled to the southern Angolan port of Mocâmedes (now Namibe) and then went inland through little-known territory. They reached the last Portuguese outpost, traveled to the headwaters of the Cunene River, and sent one more report back to Portugal before disappearing into the interior. Capelo and Ivens then hiked overland to the African village of Handa on the Okavango River. They found little food in the uninhabited region near the upper Zambezi River and were saved from starvation by the representatives of Lewanika, the king of that region. With guides furnished by Lewanika they were able to cross the Zambezi River in October.

The remaining portion of their trip would have been easier had the two Portuguese explorers gone straight down the Zambezi to the Mozambique settlements. Instead, they decided to attempt something that had never been done by Europeans—the exploration of the headwaters of the Zambezi and Congo rivers. Heading north, they reached the headquarters of Chief N'Tenke, who befriended them, replenishing their food supplies and trying to marry them to two young women from his village. Ivens went on to the town of Bunkeya—presently in southern Zaire near the mining towns of Kolwezi, Likasi, and Lubumbashi—and met the king of that area, M'Siri.

Arrival in Mozambique

Capelo and Ivens turned east to reach the Luapula River, one of the main tributaries of the Congo on February 1, 1885.

Although they were ill with scurvy and malaria, they reported on the Mambirima Falls on the Luapula. Heading east across central Zambia, they reached a small fort called Zumbo, the farthest Portuguese outpost on the Zambezi. Exhausted, they recuperated in Zumbo for 19 days. When they arrived in the coastal town of Quelimane, Mozambique, Capelo received word that his wife had died.

Capelo and Ivens telegraphed the results of their successful expedition to Portugal, confirming that it was possible to travel overland between Angola and Mozambique. They returned to Portugal in September 1885, more than a year and a half after their departure. They received recognition for their efforts from King Luis; however, Portugal was not able to make its dream of an extended colonial empire a reality. Great Britain, a much wealthier and more powerful country, was able to block the Portuguese corridor by moving in from the south and establishing the colonies of Southern Rhodesia, now Zimbabwe, and Northern Rhodesia, now Zambia.

This marked the end of Capelo's career as an explorer, but he went on to become an important official, serving as the vice-president of the Portuguese Overseas Institute. He was also aide-de-camp to King Luis and his son King Carlos. Capelo died in Lisbon in 1917 at the age of 76. Ivens remained in the navy and died aboard ship on January 28, 1898, when he was 48 years old.

Étienne Brulé

Born c. 1592,
Champigny-sur-Marne, France

Died June 1633,
Probably Ontario, Canada

Born 100 years after Christopher Columbus discovered America, Étienne Brulé was one of the French explorers and adventurers sent to the New World to carve out an empire in what is now Canada and the northeastern United States. The English had competing claims in these areas, and there were inevitable clashes between France and England, two old enemies. Brulé spent most of his life living and working with Native Americans, serving either the French or the English as it pleased him. He is credited with discovering four of the five Great Lakes and pioneering the main route west for the lucrative fur trade.

Life among the Hurons and Susquehannas

Brulé was only 16 when he accompanied **Samuel de Champlain** (see entry), the founder of New France, to the province of Quebec. He never returned to his home near Paris, where he was born in about 1592. After two years with Cham-

Étienne Brulé, a French explorer, traveled to the New World and lived among Native Americans in order to serve as an interpreter. He also made several notable journeys in the Great Lakes region, as well as in New York and Pennsylvania.

plain, Brulé requested permission to live among the Hurons so he could learn their language and serve as an interpreter between the French and Native Americans. This request was granted. He soon showed his courage and disregard for danger by becoming the first European to shoot the Lachine Rapids just upstream of Montreal. Brulé returned to Quebec on June 13, 1611, fluent in Wyandot, the Huron language.

Although there is little documentation of Brulé's trips, it is believed he discovered the main route for the lucrative fur trade by traveling west through the Ottawa River into Lake Nipissing and from there through the French River to the Georgian Bay of Lake Huron. He guided Champlain on this route in 1612. In 1615 the French and the Hurons planned a campaign against their mutual foes, the Iroquois. Brulé joined a delegation to the Susquehannas in an attempt to get them to join the Hurons in their war. They traveled from Lake Simcoe in Ontario down the Humber River, across the western end of Lake Ontario, and then down the Niagara and Genesee rivers to the headquarters of the Susquehanna at Carantouan, located in present-day upstate New York.

By the time the Susquehannas came to the aid of the Hurons, they had been defeated by the Iroquois and were in retreat. Brulé returned with the Susquehannas to their own territory and then decided to follow the Susquehanna River south for several hundred miles until it reached its destination in Chesapeake Bay. Passing the area that is now Pennsylvania, he is thought to have been the first European to set foot in that state.

Exploration of the Great Lakes

On his return to Canada, Brulé was captured and tortured by the Senecas, a member of the Iroquois confederation. After he managed to escape, he continued to live among the Hurons and explore the Great Lakes. In 1621 he became the first European to see Lake Superior and to traverse it as far as the site of Duluth, Minnesota. He is also thought to have been the first European to see Lake Erie. If so, he can be credited with the discovery of four of the five Great Lakes. It was said that

Brulé's old commander, Champlain, disapproved of Brulé's life among the Native Americans. In any event, Brulé piloted the English vessels that captured Champlain and Quebec in 1629. England's occupation of Quebec was brief.

Brulé went back to living among the Hurons. His murder in 1633 by the Hurons remains a mystery, although some speculate there was a quarrel. He was 37 years old. Brulé was one of a rare breed of rugged individualists who chose a life of freedom and hardship to the constraints and comfort of civilization. In doing so, he enlarged the limits of the known world and blazed trails for the farmers and townspeople who followed.

Robert O'Hara Burke

Born c. May 6, 1820,
St. Cerah's, Galway, Ireland
Died c. June 28, 1861,
Australia

William John Wills

Born 1834,
Devonshire, England
Died 1861,
Australia

Robert O'Hara Burke

Robert O'Hara Burke and William John Wills, two Australian explorers, were the first to cross Australia from south to north. They died on the return trip.

Robert O'Hara Burke and William John Wills were the leaders of a tragic expedition that has become a legend in Australian history. Burke was in a great hurry to achieve fame and fortune; Wills was swept up in Burke's grand ambitions. Together they lost their lives in an expedition that accomplished little but proved to be the most costly in Australia's history. Their brave and lonely deaths made them sentimental heroes. Today they are reminders of an era when climate and terrain made many parts of the country uninhabitable.

Race to find the north-south route

By the 1860s most of the Australian continent had been explored, but communication between populated districts was nonexistent. The government of South Australia offered a reward to anyone who could find a north-south route for a telegraph line from Adelaide to the northern coast. John McDouall Stuart, a Scottish-born Australian explorer, had already taken up that challenge. Not to be outdone, the rich gold-mining state of Victoria sponsored its own expedition to travel from Melbourne to the northern coast. They chose as its leader Robert O'Hara Burke, an inexperienced but flamboyant man with a colorful history. Born in Ireland and educated in Belgium, he had served in the Austrian army in 1840. In 1848 Burke joined the Irish Constabulary, emigrating to Australia in 1853 to become a police inspector in Victoria. His deputy was an Englishman, William John Wills, who had studied medicine before becoming a surveyor and meteorologist in Victoria.

The expedition set out with great fanfare from Melbourne on August 20, 1860. Public contributions and government subsidies had provided ample funds and enough supplies for two years; 25 camels and 3 drivers had been brought from India. It appeared that careful preparations had been made for a journey from Menindee on the Darling River to the Gulf of Carpentaria in the north.

William John Wills

Trek across the Australian continent

Almost immediately members of the exploring party began to quarrel. Burke replaced his second in command, George Landells, with Wills. Although the expedition was not yet fully organized, Burke was eager to leave. He recruited a local man, William Wright, to guide him, Wills, and three other men—John King, Charles Gray, and William Brahe—on a shortcut to Cooper's Creek, which was located 400 miles to the northwest. They left on October 19 and arrived 23 days later. Wright was instructed to return to Menindee for the others and guide them to Cooper's Creek as soon as the party was complete. For various reasons he actually delayed his own departure for three months.

Robert O'Hara Burke
William John Wills

Once again Burke made an impetuous decision. Unwilling to wait for the others, he set out for the northern coast on December 16, determined, as he put it, to "dash into the interior and cross the continent at all hazards." Mounted on his gray horse, he took with him Wills, Gray, and King, who all rode camels; Brahe stayed behind at Cooper's Creek with orders to wait there for three months or until the supplies ran out. The route Burke had chosen was easier to cross than the desert passage attempted by Stuart, his competitor, because much of it skirted the desert and crossed land already occupied by sheep and cattle stations.

Burke's party actually made excellent progress at first, but when the rainy season began and the land became a morass of mud, it took them eight weeks to reach the coast. They arrived at the mouth of the Flinders River at the Gulf of Carpentaria on February 9, 1861. They could see the effects of the tide on the river but were unable to see the ocean because of swamps filled with dense growths of mangrove trees. Figuring they would need another two days to cut through the swampland, they decided they could not afford the drain on their already dwindling supplies. Thus, after their difficult journey, Burke and the others left without reaching their goal.

Illness and a shortage of food

Burke and Wills calculated that they had enough supplies to last for five weeks and that the trip back would take eight. As it turned out, the trip actually took ten weeks. They left on February 13 in a thunderstorm, and the rain continued throughout their journey. They all became ill with dysentery and other diseases. When the food ran out, they ate one of the horses, and four of the six camels died. On March 25 Gray was discovered stealing rations, and Burke gave him a beating. Gray subsequently died on April 17.

Upon finally reaching Cooper's Creek a few days later, Burke, Wills, and King found no one there. Having waited six weeks longer than instructed, Brahe had given up and left just eight hours earlier. He had carved a message on a tree telling them where to dig for provisions, and he left a letter informing them of his departure. Wills recorded his disappointment: "Arrived the depot this evening just in time to find it deserted. A note left in the plant by Brahe communicates the pleasing information that they have started today for the Darling: their camels and horses all well and in good condition."

Burke's fatal decision

Before starting out again, Burke wrote a note on April 22 and put it in the tree at Cooper's Creek:

> The return party from Carpentaria, consisting of myself, Wills, and King (Gray dead), arrived here last night, and found that the depot party had only started the same day. We proceed on tomorrow slowly down the creek towards Adelaide by Mount Hopeless, and shall endeavor to follow Gregory's track; but we are very weak. The two camels are done up, and we shall not be able to travel further than four or five miles a day. Gray died on the road from exhaustion and fatigue. We have all suffered much hunger. Greatly disappointed at finding the party here gone.... The camels cannot travel and we cannot walk, or we should follow the other party. We shall move very slowly down the creek.

Wills and King wanted to follow Brahe, who was by then only 14 miles away, along their old route to Menindee. Burke, however, was convinced they would never catch up and insisted they follow a tributary of Cooper's Creek to the south in an attempt to reach the cattle ranch at Mount Hopeless, which was 150 miles away. They rested for five days before setting out. Along the way friendly Aborigines gave them food—fresh water, fish, rats, and nardoo (made from the seeds of a fern that were pounded into a kind of flour). By May 17 the three men had killed their last two camels. They wandered aimlessly and by May 28 were back near the camp at Cooper's Creek, very close to where they had started out a month before.

Ironically, Brahe had been at Cooper's Creek on May 8. He had met Wright, who was at last making his way up from

Menindee, and decided to check the camp one more time. Burke, Wills, and King had carefully covered all signs of their visit so that the Aborigines would not find and destroy the note they had left behind. Brahe found the camp apparently undisturbed. He did not discover the note and rode away, not bothering to see if the provisions he had left were still there.

Demise of Burke and Wills

Burke, Wills, and King joined a group of Aborigines in an attempt to stay alive, but they became weaker and weaker and were no longer able to gather nardoo. The constantly wandering Aborigines moved on, leaving them behind. Since he was the strongest of the three, King tried to supply the other two with food. In their desperate situation it was decided that King and Burke would try to find the band of Aborigines. They left Wills behind with eight days' supply of food. Two days later Burke collapsed. King made him a meal from a crow that he had shot and some nardoo flour. "I hope you will remain with me until I am quite dead," Burke said. "It is a comfort to know that someone is by." He died at 8:00 A.M. on June 30, 1861.

King went back to where they had left Wills and found that he had also died. "I am weaker than ever although I have a good appetite and relish the nardoo much, but it seems to give no nutriment," Wills's last journal entry reads. "I may live four or five days if the weather continues warm. Starvation on nardoo is by no means unpleasant but for the weakness one feels and utter inability to move oneself."

King was able to catch up with the band of Aborigines, who tolerated his presence and gave him food. In return, he shot crows and hawks for them. In the meantime, four different rescue parties had been sent out to find the survivors of the disastrous Burke-Wills expedition. One of them, led by Alfred Howitt, finally found King on September 18, 1861. Howitt wrote that King was "wasted to a shadow, and hardly to be distinguished as a civilized human being but by the remnants of the clothes upon him." The bodies of Burke and Wills were carried back to Melbourne, where a tremendous funeral parade was held for them. A statue honoring Burke and King was erected in Melbourne.

Expedition's lasting legacy

Burke had no time for scientific work and kept no journal. Fortunately Wills wrote a poignant record of the doomed expedition, documenting its sad and terrible disintegration. His journal was found with his body. The Burke-Wills venture did not produce the results its supporters had expected. In fact, the four search parties contributed considerably more information about the north-central area, particularly its grazing potential. Burke's rival, Stuart, who crossed the continent from north to south and successfully made the return trip, actually pioneered the principal all-weather route to the Indian Ocean. Yet, while the decisions made by Burke and Wills have been open to criticism, their expedition has earned a permanent place in Australian history.

Richard Burton

Born March 19, 1821
Torquay, England

Died October 20, 1890
Trieste, Italy

Sir Richard Burton was an English soldier and writer who led an adventurous life that took him into the Muslim holy city of Mecca and on an expedition to discover the source of the Nile River.

Sir Richard Burton was at the center of one of the greatest geographical controversies of the Victorian age—the search for the source of the Nile, the world's longest river, which nourished the civilizations of the ancient world and held an allure for Western explorers. A colorful figure, Richard Francis Burton was a soldier, writer, adventurer, and explorer. He was born in the port town of Torquay in southwest England on March 19, 1821, the son of a retired Anglo-Irish colonel in the British army.

Student at Oxford

During Burton's childhood his family lived in a castle in the Loire River Valley of France, where he received little formal education. They also spent several years wandering in England, France, and Italy. His father wanted him to become a clergyman in the Anglican church and sent him to Oxford University. Burton hated Oxford and was expelled for going to the local racetrack.

Burton did study Arabic while at Oxford, and over the course of his life he would eventually learn 29 languages—a valuable resource for an explorer. At that time he also started to study Eastern mysticism, a religious practice in which the individual places himself in direct relationship with God. Burton studied Hindi, the official language of India, as well, and later he became a Hindi scholar, translating many classic texts into English.

In 1842, at the age of 21, Burton joined the East India Company's private army in Bombay. The army's job was to protect the company's possessions. Burton's first post was in the city of Baroda; a year later he was transferred to the province of Sind in what is now Pakistan. Burton's time in Sind had a profound effect on him. He began to wear Indian clothes and converted to Islam. Later, he wrote about his love for a "Persian lady" that ended tragically. Possibly the woman was killed because she had a liaison with a Westerner.

Life as a spy

British army intelligence recruited Burton as a spy, and his command of Indian languages, along with his ability to disguise himself, was a distinct advantage. In fact, Rudyard Kipling later used Burton's adventures in his novel *Kim* (1901), which portrays the "Great Game," as the struggle for control of central Asia was called. Burton left India in 1849 because of illness, ending seven years of adventure. He chose to recuperate in the French port of Boulogne. There two things happened that would have a major influence on his life: he began writing and he met his future wife. While in Boulogne, Burton wrote four books about his Indian experiences. (He would write 50 books during his lifetime.) He also met 19-year-old Isabel Arundell, who was from a prominent English Catholic family. Arundell later wrote that when she saw Burton for the first time she realized it was her destiny to marry him.

Pilgrim at Mecca

In 1852 Burton determined he needed to fulfill his religious duty as a Muslim by making a pilgrimage to Mecca. He approached the Royal Geographical Society to sponsor his journey, stressing the fact that his trip would add to the geographical knowledge of Arabia. The Society agreed to his request, and he left England in April 1853. Drawing upon the spy disguises he had perfected in India, Burton passed himself off as an Indian-born Afghan doctor. He traveled for three months via Alexandria, Cairo, and Port Suez in Egypt to the Arab port of Yenbo'.

During the trip Burton cut his foot on a sea urchin, and a severe infection made it impossible for him to walk. Fortunately the Burton party joined a passing caravan and proceeded to the holy city of Medina, where Burton visited the tomb of the prophet Mohammed. He then traveled along the Darb-al-Shakri, the inland road that crosses lava fields, to Mecca. Burton reached the valley of the El Zaribah, where pilgrims prepare for the entry into Mecca, and entered the holy city on September 11, 1853.

In Mecca, Burton participated in Islamic religious practices. He made the required walk around the holiest spot in Islam, the Ka'abah, a huge cube-shaped building that contains a chunk of black rock, probably a meteorite. As a pilgrim he took part in a commemoration of the day of Id-al-Khabir by tossing stones to symbolize how the patriarch Abraham drove away the Devil. But Burton had little patience with the required sermons, which he found boring, so he spent his time flirting with a young Arab woman, whose face was covered with a thin veil. Having run out of money, Burton canceled his plans to see eastern Arabia. He traveled to the Red Sea port of Jidda and took a ship to Cairo, where he wrote a book about his Islamic pilgrimage.

Searcher for source of Nile

While in Cairo, Burton met a man who told him stories that would change forever his life. The man was **Johann Ludwig Krapf** (see entry), a German missionary and one of the first Europeans to explore in East Africa. Krapf told Burton about a large inland lake from which the Nile River flowed. Thus began Burton's obsession to find the source of the Nile, which, unlike most rivers, flows north. Unfortunately, Burton's leave of absence from the British army had expired. He was forced to return to Bombay against his will. He mounted a campaign to convince his superiors and the Royal Geographical Society to sponsor an expedition to locate the source of the Nile.

Although Burton's requests were not approved, future events would lead him closer to realization of his goal and to a man who would play a major role in the expedition. Burton was assigned the task of exploring the northern coast of Somalia, where the port of Berbera would make an excellent stopping point for British ships sailing from Suez to India. Once again donning a disguise, Burton sailed from the new British colony of Aden in southern Arabia in the fall of 1854. In January 1855 he reached Harar, a "forbidden holy city," which is now in eastern Ethiopia. Burton may have been the first Western visitor. He returned to the coast, where he encountered other adventurers, including **John Hanning Speke** (see entry), a British army officer on leave, whom Burton had met previously in Aden. The two men returned to Aden and then made their way back to Somalia in April. During an attack by Somali warriors on their camp, a javelin pierced through the lower part of Burton's face. Speke was captured but, though seriously wounded, he somehow managed to escape. Burton and Speke went back to England to recover.

Expedition with Speke

While in England, Burton again petitioned the Royal Geographical Society to sponsor a Nile expedition. He also briefly renewed his acquaintanceship with Isabel Arundell, but was called to Turkey by the British army to fight in the Crimean War. On his return, he finally convinced the Society to fund the Nile expedition. The obsession of his adult life was now realized, and he invited Speke to join him.

This invitation would have profound repercussions for both men. They sailed to Bombay in November 1856 and from there to Zanzibar, an East African coastal island, in December. They traveled briefly to the mainland, hiring **Sidi Mubarak**

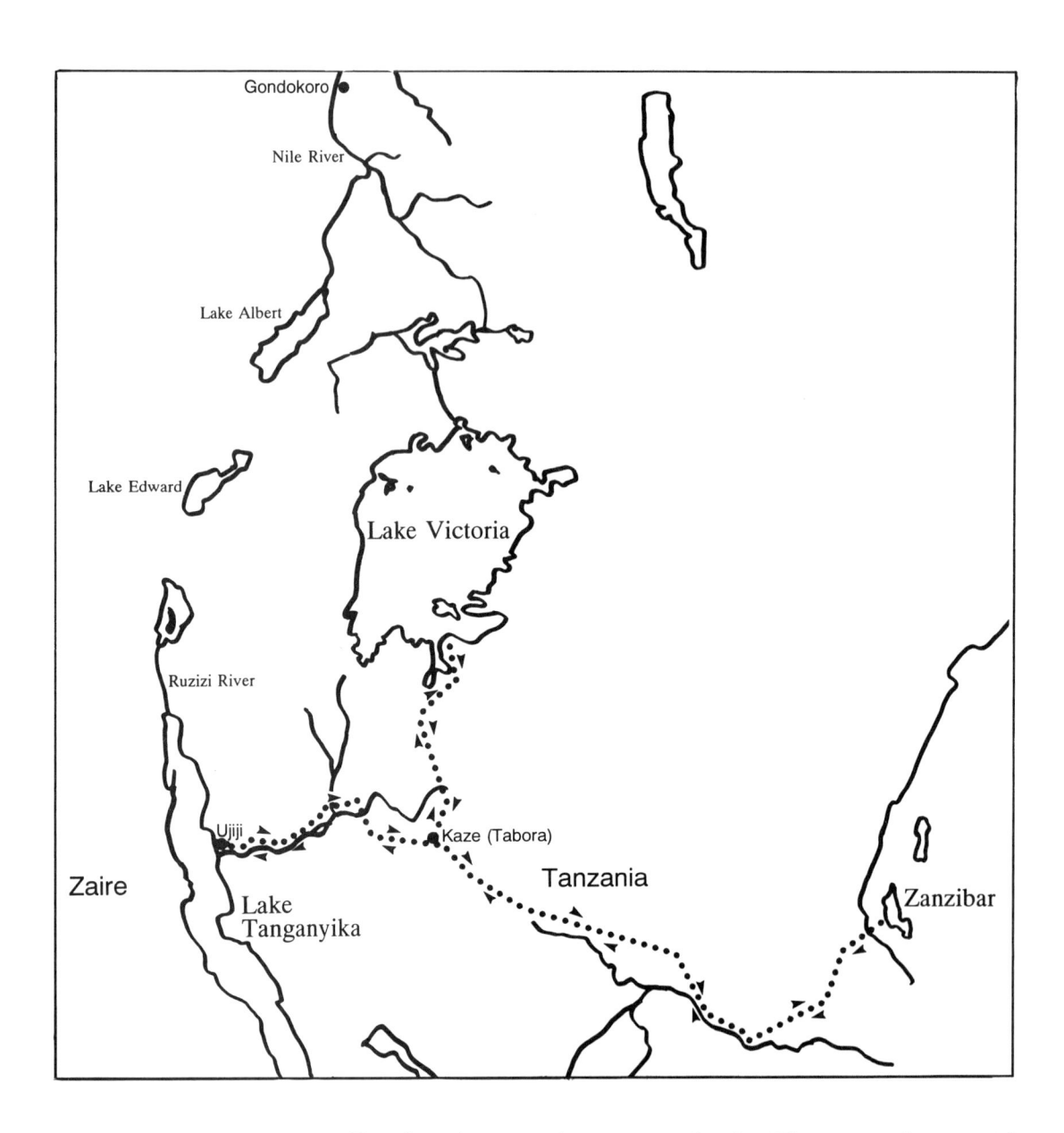

Burton and John Hanning Speke encountered surprises and hardship along their route in search of the source of the Nile River.

Bombay (see entry) as caravan leader. Then, near the start of the summer of 1857, they left Zanzibar and crossed over to the mainland.

Following one of the traditional routes of Arab slave traders into the interior, the Burton and Speke expedition soon met with hard luck. Their progress was impeded by sickness, and they averaged only ten miles a day. Because they were ill,

Burton and Speke were often too weak to walk and could barely sit on their donkeys. The explorers took more than four months to reach the trading center of Kazé (modern Tabora, Tanzania), some 500 miles inland, arriving on November 7, 1857.

Burton and Speke reorganized their expedition during a five-week rest stop. But a new disaster struck soon after they resumed. Burton became paralyzed and partially blind, and Speke went almost totally blind. Yet the intrepid explorers did not give up. Indeed, they climbed a hill so steep it killed Speke's donkey. Since both Burton and Speke were unable to see, it was Bombay who first sighted the body of water called the Sea of Ujiji, now known as Lake Tanganyika. Burton and Speke were the first Europeans to see it, insofar as they could.

Dashed hopes

Burton hoped that Lake Tanganyika would turn out to be the source of the Nile. He further speculated that a large river in the north, the Ruzizi, was in fact the Nile. The two explorers, still very ill, traveled by canoe to the north end of the lake. There Arab traders told them the Ruzizi flows into the lake, not out of it. "I felt sick at heart," Burton later wrote. They had not found the Nile source.

Burton and Speke left Lake Tanganyika on May 26, 1858. Speke was now ill with an ear infection as well. In Tabora, the men rested, partially recovering their health, and heard stories of a great lake to the north. Might this prove to be the Nile source? The event that followed is at the center of the Nile controversy. The accounts of the two men differ here: Speke says that Burton was ill and did not want to explore the northern lake. Burton says that he had more important things to do and sent Speke to verify the rumors. Whatever the reason, Speke, accompanied by Bombay, traveled north. He found the large lake, which he named after Queen Victoria, on August 3, 1858. Speke concluded that he had discovered the source of the Nile. When he returned to Tabora on August 25, Burton refused to believe him.

Controversy over findings

A strained relationship now broke down completely. By the time they reached Zanzibar, Burton and Speke were barely talking to each other. Arriving in London 12 days ahead of Burton, Speke told the president of the Royal Geographical Society that he had indeed discovered the source of the Nile. By the time Burton arrived, Speke had already given a public lecture on the expedition. Speke was now a popular hero, and Burton was livid.

A public quarrel ensued, with the Royal Geographical Society backing Speke, who then returned to Africa along with Scottish army officer James Augustus Grant. Speke and Grant proceeded north from Lake Victoria to Gondokoro in the southern Sudan. They were met by **Samuel White Baker** and his future wife **Florence** (see entry), who were traveling south on the upper Nile, thereby proving Speke's theory. Speke was unable to travel along the river for a distance of some 60 miles, thus giving Burton "evidence" to refute Speke's claim. Geographers were divided into rival camps. Some believed Speke had found the source, others supported Burton, who argued Lake Tanganyika was the Nile's source.

A public meeting was set for September 16, 1864, in the resort city of Bath, England, so that the two rivals could resolve the controversy. On the morning of the meeting, Speke went partridge hunting and shot himself in the chest while climbing over a low wall. He died within hours. Ignoring the official verdict of accidental death, many thought Speke had committed suicide out of fear of debating Burton. In fact, Speke's claim was proven to be correct, and Burton's wrong.

Marriage and later career

At the time of the Nile conflict, Burton had renewed his courtship of Isabel Arundell, whose family refused to allow her to marry him. He fled to North America, returning to England at Christmas in 1860. He threatened to go back to India if the marriage was blocked. Against the wishes of Arundell's mother, however, the couple were married on January 22, 1861, in a Catholic ceremony.

During the first year of his marriage Burton was appointed British consul of Fernando Po, an island in the Gulf of Guinea, beginning a period of government service. He led a British diplomatic mission to the African kingdom of Dahomey (now Benin). After the death of Speke, Burton, with the help of his wife, was appointed consul in Santos in Brazil, where the couple went to live in 1865. In 1868 Isabel returned to England but Burton's wanderlust took him throughout South America to Buenos Aires, Argentina, and over the Andes Mountains to Lima, Peru. He left Brazil to accept an appointment as British consul in Damascus, Syria, serving there until 1872. His last job was at the port of Trieste, Italy, on the Adriatic Sea, where he made his home for the rest of his life. Even in retirement Burton wandered ceaselessly around Europe and Africa.

During his later years Burton spent his time searching for diamonds in India and gold in Ghana. He made excursions to Egypt and what is now Jordan. In 1886 Burton was unexpectedly knighted, an honor conferred by the British monarch on citizens for civil or military achievements. From today's perspective, Burton's explorations are synonymous with the age of Victorian adventurism and are therefore worthy of knighthood. He made his last trip in 1889, to North Africa. He then returned home to Trieste, where he died on October 20, 1890, at the age of 69. Following his death, his wife burned many of his papers, thus prompting speculation about their contents. Isabel Burton wrote a biography of her husband before her own death, but it is generally considered to be a sanitized account of his life and exploits.

Richard Evelyn Byrd

*Born October 25, 1888,
Winchester, Virginia*

*Died March 11, 1957,
Boston, Massachusetts*

> Richard Evelyn Byrd was the first explorer to recognize the importance of the airplane in polar expeditions and the first to fly over both the North and South poles. He led five American expeditions to Antarctica in his quest to have the continent made a U.S. territory.

Richard Evelyn Byrd dedicated most of his life to exploring the earth's two polar caps and was celebrated in the United States for his accomplishments. Like Norwegian Arctic explorer **Roald Amundsen**, Byrd imagined himself a polar explorer from an early age. He wrote in his diary at age 14 that he wanted to be the first man to explore the North Pole, although **Robert Edwin Peary** and **Matthew A. Henson** (see separate entries) would eventually prevent Byrd from achieving that distinction.

Byrd was born in Winchester, Virginia, on October 25, 1888, into one of the state's most prominent families. He was a descendant of Lord Delaware, as well as William Byrd II, the founder of Richmond. His brother Harry served as governor of Virginia and then U.S. senator for 32 years. At age 13 Byrd traveled alone to the Philippines—which the United States had conquered in 1898 in the Spanish-American War—and lived with a family friend who had become a judge in the new administration of the Philippines. He stayed for a year before boarding a British steam ship, which took him on a journey around the world, stopping in India, Suez, England, and New York.

Service in the navy

Byrd enrolled as an undergraduate at the University of Virginia to prepare for law school. When he decided against a law career, he transferred to the U.S. Naval Academy in Annapolis, Maryland. He excelled at athletics at the academy but broke his right ankle twice—once in football and again in gymnastics. Receiving his commission in 1912, he served as a gunnery officer on U.S. Navy ships and took part in the invasion of Veracruz in 1914. Two years later, in 1916, Byrd broke his ankle again, this time so seriously he was forced out of the navy. Within two months, however, Byrd was given a second chance. The United States was preparing to enter World War I, and the navy needed his services as a training officer.

Once Byrd was back in the service, he convinced his superiors that he was sufficiently recovered to learn how to fly. He earned his wings at the navy's flight school at Pensacola, Florida, and then worked on a plan to send flying boats, or amphibious airplanes, across the Atlantic to Europe. Byrd developed two important navigational tools during these preparations, though the actual mission took place, without Byrd on board, in 1919, one year after the conclusion of the war. Following the war Byrd wrote the legislation for the navy's Bureau of Aeronautics, which the U.S. Congress passed into law. His efforts also led to the establishment of the Naval Reserve Air Force.

Polar expeditions

Fulfilling his childhood dream at age 37, Byrd made his first trip to the Arctic in 1925 on an expedition sponsored by the National Geographic Society with joint army-navy participation. Byrd was the first person to fly over the interior of Ellesmere Island and over the Greenland Ice Cap; he decided he also wanted to be the first person to fly over the North Pole. He knew he had to act quickly since other explorers, including Amundsen, were attempting the same feat. With financial assistance from John D. Rockefeller and Henry Ford's son Edsel, Byrd flew the *Josephine Ford* to Spitsbergen Island in the Arctic Ocean on April 29, 1926. From there he flew to the North Pole, reaching it at 9:02 A.M. on May 9, 1926. Byrd was successful in spite of a difficult takeoff and an oil leak in one of the engines of his Fokker monoplane. Warrant officer Floyd Bennett accompanied Byrd; on their return to Spitsbergen they met Amundsen.

Byrd received a hero's welcome in the United States; both he and Bennett were awarded the Congressional Medal of Honor. Although **Charles Lindbergh** (see entry) had made a solo flight across the Atlantic Ocean in May 1927, Byrd decided next to fly nonstop across the North Atlantic. Byrd pursued another record, however, by carrying the first transatlantic mail. Departing in June 1927, he flew with a three-man crew, crash-landing on the coast of France at Ver-sur-Mer. Byrd returned to his original dream of polar conquest, except now he looked to Antarctica, where he saw the opportunity to become the first man to fly over the South Pole.

With funding from private sources, his new expedition set out from the United States for Antarctica in August 1928 on a steamer and a sailing ship. They reached New Zealand without undue difficulty, but from New Zealand to Antarctica the ships had to cut through 600 miles of ice. When they finally landed at Antarctica, Byrd established his base camp at a place he named Little America, which was located in the Bay of Whales, a wide opening in the Ross Ice Barrier. This spot became the main scientific camp for American expeditions. Byrd named a nearby region Marie Byrd Land after his wife.

The expedition faced several obstacles before reaching its goal. One of Byrd's two planes was wrecked in a storm; the other, named the *Floyd Bennett* in tribute to Byrd's former copilot, who had died in a crash, failed to reach the required altitude and damaged its engine in a forced landing. Byrd tried again, taking off at 3:29 P.M. on November 28, 1929. At one point Byrd, the navigator, and his four-man crew were forced to throw 250 pounds of emergency rations out of the plane in order to gain the 20 feet needed to clear Liv's Glacier. At 1:14

A.M. on November 29, 18 hours and 39 minutes after takeoff, the *Floyd Bennett* reached the South Pole. Circling twice, the plane landed back at the base, having covered 1,600 air miles. For this feat Congress named Byrd a rear admiral on the retired list. Byrd returned to New York from Antarctica on February 19, 1930, again receiving a hero's welcome.

Leader of Little America project

Three years later Byrd returned to Little America as head of a major scientific expedition. The purpose of the expedition was to establish a small advance weather post, named the Bolling Advanced Weather Station, and to chart the surrounding area of 200,000 square miles. The weather station was located 125 miles south of Little America in a tiny prefabricated hut buried in the snow. In March 1934 Byrd was left by himself to man the "station," where temperatures reached -80°F. He stayed there alone for five months.

The following May Byrd was caught outside the hut during a blizzard and nearly became stranded. Miraculously, he found a shovel and dug his way back. In *Little America,* one of four books in which Byrd wrote about his polar explorations, he described his predicament: "It is more than just wind, it is a solid wall of snow moving at gale force, pounding like surf ... you can't see, you can't hear, you can hardly move." By May Byrd's radio transmissions to Little America had become increasingly irrational; although he was unaware of it at the time, carbon monoxide was poisoning him. One reason was that the sole entry hatch to the station had not been closing properly, but, more crucially, the heat stove was also defective. His condition steadily worsened. Dr. Poulter, the second in command at Little America, sent out a rescue mission in July, yet it did not reach Byrd until August. By then Byrd was so seriously ill that he could not be transported back to Little America for two months. When he was able to travel, the expedition left Little America on February 7, 1935, carrying valuable scientific information.

Byrd's third Antarctic expedition, which was funded by the U.S. government, took place in November 1939, soon after

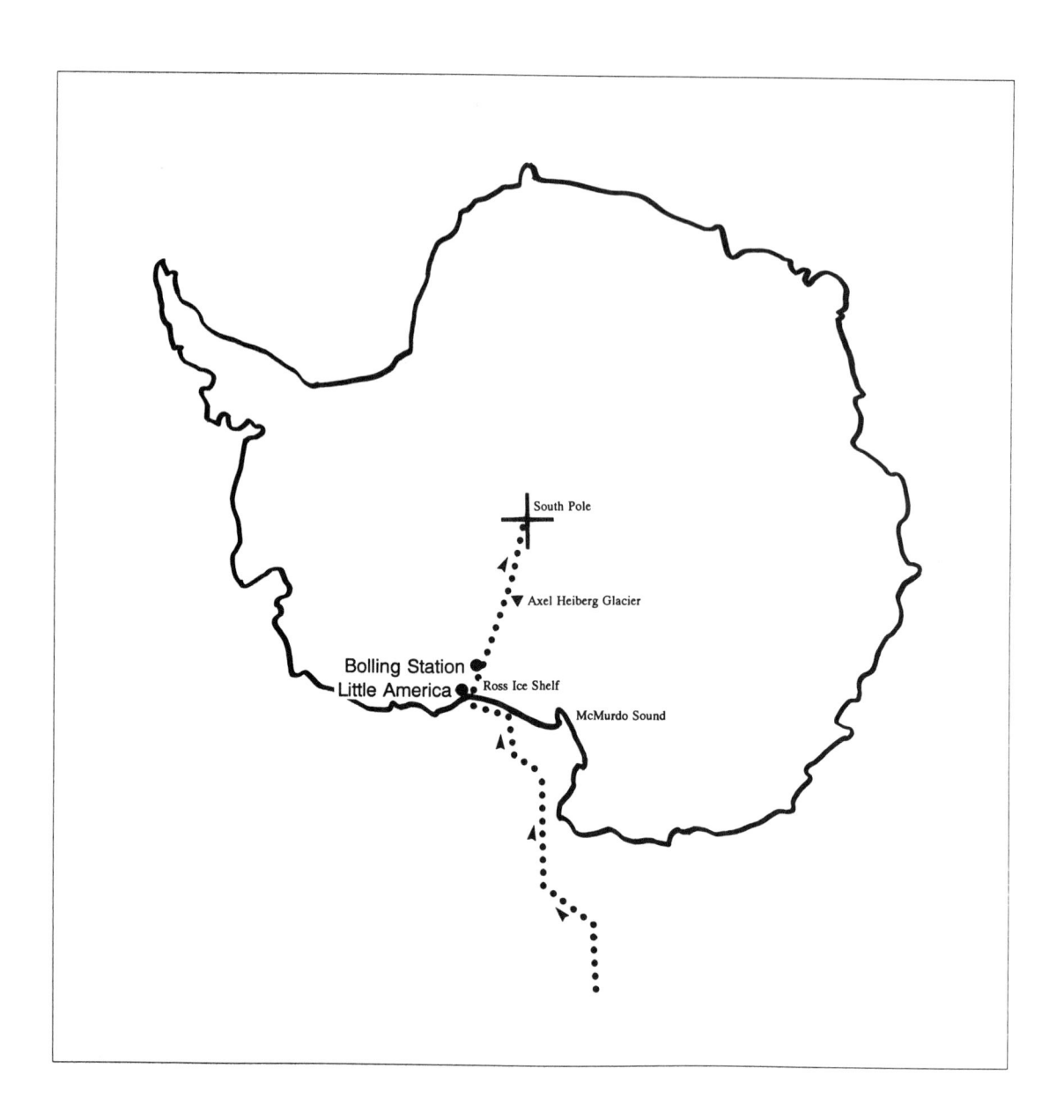

Byrd headed the Bolling Advanced Weather Station, 125 miles south of Little America, in Antarctica, from 1930 to 1934.

the outbreak of World War II in Europe. The aim was to map parts of the continent in case the United States decided to join other countries in claiming Antarctic territory. After supervising the construction of two new bases, Byrd returned to the United States at the end of 1940 because the government decided not to fund a second year of research. During World War II Byrd helped plan U.S. strategy in the Pacific Ocean, where he surveyed uncharted islands. He also flew missions behind German lines in France.

Last expeditions

After the war, in 1946, Byrd commanded the largest expedition sent to Antarctica up to that time. Called Operation Highjump, it consisted of 4,100 men (including 300 scientists), 13 ships, 19 airplanes, 4 helicopters, and a submarine. The primary task of the large expedition was to make an aerial map of Antarctica and test military weapons in extreme cold. Byrd participated in a two-plane flight over the South Pole and the unknown land beyond; these were the second and third planes ever to reach the pole. He returned to the United States in March 1947. Operation Highjump was a success, having explored vast regions of new territory and mapped and photographed 1,400 miles of the Antarctica coast.

Byrd made one last flight over the South Pole, accompanied by Dr. Paul A. Siple, on January 8, 1956. The men discovered two mountain ranges west of the Victoria Land peaks, as well as two ranges inland from Weddell Sea. A year later, on March 11, 1957, Byrd died peacefully at his Boston home at the age of 68.

Byrd made major contributions to the study of how humans can live in extreme cold. He was also instrumental in showing how the airplane could be used successfully in exploration. Although Byrd failed in his attempt to have Antarctica made a U.S. territory, his expeditions produced valuable scientific data and opened the region to further exploration.

Álvar Núñez Cabeza de Vaca

*Born c. 1490,
Jerez de la Frontera, Spain*

*Died c. 1560,
Seville, Spain*

Álvar Núñez Cabeza de Vaca, a Spanish explorer, sailed to the New World and was shipwrecked on the coast of what is now Texas. He spent many years in this region and also traveled overland to Mexico. Later he explored the area along the Paraguay River in South America.

Although Álvar Núñez Cabeza de Vaca could have lived an easy life as a member of one of Spain's noble families, he chose the hard and uncertain existence of an explorer. During his career he experienced triumph and disgrace. He had a unique ability to adapt to his surroundings, living for years among Native Americans as a medicine man and trader. His stories about the Seven Golden Cities of Cíbola probably inspired the explorations of **Hernando de Soto** and **Francisco Vásquez de Coronado** (see separate entries). Cabeza de Vaca blazed new trails for the Spanish in the New World.

Cabeza de Vaca was born in the town of Jerez de la Frontera, the center of Spanish sherry wine production. His family had earned its title of nobility, Cabeza de Vaca (literally "head of a cow"), in 1212, when a peasant ancestor used the skull of a dead cow to mark a pass for a Christian army. The army went on to defeat the Muslim Moors in a fierce battle during the Crusades. Brought up by a paternal grandfather in the Canary Islands (located off the northwestern coast of Africa), Cabeza de Vaca joined the Spanish army in 1511 and served in Italy and Spain.

Arrival in Florida

Cabeza de Vaca's ventures into the New World began in 1527, when he was appointed royal treasurer for an expedition commanded by Pánfilo de Narvárez. The expedition, which was to be an ill-fated one, consisted of 600 men and five ships. It made stops in Santo Domingo and Cuba before crossing over to Florida and landing at present-day Tampa Bay on April 14, 1528.

Unwisely splitting his land and sea forces, Narvárez led a force of 250 to 300 men inland to pursue reports from Native Americans about an abundance of gold at a place called Apalachen (on the site of Tallahassee). Corn was the only gold they found in Apalachen. Disappointed, the Spaniards returned to the coast, only to learn that their ships had sailed to Cuba. Since they were short of supplies and had come under attack by hostile Native Americans, it was thought that their best chance for survival might be to sail to the Spanish settlement of Pánuco in northeastern Mexico.

Disaster at sea

The Spaniards constructed five barges out of materials at hand. They melted down metal to make nails, fashioned sails out of clothing, wove horsehair into ropes, and used horsehides to make water containers. In September 1528 a total of 242 men sailed in the barges from a bay somewhere in the present-day Florida panhandle. Cabeza de Vaca and his men called it the Bay of the Horses because they had killed and eaten the last of their horses there.

The trip became a nightmare as they sailed west, keeping close to the shore. Along the way they suffered from lack of food and water. While passing into the mouth of the Mississippi River, the barges were separated by winds and currents. Cabeza de Vaca's barge was wrecked on Galveston Island on November 6; a few days later it was joined by another barge captained by Alonso de Castillo and Andres Dorantes. The other three barges sank at sea. The 80 surviving Spaniards found themselves among a group of Native Americans who were friendly but did not have any spare food for the men. Many of the Spanish died during the severe winter that followed. By the spring only 15 men remained. They headed for the Texas mainland without Cabeza de Vaca, who was too ill to travel. Among them were Castillo, Dorantes, and the Muslim slave **Estevanico** (see entry).

Life among the Native Americans

Cabeza de Vaca later crossed to the mainland and traveled west, attempting to reach by foot the town of Pánuco in eastern Mexico. For several years he lived among the Native Americans in eastern Texas as a trader, wandering along the coast and sometimes going inland. Cabeza de Vaca also gained a considerable reputation as a healer. According to some accounts, he was held as a slave.

During Cabeza de Vaca's travels he became the first European to see the North American bison, or buffalo. In the early winter of 1533 he was surprised to meet the only survivors of the party that had left Galveston Island in 1529. Having spent the intervening years as the slaves of various tribes, Castillo, Dorantes, and Estevanico had been brought to a place along the Colorado River in Texas where the Native Americans traditionally celebrated the pecan harvest.

The four men planned an escape for the following summer at a place where they knew the Native Americans would again rendezvous to eat prickly pears. They successfully broke away in September 1534 from a site near the modern city of San Antonio and headed for Mexico. After wintering with a tribe they called the Avavares, they continued their westward journey using Native Americans as guides. Surviving by skills learned from years of living in the hot, arid climate and using a good bit of diplomacy, they were led from one tribe to the next, maintaining the goodwill of all. Cabeza de Vaca apparently grew tired of his role of healer and medicine man, reporting that "it was very tiresome to have to breathe on and make signs of the cross over every morsel they [Native Americans] ate or drank."

Warm welcome in Mexico

At last the survivors crossed the Rio Grande near Rincon, New Mexico, where they saw members of the Yaqui tribe wearing items of Spanish origin. The Native Americans said they had been driven off their land by Europeans. Realizing they were near Mexico, Cabeza de Vaca and his three companions headed south into the modern Mexican state of Sonora. In early 1536 they made contacts with Spanish settlers near the city of Culiacán, where they planned to rest for several weeks before going on to Mexico City.

The party was warmly welcomed by Viceroy Antonio de Mendoza. Although Cabeza de Vaca had experienced only poverty and hardship on his long trip, he told tales of the fabulous riches that were to be found in the "Seven Golden Cities of Cíbola." He indicated they were somewhere beyond the region where he had traveled. Always eager to find new wealth for Spain, the viceroy sent out an expedition under Fray Marcos de Niza. The guide was Estevanico, who had accompanied Cabeza de Vaca on his journey to Mexico. When Estevanico was killed, Marcos returned, and another expedition, headed by Francisco Vásquez de Coronado, resumed the search. Although Coronado found no gold, he opened the southwestern part of the United States for exploration.

Return to Spain

Cabeza de Vaca returned to Spain in 1537. Not surprisingly, he declined an opportunity to go back to Florida with the expedition of Hernando de Soto. On March 8, 1540, he was named captain general of Spanish settlements on the Río de la Plata, headquartered at Asunción in what is now the South American country of Paraguay.

The journey to Asunción was another test for Cabeza de Vaca and his force of 280 men. The Spanish survived by bartering with the villages of the Guaraní tribe. Cabeza de Vaca was so honest in his dealings that the Spaniards maintained good relations with the local people throughout the trip. In January 1542 they became the first Europeans to see the

Iguaçu Falls, one of the world's greatest waterfalls. Continuing down the Paraná River to where it meets the Paraguay River, Cabeza de Vaca then took several members of his party and traveled by land to Asunción. They arrived on March 11, 1542, to the great joy of the settlers, who thought they had been abandoned.

Believing it would be possible to open a route from the Paraguay River to the rich gold mines and cities in Peru, Cabeza de Vaca set off once again in September 1543. He led about 400 Spaniards and 800 members of the Guaraní tribe up the river to a place he christened Puerto de los Reyes, or "Port of the Kings." He had traveled only a short distance before he was forced to return by his followers, who did not want to risk the hazards of the jungle.

Imprisonment and deportation

Two weeks after he returned to Asunción, Cabeza de Vaca was thrown out of office by a rebel governor, who imprisoned him and deported him to Spain in 1545. Cabeza de Vaca was charged with a variety of offenses, among them trying to subvert the authority of the king. He was found guilty by the Council of the Indies and condemned to exile in Africa.

There are conflicting reports of how Cabeza de Vaca fared after the trial. One source states that he was cleared of all charges by King Charles I and lived out his life in well-deserved honor until his death in 1557. According to another account, the verdict was upheld, but Cabeza de Vaca received a lightened sentence after he appealed. This same source indicates that he died in poverty sometime after the year 1556 (probably in 1560). Whatever the circumstances of his final years, it is apparent that he was an honest and fair person in his dealings with the indigenous peoples he encountered.

Cabeza de Vaca's books and reports about his trips are still being read today. Among them are *Naufragios* (The Shipwrecked Men), published in 1542, and *La Relación y Comentarios* (1555), an account of his experiences in South America, which is a valuable geographic work.

John Cabot

*Born c. 1450,
Genoa, Italy
Died c. 1499,
Possibly in Newfoundland*

Giovanni Caboto (John Cabot) was born in the Italian port city of Genoa. In 1476 he was granted citizenship in Venice, which at the time was the major trading center for all the Mediterranean region. Cabot worked as a merchant and navigator, and it is thought that from 1490 to 1493 he lived in the Spanish city of Valencia. There is speculation that he may have been in Valencia in April 1493, the month when **Christopher Columbus** (see entry) traveled through the city on his way to report to the king and queen of Spain about his successful voyage to America.

Search for the Northwest Passage

Columbus had, in fact, announced he found a new route to Asia, not a new landmass. Cabot was skeptical of this claim, concluding the distance was much greater than that traveled by Columbus. Instead, he believed it was possible to reach Asia by sailing around the northern end of the body of land

John Cabot, an Italian navigator in the service of the king of England, was the first European known to have reached the mainland of North America following the Vikings.

discovered by Columbus, later called the North American continent. Cabot's theory gave rise to the search for a "Northwest Passage," which would involve many voyages of exploration over the next 350 years.

In 1495 Cabot went to England, where he tried to sell his plan for reaching Asia to King Henry VII. On March 5, 1496, the king issued "letters of patent" that granted to "John Cabotto, Citezen of Venice" the right to sail with five ships "to all parts, countries and seas of the East, of the West, and of the North," where he was to "discover and find whatsoever isles, countries, regions or provinces of heathens and infidels, in whatsoever part of the world they be, which before this time were unknown to all Christians." Cabot made a first attempt to sail to North America in 1496 but was forced to turn back because of a shortage of food, bad weather, and problems with the crew.

Discovery of the North American mainland

On May 20, 1497, he sailed again from the port of Bristol, this time in a small ship named the *Matthew* with a crew of 20 that included his son **Sebastian Cabot** (see entry). Initially sailing along the south of Ireland, they headed west into the ocean, and 35 days later, on June 24, they sighted land. Cabot went ashore and saw signs of human habitation but did not meet anyone. He then explored the coastline from his ship before turning back and heading for Ireland. It took Cabot 15 days to cross the Atlantic to Brittany and from there to Bristol, where he landed on August 6. On August 11 he arrived in London to report to the king, who gave him a reward. He was back home in Bristol with his family by August 23.

Since Cabot's voyage people have speculated about where he actually landed in North America. Most likely he touched land somewhere on the coast of Maine and then headed north along the coast of Nova Scotia and Cape Breton Island as far as Cape Race in Newfoundland. From there he probably sailed back to Europe. Like Columbus, however, he claimed to have reached Asia.

Lost at sea

Having found land that was unknown to Europeans, Cabot was able to secure backing from the king for a new expedition. This time he commanded five ships and a larger crew. The ships sailed from Bristol in May 1498 but were never heard from again. Evidence obtained by later explorers suggests this second expedition may have reached the coast of Newfoundland. It is possible that some of the ships or survivors fell into the hands of the Spanish. Later explorers—such as Gaspar Corte-Real, the Portuguese adventurer, and **Alonso de Ojeda** (see entry), the Spaniard who founded a colony in Colombia—seem to have sailed with some knowledge of previous discoveries made by the English.

Sebastian Cabot

*Born c. 1476,
Venice, Italy*

*Died 1557,
London, England*

Sebastian Cabot, a navigator of Venetian origin, explored the coast of North America for the king of England. In the service of the king of Spain he explored and named the Río de la Plata, a river in Argentina.

The urge to travel and pursue adventure in strange lands came to Sebastian Cabot quite naturally. Born in Venice, Italy, in 1476, he was the son of Giovanni Caboto, better known as **John Cabot** (see entry), the famous explorer. When Sebastian was a young boy, he accompanied his father to England. He was also present when the elder Cabot sailed west from Bristol, England, in 1497. Although he was probably seeking the riches of the Far East, John Cabot instead landed on the North American coast. England's claims to North America were based on this voyage.

After John Cabot's second expedition was lost at sea, King Henry VII of England granted Sebastian an annual income in recognition of his father's services. Sebastian Cabot went on to serve two rival countries, exploring the coast of North America for England and the Río de la Plata in Argentina for Spain. Later in life he became a respected mapmaker and organized expeditions that eventually resulted in increased trade with Russia.

Search for the Northwest Passage

During the sixteenth century the major European maritime powers were devoted to finding a Northwest Passage, a water route across the North American continent that would shorten the long, arduous journey to India and China. Believing that such a route existed, many explorers attempted to find it, but expedition after expedition was either turned back by the cold or lost in vicious Arctic storms.

Sometime during the spring of 1508 it was Cabot's turn to search for the Northwest Passage. Although Cabot kept no written records of this voyage, it has been reconstructed from reports of others who sailed with him. An Italian monk named Peter Martyr reported eight years later that two ships, equipped at Cabot's expense, headed north from England with 300 men. They were surprised to find great icebergs floating in the sea as early as July and to experience days of almost unending sunlight. If the complete report is accurate, it would seem that Cabot had sailed from England to Greenland and from there to the coast of Labrador in eastern Canada. He probably continued north until his crew refused to go farther and then headed south along the coast of North America. From maps Cabot drew later in his life, it also seems possible he found the entrance to Hudson Bay and thought it was the passage to Asia.

Voyage to South America

Following his return to England, Cabot found work in southern France. In 1512 he settled in Spain, where he was appointed pilot major to King Philip I, succeeding Juan Díaz de Solís, who had explored Central and South America. In this position Cabot kept the records of all the Spanish voyages of discovery and was the official examiner of pilots, or helmsmen.

He made plans for expeditions to the New World in 1516 and 1521, but neither of these materialized. In 1524, however, Cabot managed to interest Philip I and a group of merchants from Seville in testing the theory that there was an easier passage to the Pacific Ocean than the Strait of Magellan, found by **Ferdinand Magellan** (see entry) in 1520. This was a difficult and dangerous waterway around the southern tip of South America, where many Spanish ships had been lost. Cabot's assignment was to find a new passage and sail to the Moluccas, or Spice Islands. Spices were almost priceless in Europe in the sixteenth century, and a direct route to these islands would have meant a fortune to the country that found it first. Cabot's expedition left Spain with three ships and about 200 men on April 3, 1526. They stopped at the Canary and Cape Verde islands and on June 3, 1526, landed on the coast of Brazil at present-day Recife.

Treasure hunting in Argentina

At Recife the voyage took a different turn. Cabot picked up an abandoned sailor, who reported on the results of a previous Spanish expedition to the interior of South America. It had returned with a large supply of silver, most of which was lost in a shipwreck. Several of the sailor's companions were also rescued farther south, and they verified the story of "a mountain two hundred leagues inland containing many mines of gold and silver and other metals." These stories were the first hints to reach the Spanish of the fabulous wealth of the Inca empire.

Impressed by these reports and deciding he could not pass up this opportunity for riches, Cabot sailed toward Argentina to begin his quest. Cabot explored the great river that Magellan had reported seeing in 1519 and named it the Río de la Plata, or "Silver River." He then traveled along two large tributaries of the Río de la Plata, the Uruguay and the Paraná rivers.

In 1527 he built a small fort, called the Sancti Spiritus, near the present-day city of Rosario, Argentina. From there exploring parties traveled up the Paraná as far as the foothills of the Andes; however, they did not find precious metals of any kind. To make matters worse, local Native Americans, who were antagonized by the actions of the Spaniards, destroyed the fort during Cabot's absence. After three years of fruitless searching, Cabot's party set out for Spain on October 6, 1529. With only one ship and 24 men remaining, they arrived in Spain on July 22, 1530.

Upon Cabot's return the Spanish accused him of failing in the expedition. He was tried and sentenced to banishment in Africa for four years. King Charles I pardoned Cabot in 1532, however, allowing him to resume his activities as pilot major.

Return to England

In 1548 Cabot was offered a naval post and a pension in England by King Edward VI. He became governor of the Merchant Adventurers, which attempted to organize expeditions to find a Northeast Passage from Europe to the Orient (by sailing east along the northern coast of Europe and Asia). This objective was not realized, but it resulted in increased trade with Russia.

Cabot died in London sometime before December 1557. He was 73 years old, an advanced age for an explorer in the 1500s. Although Cabot had only mixed success, he is remembered for his accomplishments in pushing beyond the boundaries of the known world, serving two countries in the process. A copy of his map of the world in 1544 is in the Bibliothèque Nationale (National Library) in Paris.

João Rodrigues Cabrilho

Lived sixteenth (and possibly fifteenth) century, Portugal

Died January 3, 1543, San Miguel Island, California

João Rodrigues Cabrilho, a Portuguese soldier and explorer in the service of Spain, was the first European to explore the coast of California.

The first recorded reference to the Portuguese explorer João Rodrigues Cabrilho dates from 1520, when he was a soldier under the command of Pánfilo de Narváez during the conquest of Mexico by **Hernán Cortés** (see entry). He is credited with founding Oaxaca, a district of southeastern Mexico. Later he went to Guatemala, probably at the same time as Pedro de Alvarado, who conquered part of present-day San Salvador. Following the conquest of Guatemala, Cabrilho stayed in the country and seems to have prospered there.

Commander of expedition

In the meantime, the first Spanish viceroy of New Spain (Mexico), Antonio de Mendoza, began to send exploring expeditions in various directions. For instance, he dispatched a fleet across the Pacific Ocean to the Philippines, and he ordered overland expeditions, headed by Fray Marcos and **Francisco Vásquez de Coronado** (see entry), into what is now the southwestern part of the United States. Mendoza chose Cabrilho to lead an expedition of two ships north along the Pacific coast of Mexico in search of a passage between the Atlantic and Pacific Oceans.

Cabrilho left from the Mexican port of Navidad on June 27, 1542. He sailed along Baja ("Lower") California, the outer coast of the southern part of California, which was already known to the Spanish as a result of several expeditions sent out by Cortés. The Spanish had named the region California after a mythical island—ruled by Califia, queen of the Amazons—which was described in a popular Spanish tale published around 1510 by Garci-Rodriguez de Montalvo.

Exploration of the California coast

On September 28, 1542, Cabrilho sailed into San Diego Bay. From there he continued north along the California coast, stopping frequently. The first Native Americans he met were fishermen, who told him about the people who lived on the mainland and subsisted by growing corn (maize). Cabrilho continued to have friendly encounters with the Native Americans. Just north of present-day Los Angeles he saw a large village, where he landed and took possession of the area in the name of King Charles I of Spain.

Leaving the coast in October, Cabrilho's ships sailed through the Santa Barbara Channel, visiting Santa Catalina and other islands. They then regained the mainland at Point Conception, where they were caught in heavy storms. They continued north, but because of the bad weather they did not sight either Monterey Bay or San Francisco Bay, places where they could have found shelter. Cabrilho's party turned south and anchored at San Miguel, one of the islands in the Santa Barbara Channel, where they decided to wait for better weather.

Fatal accident

Cabrilho died at San Miguel after a serious fall on January 3, 1543. The captain of the second ship, Bartolomé Ferrelo, took command of the expedition. He decided to try sailing north again. He made a first attempt on January 19, but both ships were forced to turn back by bad weather. They stayed among the Channel Islands for another month and then set out again, this time heading farther out to sea before turning north. Ferrelo spotted land at Point Arena, about 100 miles north of San Francisco.

The ships rounded Cape Mendocino and then went as far north as the mouth of the Rogue River in southern Oregon, which they reached on March 1, 1543. Heading south, the party encountered more bad weather. They were separated for a while but eventually met again and sailed safely into Navidad harbor on April 14, 1543.

Cabrilho's discoveries had no immediate results in either New Spain or Spain itself. Exploration did not take place again until the seventeenth century, when Spanish friars began to push up the coast of California, effectively bringing that part of the world into the Spanish empire. Point Loma Head, the spot at the entrance to San Diego Harbor where Cabrilho landed in 1542, is now part of a national monument dedicated to the explorer.

René Caillié

*Born November 19, 1799,
Mauze, France*

*Died c. 1838,
La Badere, France*

René Caillié, a Frenchman, was the first European to reach the fabled city of Timbuktu in West Africa and to make the return trip.

"Dead or alive, the prize shall be mine," so wrote 17-year-old René Caillié in his journal when he heard in 1826 that the French Geographical Society was offering a prize of 10,000 francs for the first European who could travel to the fabled city of Timbuktu. He fulfilled that vow, but skeptics and doubters made it difficult for him to collect his prize. The difficulties Caillié endured to reach his goal were typical of those many explorers encountered, whatever the prize. More often than not, as in Caillié's case, the personal victory proved to be hollow.

René-Auguste Caillié was the son of a poor Parisian baker. At an early age he started reading travel books, which inspired him to become an explorer. It was a good time to seek adventure because Europe was expanding its territories. The New World was still being explored and fought over, claims were being made in many areas of the Far East, and Africa was being divided up among the European powers. At the age of 16 Caillié got a job as a servant on a French ship sailing to

Senegal, West Africa, where he was able to travel some distance inland. He made a return trip in 1824 and lived in Senegal until 1827. While living in Senegal, Caillié began planning his trip to Timbuktu.

Dangerous journey across Africa

Realizing it was dangerous for a French Christian to travel through Arab lands, he disguised himself as an Arab and spent nine months with a Muslim tribe studying the Koran and learning to speak Arabic. In March 1827 he traveled to Freetown, a seaport in Sierra Leone, and then went north in a coastal vessel to the Rio Nunez, where he joined a caravan to the interior. He told his companions he had been born in Cairo and had been taken as a child by the French to Senegal. While the Arabs may have doubted his story, he was so poor that no one robbed him or prevented him from continuing his journey.

When the caravan reached the town of Kouroussa in June, Caillié joined another caravan traveling to the important trading town of Djenné. Along the way he became ill with malaria and scurvy; he rested for five months in the town of Tieme, where a local woman nursed him back to health. In March 1828 he reached Djenné on the shores of the Niger River and took a boat from there to Timbuktu. Because he was so poor, he had to book passage in the slave quarters below deck, where he suffered from the intense heat during the 500-mile journey. At one point the boat was boarded by pirates from the Tuareg tribe, who demanded tribute at every Tuareg camp it passed.

Arrival in Timbuktu

On April 20 Caillié reached Timbuktu, only to find the city did not meet his expectations:

> I had formed a totally different idea of the grandeur and wealth of Timbuctoo. The city presented, at first view, nothing but a mass of ill-looking houses, built of earth. Nothing was to be seen in all directions but immense plains of quicksand of a yellowish white

colour. The sky was a pale red as far as the horizon: all nature wore a dreary aspect, and the most profound silence prevailed; not even the warbling of a bird was to be heard. Still, though I cannot account for the impression, there was something imposing in the aspect of a great city, raised in the midst of sands, and the difficulties surmounted by its founders cannot fail to excite admiration.

Some 900 miles northeast from the mouth of the Rio Nunez—the starting point of Caillié's journey—Timbuktu lies within the present-day country of Mali. Founded in the eleventh century, the city had been a trading hub for the nomads of the Sahara Desert. By the fourteenth century, when **Abu Abdallah Ibn Battutah** (see entry) wrote about it, Timbuktu had become a capital of Mali culture and was famous for its gold trade. The city later became a center for Muslim learning but had been in a long period of decline by the time Caillié visited in 1828. He stayed for two weeks, living in a house across the street from the former home of Alexander Gordon Laing, the Scottish explorer who was murdered in Timbuktu in 1826. Caillié began to worry that his identity would be discovered and that he would meet the same fate.

Caravan trek to Morocco

In May 1828 Caillié joined a caravan of 1,400 camels and 400 men that was heading north from Timbuktu across the great Sahara Desert. His companions pointed out the place where Laing had been killed; however, it was not the possibility of death by human hands that he needed to worry about. It was the desert itself. Caillié suffered from the intense heat and constant thirst. He wrote: "My throat was on fire and my tongue clove to the roof of my mouth. I thought only of water—rivers, streams, rivulets were the only ideas that presented themselves to my mind." Caravan travelers were permitted only one drink at the end of the day, so Caillié was always thirsty:

It is difficult to describe with what impatience we longed for this moment. To enhance the pleasure which I expected from my portion, I thrust my head into the vessel and sucked up the water in long draughts. When I had drunk, I had an unpleasant sensation all over me, which was quickly succeeded by fresh thirst.

After the caravan reached the Atlas Mountains in Morocco in mid-June, Caillié journeyed six more weeks to Fez and then to the city of Tangier, located on the Strait of Gibraltar between the Atlantic Ocean and the Mediterranean Sea. In Tangier he sought help from the French consul in returning to France. Refusing at first to believe Caillié's story, the consul later smuggled him aboard a ship bound for the French port of Toulon. When Caillié arrived in Toulon, the French Geographical Society sent him a small sum of money for passage to Paris, where a special commission had been formed to examine his claims.

Fall from honor to poverty

The commission eventually decided Caillié was telling the truth and awarded him the Legion of Honor, a gold medal, and an annual pension. Shortly thereafter he wrote *Caillié Travels through Central Africa to Timbuktoo,* which was published in three volumes in 1830. Translated from the original French into English that same year, the book became very popular in England.

Doubts remained among the French about Caillié's honesty, however, and his pension was discontinued in 1833. Suffering from diseases he had contracted on his travels, he died in poverty in 1838. Later the truth of his story was confirmed. Although Caillié's achievements were questioned during his lifetime, he is remembered for his courage and imagination. His books provide an accurate description of travel conditions for Europeans in Africa during the early 1800s.

Giovanni da Pian del Carpini

*Born c. 1180,
Pian del Carpini, Tuscany*

*Died August 1, 1252,
Italy*

The Mongol invasions of the thirteenth century frightened all the countries of Europe and Asia. In an attempt to avoid war, many leaders sent diplomats to the court of the Mongol khans. One of the most important delegations, sent in 1245 by Pope Innocent IV, was headed by Giovanni da Pian del Carpini.

Born in Pian del Carpini, a village near the city of Perugia (in present-day Italy), Carpini was a contemporary of St. Francis of Assisi, founder of the Franciscan order of monks. Carpini became one of the earliest members of the Franciscans. When he was chosen by the pope to lead a mission to the Mongols, he was almost 65 years old and had extensive negotiating experience, having already been sent to Germany, Spain, Hungary, Poland, Scandinavia, and elsewhere. Carpini was also very fat and could not walk well, often having to be carried by a donkey; however, he never complained about his own sufferings during his long journey.

Giovanni da Pian del Carpini, a Franciscan monk, was sent by Pope Innocent IV to head the first European diplomatic mission to the Mongol court in central Asia.

The Mongol invasions

The conquests of the Mongols form one of the great chapters of world history. Their center of power was Karakorum, a city in central Asia and the capital of Mongolia; their leader was Genghis Khan, who was proclaimed Great Khan, or supreme ruler, in 1206. Led by Genghis Khan, the Mongols captured Peking (now known as Beijing, China) in 1215 and then Bukhara, thousands of miles to the west in central Asia, in 1220. Under Genghis Khan's son Ögedei, all of China was conquered by 1234.

The Mongols then turned westward again, taking Moscow in 1238 and Kiev in 1240 before advancing as far as Vienna and the Adriatic Sea. In April 1241 they defeated two large Christian armies, one at Liegnitz (in what is now western Poland) and one at Mohi (in Hungary). They could have conquered all of Europe, but they suddenly turned back during the winter of 1242-43 on receiving news of the death of Ögedei.

The next Mongol ruler, Möngkhe, concentrated his attacks on the Muslim lands of the Middle East, invading Persia and capturing Baghdad in 1258. It looked as though all of the Arab-ruled lands would fall, but once again the Mongols retreated, this time in 1260, when Möngkhe died. His successor was Khubilai Khan, who ruled from the city of Khanbaligh (as Peking was then called) from 1260 to 1294. Khubilai was the Great Khan during the visit of **Marco Polo** (see entry) to China.

Journey to the Mongol court

Carpini and his companions left Lyons, France, on Easter Sunday, April 16, 1245, and traveled by way of Bohemia, Poland, and Ukraine, arriving on April 6, 1246, at the encampment of the Mongol general Batu on the banks of the Volga River. Much to Carpini's surprise, the Mongols were unimpressed by his papal letters and paid no attention to his appeals for peace, his desire to send missionaries to convert the Mongols to Christianity, and his requests that they cease their attacks on the West. In fact, the Western visitors were subjected to demands for gifts and were forced to undergo a purification ceremony in which they had to walk between two great fires. The only food they were given was boiled millet and melted snow for drinking.

In April 1246 Batu sent the Carpini mission to the court of the Great Khan. Carpini wrote, "most tearfully we set out, not knowing whether it was for life or for death." They traveled through the plains of southern Russia and the desert regions north of the Caspian Sea to the Syr Darya River. By then Carpini was in lands inhabited by Muslims, all of whom had been conquered by the Mongols. He headed eastward to Lake Alakol, which is now in the easternmost part of Kazakhstan. He then had to traverse the Altai Mountains, where, even at the end of June, the party encountered snow and high winds.

Finally, on July 22, 1246, Carpini and his fellow travelers reached the court of the Great Khan near Karakorum, which is now in ruins in north-central China near the Mongolian border. They had traveled approximately 3,000 miles on horseback in 106 days. They arrived just when the Mongols were engaged in electing Güyük as Great Khan to succeed Ögedei, who had died five years earlier. Carpini was not allowed to see the new khan until after the election took place, but he joined in the festivities along with "more than 4,000 ambassadors"—from all over Asia, the Middle East, and eastern Europe—who had come to recognize the new ruler.

Meeting with the Great Khan

Carpini was present at the enthronement of the Great Khan on August 24 and reported on the multitudes in attendance, the rich clothes of the Mongol leaders, the obeisance and lavish gifts given to the new ruler, and the feasting and drunkenness that followed the coronation. During the ceremonies one of the other visitors, Prince Yaroslav of Suzdal (in Russia), was fatally poisoned, apparently by the new khan's mother, the empress Töregene. Carpini was no doubt alarmed when he was instructed to stay in the court of this woman.

The mission from the pope was finally allowed to present its letters. These were translated, and in November 1246 a response from the Great Khan was drafted for the mission to take back to Rome. Güyük's letter, later found in the Vatican archives, insultingly demanded that the pope travel to Khanbaligh himself and submit to the khan. Carpini was able, however, to resist an offer to take back ambassadors from Güyük, thinking they would be spies and might seek to come up with excuses for war.

Carpini left Mongolia on November 13, 1246, and suffered much hardship while traveling during the winter. Carpini wrote about sleeping on the ground at night and waking to find himself covered in snow. On May 9, 1247, he returned to the court of Batu, where, now under the protection of the Great Khan, he was received with greater respect. On June 9 the mission arrived in the Christian city of Kiev, where they were received "with great joy." Carpini delivered his report to the pope in Lyons on November 18, 1247.

Final mission

In 1248 Carpini was sent as papal legate, or ambassador, to the court of King Louis IX of France, who would later be recognized as a saint by the Roman Catholic church. Carpini's mission was to try to convince the king to delay his Crusade against the Muslim armies of the Middle East, but his efforts were unsuccessful. He was then named bishop of Antivari, a town on the coast of the Adriatic Sea. When his appointment was disputed by the local archbishop, he was forced to return to Italy, where he died on August 1, 1252. Carpini's account of his travels, *Liber Tatarorum* (Book of the Tatars)—the first study of this kind to be published in Europe—gives a detailed description of the history, as well as the social, political, and military customs, of the Mongols.

Philip Carteret

Born 1734
Died July 21, 1796,
Southampton, England

Samuel Wallis

Born April 23, 1728,
Cornwall, England
Died January 21, 1795,
London, England

L ittle is known about Philip Carteret's early life. Apparently the only source of information is his journal, which was published in 1773. In it Carteret gives an account of his voyage around the world in 1764-66, when he sailed with an expedition led by John Byron, the English navigator who laid claim to the Falkland Islands for Great Britain. Carteret served as first lieutenant on both ships in Byron's expedition. Soon after his return to England, Carteret embarked on a new expedition under the command of Samuel Wallis.

Wallis, born in Cornwall, England, on April 23, 1728, went to sea as a young boy. He served in the Royal Navy during the War of the Austrian Succession (1740-48) and was promoted to lieutenant at the end of the war. For the next eight years he steadily advanced in rank, securing his first command on June 30, 1756. He commanded various ships in North America and the English Channel during the Seven Years' War (1756-63) between Great Britain and France.

Philip Carteret, as part of Samuel Wallis's expedition to find the great southern continent, became the first European to see many of the Pacific islands; Wallis, meanwhile, was the first European to visit the South Pacific island of Tahiti.

Search for the great southern continent

In 1766 Wallis was appointed head of an expedition to find the so-called great southern continent, or Terra Australis, which explorers were led to believe existed off the coast of South America. Under Wallis's command were two ships, the *Dolphin* and the *Swallow*. Taking the helm of the *Dolphin* himself, Wallis entrusted Carteret with the *Swallow,* a leaky old vessel with few repair facilities on board. Carteret's later reputation would be made by his success in navigating the *Swallow*.

The *Swallow* followed the *Dolphin* south through the Atlantic Ocean to the Strait of Magellan, a narrow waterway at the tip of South America connecting the Atlantic and Pacific oceans. Hindered by bad weather, the two ships took four months just to get through the strait. They reached the Pacific Ocean on April 11, 1767, but then became separated, and the *Dolphin* sailed on without the *Swallow*. According to Carteret's entry in his ship log, he felt Wallis purposely left him behind in order not to be burdened by the *Swallow*.

Early problems with the *Swallow*

Despite being in charge of a ship that was close to unseaworthy, Carteret wrote in his journal, "I determined at all events to perform ... in the best manner I was able." He sailed north to the Juan Fernandez Islands in the South Pacific, navigating through a storm that split the *Swallow*'s sails and tore off its rigging. Carteret's party reached Juan Fernandez on May 8, only to find the Spanish already occupying the island. The Spanish barred the *Swallow* from landing, so Carteret sailed west to a smaller island, Mas Afuera, where he was able to obtain a supply of water and make repairs to the ship.

Battling continued bad weather, Carteret sailed due west in search of the great southern continent, which, according to speculation, existed in that area. The first land he saw was the tiny, isolated island of Pitcairn, named after one of the crewmen who had first sighted it. At that time the island was uninhabited—it would be settled 23 years later by mutineers on a ship named the *Bounty*.

Carteret's rediscoveries

From Pitcairn the *Swallow* sailed northwest and passed some of the small uninhabited islands of the Tuamotu Archipelago in what is now French Polynesia. Farther north toward the equator, the ship finally encountered favorable winds and proceeded due west. But good luck did not last long for the *Swallow*. The entire crew became ill with scurvy, a disease caused by a lack of vitamin C; the ship could not be steered; and it had sprung a leak below the waterline. Before inevitable disaster struck, Carteret and his crew sighted the Santa Cruz Islands, which had last been seen by Westerners when an expedition led by Alvaro de Mendaña, a Spanish explorer, had reached them 200 years earlier.

Carteret sent a landing party, headed by one of his two subordinate officers, to search for food and assistance. At first the islanders were friendly, but then the officer started to cut down a coconut tree, even though the islanders tried to stop him. The natives attacked; by the time the British retreated to the ship, the officer and three other men were dead, and the rest were wounded. The *Swallow*'s survival was now in question, since Carteret and his first lieutenant were the only two men left alive who knew how to navigate the ship.

The *Swallow* remained anchored long enough for the leak to be repaired. An armed party went ashore to get fresh water; however, trade with the natives for any other provisions was impossible. Carteret headed west and found the Solomon Islands, which Mendaña had discovered around 1567 and which seamen had been looking for ever since. The Spanish

The *Bounty* mutiny

The *Bounty* was a British navy ship, commanded by Captain William Bligh, that left England for the West Indies in December 1787. In April 1789, when the *Bounty* was on the high seas, first mate Fletcher Christian led a mutiny against Bligh. The mutineers set Bligh and 18 members of his crew adrift in a small open boat. Yet, because of their determination and expert seamanship, the party survived. They traveled 3,618 miles by sea, reaching Timor, an island in the Malay Archipelago northwest of Australia, in June. From Timor they continued safely to England.

The fate of some of the mutineers was not so fortunate. Several returned to England, where they were captured and court-martialed; three were subsequently executed. A group led by Christian, however, landed on Pitcairn Island, which had been discovered by Carteret. They burned the *Bounty* and stayed on the island, becoming its first inhabitants and founding a colony where their descendants still live today. Three Hollywood films (1936, 1962 and 1984) were made about the *Bounty* mutiny.

explorers had provided such poor locations on their maps that Carteret did not realize he had rediscovered the lost islands.

Carteret's discovery of the Admiralty Islands

From the Solomon Islands Carteret sailed northwest to the island of New Britain, where he found a cove in which he could anchor the *Swallow* to make further repairs and take on fresh supplies. From there the *Swallow* sailed along the coast of the island of New Ireland and then headed west, where Carteret discovered and named the Admiralty Islands. Passing the northern coast of New Guinea, he eventually reached Celebes, an island in the Dutch East Indies (now Indonesia). Again Carteret encountered difficulties, this time with the Dutch; however, the Dutch permitted him to stay from December 21, 1767, to May 22, 1768, when he moved on to Batavia (now Djakarta), a city on the coast of Java, to make repairs to the *Swallow*. The ship was in such poor condition that the Dutch carpenters were convinced it would not withstand the voyage back to England.

Carteret had little choice but to sail on. He left Batavia in September 1768, and at the end of November he reached the Cape of Good Hope, located on the southern tip of Africa, where he stayed for six weeks. Three weeks after passing Ascension Island in the South Atlantic, the *Swallow* was overtaken by the *Boudeuse,* a French ship commanded by **Louis Antoine de Bougainville** (see entry). Bougainville knew about the *Swallow*. Wallis had long since returned to England and had reported the ship missing. When the *Boudeuse* sailed away, Carteret recorded: "She shot by us as if we had been at anchor, notwithstanding we had a fine fresh gale and all our sails set." The *Swallow* faced one more storm, during which it lost one of its sails. But on May 20, 1769, the ship anchored off Portsmouth in England. The completion of the voyage was "to our great joy," Carteret wrote in his journal.

Wallis's discovery of Tahiti

After separating from Carteret, Wallis had sailed the *Dolphin* northwest across the Pacific Ocean. The ship's progress was hindered, however, by severe storms and illness among the crew; Wallis himself had also become sick. On June 10, 1767, the ship came in sight of some of the small outlying islands of the Tuamotu Archipelago. There the *Dolphin* stopped briefly to load on fresh water and coconuts before sailing west. On June 18 Wallis and his crew were rewarded with the sight of the large, mountainous island of Tahiti, where they anchored offshore at twilight.

The next day, to the surprise of the crew, the *Dolphin* was surrounded by hundreds of canoes manned by the Tahitians, who had come to see the first Europeans to land at their island. The crew made indications that they would not harm the Tahitians, and a few of the Tahitians came on board. One of the Tahitians was butted by a goat and, according to an eyewitness account, "the appearance of this animal, so different from any he had ever seen, struck him with such terror, that he instantly leaped overboard; and all the rest, upon seeing what had happened, followed his example."

After a few days of hostile gestures on both sides—the *Dolphin* crew even fired a cannon at a Tahitian chief in his canoe—the two groups decided that it was more advantageous for them to trade. The Englishmen bartered nails, the first metal tools the Tahitians had ever seen, for all the fresh fruit and other provisions they needed. In fact, the Tahitians were so anxious to get the nails, and the crew so willing to trade, that the crew started pulling the nails out of the ship itself. Fearing for the ship's safety, Wallis limited the number of men who went ashore and the supply of the nails they took.

During Wallis's audience with one of the local queens, the English officers were massaged by young Tahitian women until the ship's doctor took off his wig and frightened them all away. The crew sent out small parties to explore the island; they came back with enthusiastic tales about the wealth and fertility of the land and the beauty and friendliness of the people. From that day, when it first became known to Westerners, Tahiti has been considered by many to be paradise on Earth.

Wallis wanted to stay in Tahiti, and the queen begged him not to leave, but he felt it was his duty to continue his explorations. He weighed anchor on July 26 and sailed northwest, passing many of the islands of Polynesia and discovering the group of islands that were later named for him. The Wallis Islands are now a French territory. The *Dolphin* stopped at the island of Tinian, a Spanish possession in the Marianas in well-charted seas, on September 19, 1767. Wallis then sailed on to Batavia in the Dutch East Indies, where many of the crew members came down with smallpox and dysentery. The *Dolphin* continued its journey, but crossing the Indian Ocean was so difficult that the party spent a month at the Cape of Good Hope so the crew could recuperate. The *Dolphin* reached England on May 20, 1768, after a voyage of 21 months.

Rewards for the expedition

For his successful voyage, Wallis was rewarded with the command of several other ships. In 1782 he was appointed to a high administrative position in the Royal Navy, where he remained until his death at his home in London on January 21, 1795. Upon his return to England, Carteret was also rewarded with a promotion. During the American Revolution he commanded ships in the Caribbean but missed the naval engagements that took place during the war. When his health began to deteriorate, he returned to England in 1781. Carteret retired from active service in 1794 and died in the port of Southampton on July 21, 1796. According to his obituary, he had "long been afflicted with loss of speech."

Jacques Cartier

*Born 1491,
Saint-Malo, France*

*Died September 1, 1557,
Saint-Malo, France*

> Jacques Cartier, a French explorer, made three voyages to Canada and discovered the Gulf of St. Lawrence and the St. Lawrence River.

During the sixteenth century European navigators had determined that the continents of North and South America were a barrier to a direct sea route from Europe to Asia. Nevertheless, it was still believed that a natural waterway could be found through this landmass, so numerous explorers continued to search for the route, which became known as the Northwest Passage. Among them was Jacques Cartier, a French navigator.

Royal commission to explore the New World

Cartier was born in 1491 in the French port of Saint-Malo in the province of Brittany. Little is known about his early life, but it is clear that he made several sea voyages. According to some accounts, he may have been a crew member in two expeditions to America led by **Giovanni da Verrazano** (see entry) in 1524 and 1528.

In 1532 the Bishop of Saint-Malo proposed to King

François I of France that the king sponsor an expedition to the New World and that Cartier be chosen to lead it. Cartier, the bishop pointed out, had already been to Brazil and the island of Newfoundland. The king approved the nomination, and on April 20, 1534, Cartier set off from Saint-Malo with two ships and 61 men. His mission was "to discover certain islands and lands where it is said that a great quantity of gold, and other precious things, are to be found." It was clear from the start that Cartier was expected to find mineral wealth.

Exploration of the Gulf of St. Lawrence

Cartier's fleet sailed to the northern tip of Newfoundland and there entered the Strait of Belle Isle, which was known to lead to open waters beyond. Avoiding the barren northern coast, Cartier headed south along the western shore of Newfoundland, naming many of the rivers and harbors he saw. The party continued along the western coast until they came to the channel, now called Cabot Strait, that connects the Gulf of St. Lawrence with the Atlantic Ocean. Since Cartier did not enter Cabot Strait, he did not discover that it separates Newfoundland from Cape Breton Island and is a better route than the Strait of Belle Isle for entering the Gulf of St. Lawrence.

In the course of exploring the Gulf of St. Lawrence, Cartier was the first European to report on the Magdalen Islands (or, in French, Iles de la Madeleine) and Prince Edward Island. Cartier then sailed on to the coast of New Brunswick, where he explored Chaleur Bay, and headed north along the coast to Gaspé Bay, where he claimed the Gaspé Peninsula for France. From Gaspé Cartier continued to Anticosti Island, but he did not travel far enough beyond Anticosti to discover the St. Lawrence River. When Cartier went ashore to claim the land for France, he encountered the Iroquois chief Donnacona; when he left, he took two of the chief's sons with him as guests (some historians say as prisoners) on the return trip to France.

Second voyage to Canada

Upon his arrival in Saint-Malo on September 5, 1534, Cartier received a great welcome. Although he did not find any gold, he brought reports of a warm climate and fertile land in New Brunswick and the Gaspé Peninsula, a region previously considered suitable for fishing but certainly not for settlement and commercial trade. Intrigued by Cartier's report, the king began planning a second voyage. The following year François provided Cartier with three ships for a return trip to Canada. Cartier left Saint-Malo on May 15, 1535, taking with him Donnacona's two sons, who had learned French in order to serve as translators.

This was Cartier's most important voyage. Guided by the Iroquois, he sailed west from Anticosti and, on August 13, entered the great estuary of the St. Lawrence, which would become the main gateway for French exploration in North America for the next two centuries. Cartier sailed up the St. Lawrence past the Saguenay River to the village of Stadacona, on the site of present-day Quebec City. After meeting with Donnacona he traveled farther up the river to the village of Hochelaga, where the city of Montreal is now located.

Harsh winter in Canada

During his stay in Hochelaga, Cartier climbed Mount Royal to view the St. Lawrence valley, which contained fertile land; he also sighted the Lachine Rapids and the Ottawa River. After planting a cross at Hochelaga, Cartier's party returned in October to Stadacona, where they settled for the winter. Cartier and his men were the first Europeans to spend the winter in Canada, and they were surprised at the extreme cold.

They also noted that the Iroquois were becoming less friendly toward the French, a fact that would later have significance. Relations, however, were still amicable, and during the winter the Iroquois would save the Europeans' lives. The Frenchmen were suffering from scurvy, a disease caused by a lack of vitamin C, and were able to survive only because the Iroquois taught them how to make a tea out of white cedar, which was a source of that vitamin. When Cartier left Stadacona for France on May 6, 1536, he took Chief Donnacona back with him. They arrived in France on July 16.

Cartier's second voyage was a great success. He had found a great waterway that might be the sought-after route to Asia, and he even brought back a few pieces of gold. François wanted to send him back to Canada immediately, but war broke out between France and the Holy Roman Empire, so Cartier was not able to leave the country. In the meantime, the rights to colonize Canada had been granted to a French nobleman, Jean-François de La Rocque, Sieur de Roberval; Cartier was assigned to conduct reconnaissance work for Roberval's voyage the following year.

Last voyage to the New World

On this third voyage Cartier reached Stadacona on August 23, 1541. Donnacona had died in France, but this probably made it easier for Cartier to deal with Donnacona's successor, Agona, who now did not have to worry about his rival. While building a camp at the present-day town of Charlesbourg, north of Quebec, Cartier found some stones that he thought were diamonds. After making a brief trip back to Hochelaga, he returned to spend the winter at Charlesbourg. Once again the Frenchmen suffered through a harsh winter. They were also faced with the hostility of the Iroquois, so in the spring Cartier and his party decided to leave the camp and head back to France.

He left Stadacona in June 1542 and traveled to the port of St. John's, Newfoundland. During the entire trip Cartier had not seen Roberval, but the two men met as Cartier was preparing to sail. Cartier received instructions to return to Canada with Roberval and help him found the new colony; however, in the dark of night he slipped away and sailed for France, leaving Roberval to fend for himself. When Cartier arrived back in Saint-Malo, he found that the "gold" he was carrying was iron pyrite and the "diamonds" were quartz crystals.

Cartier was not disciplined for leaving Roberval behind, but he was never given another expedition to command. His book about his second voyage to Newfoundland was published in 1545. Cartier retired in Saint-Malo, where he was a prosperous businessman until his death on September 1, 1557.

Chronology of Exploration

As an aid to the reader who wishes to trace the history of exploration or the explorers active in a particular location, the major expeditions within a geographical area are listed below in chronological order.

Africa: across the continent

1802-14	Pedro João Baptista and Amaro José
1854-56	David Livingstone
1858-64	David Livingstone
1872-73	David Livingstone
1873-77	Henry Morton Stanley
1877-80	Hermenegildo de Brito Capelo and Roberto Ivens
1884-85	Hermenegildo de Brito Capelo and Roberto Ivens
1888-90	Henry Morton Stanley
1896-98	Jean-Baptiste Marchand
1924-25	Delia Akeley

Africa: coast

1416-60	Henry the Navigator
1487-88	Bartolomeu Dias

Africa: east

1490-1526	Pero da Covilhã
1848	Johannes Rebmann
1848-49	Johann Ludwig Krapf
1848-49	Johannes Rebmann
1849	Johannes Rebmann
1851	Johann Ludwig Krapf
1857-59	Richard Burton and John Hanning Speke (with Sidi Mubarak Bombay)
1860-63	John Hanning Speke and James Augustus Grant (with Sidi Mubarak Bombay)
1862-64	Samuel White Baker and Florence Baker
1865-71	David Livingstone
1870-73	Samuel White Baker and Florence Baker

1871-73	Henry Morton Stanley (with Sidi Mubarak Bombay)
1883-84	Joseph Thomson
1905-06	Delia Akeley
1909-11	Delia Akeley

Africa: south

1849	David Livingstone
1850	David Livingstone
1851-52	David Livingstone

Africa: west

1352-53	Abu Abdallah Ibn Battutah
1795-99	Mungo Park
1805	Mungo Park
1827-28	René Caillié
1850-55	Heinrich Barth
1856-60	Paul Du Chaillu
1861-76	Friedrich Gerhard Rohlfs
1863	Paul Du Chaillu
1867	Paul Du Chaillu
1875-78	Pierre Savorgnan de Brazza
1879	Henry Morton Stanley
1879-81	Pierre Savorgnan de Brazza
1883-85	Pierre Savorgnan de Brazza
1891-92	Pierre Savorgnan de Brazza
1893	Mary Kingsley
1894	Mary Kingsley

Antarctica

1819-21	Fabian Gottlieb von Bellingshausen
1837-40	Jules-Sébastien-César Dumont d'Urville
1839-40	Charles Wilkes
1907-09	Ernest Shackleton
1910-12	Roald Amundsen
1914-16	Ernest Shackleton
1921-22	Ernest Shackleton
1928	Hubert Wilkins
1928-29	Richard Evelyn Byrd
1929	Hubert Wilkins
1933-34	Lincoln Ellsworth
1933-35	Richard Evelyn Byrd
1935-36	Lincoln Ellsworth
1937	Lincoln Ellsworth
1939-40	Richard Evelyn Byrd
1946-47	Richard Evelyn Byrd
1956	Richard Evelyn Byrd
1956-58	Vivian Fuchs
1989-90	Will Steger

Arabia

25 B.C	Aelius Gallus
1812-13	Hester Stanhhope
1854-55	Richard Burton
1877-78	Anne Blunt and Wilfrid Scawen Blunt
1879-80	Anne Blunt and Wilfrid Scawen Blunt
1913	Gertrude Bell

Arctic (see also North America: Northwest Passage)

1827	Edward Parry
1893-96	Fridtjof Nansen
1902	Robert Edwin Peary
1905-06	Robert Edwin Peary (with Matthew A. Henson)
1908-09	Robert Edwin Peary (with Matthew A. Henson)
1925	Roald Amundsen
1925	Richard Evelyn Byrd

1926	Roald Amundsen and Umberto Nobile
1926	Louise Arner Boyd
1926	Richard Evelyn Byrd
1926-27	Hubert Wilkins
1928	Louise Arner Boyd
1928	Hubert Wilkins
1931	Hubert Wilkins
1940	Louise Arner Boyd
1955	Louise Arner Boyd
1958	U.S.S. *Nautilus*
1986	Will Steger

Asia; interior

1866-68	Francis Garnier
1870-72	Nikolay Przhevalsky
1876	Nikolay Przhevalsky
1883-85	Nikolay Przhevalsky
1893-95	Sven Hedin
1895-97	Isabella Bird
1899	Fanny Bullock Workman
1899-1901	Sven Hedin
1900	Aurel Stein
1903-05	Sven Hedin
1906	Fanny Bullock Workman
1906-08	Aurel Stein
1913-15	Aurel Stein
1927-33	Sven Hedin
1934-36	Sven Hedin
1953	Edmund Hillary
1977	Edmund Hillary

Asia/Europe; link (see Europe/Asia; link)

Asia, south/China; link

629-45 B.C.	Hsüan-tsang
138-26 B.C.	Chang Ch'ien

1405-07	Cheng Ho
1407-09	Cheng Ho
1409-11	Cheng Ho
1413-15	Cheng Ho
1417-19	Cheng Ho
1421-22	Cheng Ho
1433-35	Cheng Ho

Australia

1605-06	Willem Janszoon
1642	Abel Tasman
1644	Abel Tasman
1770	James Cook
1798-99	Matthew Flinders
1801-02	Matthew Flinders
1801-02	Joseph Banks
1802-03	Matthew Flinders
1839	Edward John Eyre
1840-41	Edward John Eyre
1860-61	Robert O'Hara Burke and William John Wills

Aviation

1927	Charles Lindbergh
1928	Amelia Earhart
1930	Beryl Markham
1930	Amy Johnson
1931	Amy Johnson
1931	Wiley Post
1932	Amelia Earhart
1932	Amy Johnson
1933	Wiley Post
1935	Amelia Earhart
1936	Amelia Earhart
1936	Beryl Markham
1947	Chuck Yeager
1986	Dick Rutan and Jeana Yeager

Europe/Asia: link

454-43 B.C.	Herodotus
401-399 B.C.	Xenophon
334-23 B.C.	Alexander the Great
310-06 B.C.	Pytheas
1159-73	Benjamin of Tudela
1245-47	Giovanni da Pian del Carpini
1271-95	Marco Polo
1280-90	Rabban Bar Sauma
1487-90	Pero da Covilhã
1492-93	Christopher Columbus
1497-99	Vasco da Gama
1502-03	Vasco da Gama
1537-58	Fernão Mendes Pinto
1549-51	Saint Francis Xavier
1595-97	Cornelis de Houtman
1598-99	Cornelis de Houtman
1697-99	Vladimir Atlasov
1787	Jean François de Galaup, Comte de La Pérouse

Greenland

982	Erik the Red
1886	Robert Edwin Peary
1888	Fridtjof Nansen
1891-92	Robert Edwin Peary (with Matthew A. Henson)
1893-95	Robert Edwin Peary (with Matthew A. Henson)
1931	Louise Arner Boyd
1933	Louise Arner Boyd
1937	Louise Arner Boyd
1938	Louise Arner Boyd

Muslim World

915-17	Abu al-Hasan 'Ali al-Mas'udi
918-28	Abu al-Hasan 'Ali al-Mas'udi
943-73	Abu al-Kasim Ibn Ali al-Nasibi Ibn Hawkal
1325-49	Abu Abdallah Ibn Battutah

North America: coast

1001-02	Leif Eriksson
1493-96	Christopher Columbus
1497	John Cabot
1498	John Cabot
1502-04	Christopher Columbus
1508	Sebastian Cabot
1513	Juan Ponce de León
1513-14	Vasco Núñez de Balboa
1518-22	Hernán Cortés
1524	Giovanni da Verrazano
1534	Jacques Cartier
1534-36	Hernán Cortés
1535-36	Jacques Cartier
1539	Hernán Cortés
1541-42	Jacques Cartier
1542-43	João Rodrigues Cabrilho
1584	Walter Raleigh
1585-86	Walter Raleigh
1587-89	Walter Raleigh
1603	Samuel de Champlain
1604-07	Samuel de Champlain
1606-09	John Smith
1608-10	Samuel de Champlain
1609	Henry Hudson
1610	Samuel de Champlain
1614	John Smith
1792-94	George Vancouver

North America: Northwest Passage

1610-13	Henry Hudson
1776-79	James Cook
1819-20	Edward Parry

1821-23	Edward Parry		1621-23	Étienne Brulé
1824-25	Edward Parry		1657	Pierre Esprit Radisson
1845-47	John Franklin		1659-60	Médard Chouart des Groselliers
1850-54	Robert McClure		1659-60	Pierre Esprit Radisson
1903-06	Roald Amundsen		1669-70	René-Robert Cavelier de La Salle

North America: sub-Arctic

1654-56	Médard Chouart des Groselliers		1672-74	Louis Jolliet
1668	Médard Chouart des Groselliers		1678-83	René-Robert Cavelier de La Salle
1668	Pierre Esprit Radisson		1684-87	René-Robert Cavelier de La Salle
1670	Pierre Esprit Radisson		1769-71	Daniel Boone
1679	Louis Jolliet		1775	Daniel Boone
1682-83	Médard Chouart des Groselliers		1792-94	Alexander Mackenzie
1684	Pierre Esprit Radisson		1792-97	David Thompson
1685-87	Pierre Esprit Radisson		1797-99	David Thompson
1689	Louis Jolliet		1800-02	David Thompson
1694	Louis Jolliet		1804-06	Meriwether Lewis and William Clark
1789	Alexander Mackenzie		1805-06	Zebulon Pike
1795	Aleksandr Baranov		1806-07	Zebulon Pike
1799	Aleksandr Baranov		1807-11	David Thompson
1819-22	John Franklin		1811-13	Wilson Price Hunt and Robert Stuart
1825-27	John Franklin		1823-25	Jedediah Smith
			1824-25	Peter Skene Ogden

North America: west

			1825-26	Peter Skene Ogden
1527-36	Álvar Núñez Cabeza de Vaca (with Estevanico)		1826-27	Peter Skene Ogden
			1826-28	Jedediah Smith
1538-43	Hernando de Soto		1828-29	Peter Skene Ogden
1539	Estevanico		1829-30	Peter Skene Ogden
1540-42	Francisco Vásquez de Coronado		1842	John Charles Frémont
			1843-44	John Charles Frémont
1611-12	Samuel de Champlain		1845-48	John Charles Frémont
1613-15	Samuel de Champlain		1848-49	John Charles Frémont
1615-16	Samuel de Champlain		1850-51	Jim Beckwourth
1615-16	Étienne Brulé		1853-55	John Charles Frémont

Northeast Passage

1607	Henry Hudson
1918-20	Roald Amundsen
1931	Lincoln Ellsworth

North Pole (see Arctic)

Northwest Passage (see North America; Northwest Passage)

Oceans

1872-76	H.M.S. *Challenger*
1942-42	Jacques Cousteau
1948	August Piccard
1954	August Piccard
1960	Jacques Piccard
1968-80	*Glomar Challenger*
1969	Jacques Piccard

Pacific: south

1519-22	Ferdinand Magellan
1577-80	Francis Drake
1642-43	Abel Tasman
1721-22	Jacob Roggeveen
1766-68	Samuel Wallis
1766-69	Philip Carteret
1767-69	Louis-Antoine de Bougainville
1768-71	James Cook (with Joseph Banks)
1772-75	James Cook
1776-79	James Cook
1785-88	Jean François de Galaup, Comte de La Pérouse
1791	George Vancouver

1826-29	Jules-Sébastien-César Dumont d'Urville
1834-36	Charles Darwin
1838-39	Jules-Sébastien-César Dumont d'Urville
1838-42	Charles Wilkes
1930	Michael J. Leahy
1931	Michael J. Leahy
1932-33	Michael J. Leahy

South America: coast

1498-1500	Christopher Columbus
1499-1500	Alonso de Ojeda
1499-1500	Amerigo Vespucci
1501-1502	Amerigo Vespucci
1502	Alonso de Ojeda
1505	Alonso de Ojeda
1509-10	Alonso de Ojeda
1519-20	Ferdinand Magellan
1526-30	Sebastian Cabot
1527	Giovanni da Verrazano
1528	Giovanni da Verrazano
1594	Walter Raleigh
1595	Walter Raleigh
1617-18	Walter Raleigh
1831-34	Charles Darwin

South America: interior

1524-25	Francisco Pizarro
1526-27	Francisco Pizarro
1531-41	Francisco Pizarro
1540-44	Álvar Núñez Cabeza de Vaca
1541-42	Francisco de Orellana
1769-70	Isabel Godin des Odonais
1799-1803	Alexander von Humboldt
1903	Annie Smith Peck
1904	Annie Smith Peck
1908	Annie Smith Peck

1911	Hiram Bingham
1912	Hiram Bingham
1915	Hiram Bingham

Space

1957	*Sputnik*
1958-70	*Explorer 1*
1959-72	*Luna*
1961	Yury Gagarin
1962	John Glenn
1962-75	*Mariner*
1963	Valentina Tereshkova
1967-72	*Apollo*
1969	Neil Armstrong
1975-83	*Viking*
1977-90	*Voyager 1* and *2*
1983	Sally Ride
1990-	Hubble Space Telescope

Tibet

1624-30	Antonio de Andrade
1811-12	Thomas Manning
1865-66	Nain Singh
1867-68	Nain Singh
1879-80	Nikolay Przhevalsky
1892-93	Annie Royle Taylor
1898	Susie Carson Rijnhart
1901	Sven Hedin
1915-16	Alexandra David-Neel
1923-24	Alexandra David-Neel

Explorers by Country of Birth

If an expedition were sponsored by a country other than the explorer's place of birth, the sponsoring country is listed in parentheses after the explorer's name.

Angola
Pedro João Baptista (Portugal)
Amaro José

Australia
Michael J. Leahy
Hubert Wilkins

Canada
Louis Jolliet
Peter Skene Ogden
Susie Carson Rijnhart

China
Rabban Bar Sauma
Chang Ch'ien
Cheng Ho
Hsüan-tsang

Ecuador
Isabel Godin des Odonais

England
Samuel White Baker
Joseph Banks
Gertrude Bell
Isabella Bird
Anne Blunt
Wilfrid Scawen Blunt
Richard Burton
Philip Carteret
H.M.S. *Challenger*

James Cook
Charles Darwin
Francis Drake
Edward John Eyre
Matthew Flinders
John Franklin
Vivian Fuchs
Henry Hudson (Netherlands)
Amy Johnson
Mary Kingsley
Thomas Manning
Beryl Markham (Kenya)
Edward Parry
Walter Raleigh
John Smith
John Hanning Speke
Hester Stanhope
Annie Royle Taylor
David Thompson
George Vancouver
Samuel Wallis
William John Wills (Australia)

Estonia

Fabian Gottlieb von Bellingshausen (Russia)

France

Louis-Antoine de Bougainville
Étienne Brulé
René Caillié
Jacques Cartier
Samuel de Champlain
Médard Chouart des Groselliers
Paul Du Chaillu (United States)
Jacques Cousteau
Alexandra David-Neel
Jules-Sébastien-César Dumont d'Urville
Francis Garnier

Jean François de Galaup, Comte de La Pérouse
René-Robert Cavelier de La Salle
Jean-Baptiste Marchand
Pierre Esprit Radisson

Germany

Heinrich Barth (Great Britain)
Alexander von Humboldt
Johann Ludwig Krapf
Johannes Rebmann
Friedrich Gerhard Rohlfs

Greece

Herodotus
Pytheas
Xenophon

Hungary

Aurel Stein (Great Britain)

Iceland

Leif Eriksson

India

Nain Singh

Iraq

Abu al-Kasim Ibn Ali al-Nasibi Ibn Hawkal
Abu al-Hasan `Ali al-Mas`udi

Ireland

Robert O'Hara Burke (Australia)
Robert McClure
Ernest Shackleton

Italy

Pierre Savorgnan de Brazza (France)
John Cabot (Great Britain)
Sebastian Cabot (England, Spain)
Giovanni da Pian del Carpini
Christopher Columbus (Spain)
Marco Polo
Giovanni da Verrazano (France)
Amerigo Vespucci (Spain, Portugal)

Macedonia

Alexander the Great

Morocco

Abu Abdallah Ibn Battutah
Estevanico

Netherlands

Cornelis de Houtman
Willem Janszoon
Jacob Roggeveen
Abel Tasman

New Zealand

Edmund Hillary

Norway

Roald Amundsen
Erik the Red (Iceland)
Fridtjof Nansen

Nyasaland

Sidi Mubarak Bombay (Great Britain)
James Chuma (Great Britain)

Portugal

Antonio de Andrade
Hermenegildo de Brito Capelo
João Rodrigues Cabrilho (Spain)
Pero da Covilhã
Bartolomeu Dias
Vasco da Gama
Henry the Navigator
Roberto Ivens
Ferdinand Magellan (Spain)
Fernão Mendes Pinto

Romania

Florence Baker

Rome

Aelius Gallus

Russia

(*see also* Union of Soviet Socialist Republics)

Vladimir Atlasov
Aleksandr Baranov
Nikolay Przhevalsky

Scotland

David Livingstone
Alexander Mackenzie
Mungo Park
Robert Stuart (United States)
Joseph Thomson

Spain

Benjamin of Tudela
Álvar Núñez Cabeza de Vaca

Francisco Vásquez de Coronado
Hernán Cortés
Vasco Núñez de Balboa
Alonso de Ojeda
Francisco de Orellana
Francisco Pizarro
Juan Ponce de León
Hernando de Soto
Saint Francis Xavier

Sweden
Sven Hedin

Switzerland
Auguste Piccard
Jacques Piccard

Union of Soviet Socialist Republics
Yury Gagarin
Luna
Sputnik
Valentina Tereshkova

United States of America
Delia Akeley
Apollo
Neil Armstrong
Jim Beckwourth
Hiram Bingham
Daniel Boone
Louise Arner Boyd
Richard Evelyn Byrd
William Clark
Amelia Earhart

Lincoln Ellsworth
Explorer 1
John Charles Frémont
John Glenn
Glomar Challenger
Matthew A. Henson
Hubble Space Telescope
Wilson Price Hunt
Meriwether Lewis
Charles Lindbergh
Mariner
U.S.S. *Nautilus*
Robert Edwin Peary
Annie Smith Peck
Zebulon Pike
Wiley Post
Sally Ride
Dick Rutan
Jedediah Smith
Will Steger
Viking
Voyager 1 and *2*
Charles Wilkes
Fanny Bullock Workman
Chuck Yeager
Jeana Yeager

Wales
Henry Morton Stanley (United States)

Index

Bold denotes figures profiled

A

Abd al-Hamid II 105
Abominable Snowman 453
Aborigines 147-148, 260, 302, 356-357, 367, 487, 857
Abyssinia 287, 289, 503, 789
Académie Française 286
Acadia 212, 214-215
Acapulco, Mexico 481
Accra, Ghana 416
Acoma, New Mexico 271
Aconcagua, Mount 99, 101
Acre, Israel 786
Acropolis 656
Across the Tian Shan to Lop-Nor 706
Adam's Peak 79
Adelaide, Australia 144, 355, 357, 362
Adelaide Island 853
Adélie Coast 328-329
Aden, Yemen 289, 290, 503-504, 772-773, 775
Admiralty Islands 127, 190
Adriatic Sea 157, 184, 186
Adventure 261-264, 298, 300
Adwa 503
Aegean Islands 433
Aegean Sea 6, 96, 325
A-erh-chin Shan-mo mountains 421, 706
"Aeroplane Girl" 492
Afghanistan 78, 462, 808
African Association 52, 54-55, 632, 635
African Society 501
Agadez, Niger 71
Agena 36-37
Agesilaus II 870
Agona 196
Agra, India 23
Aguarico River 629
Aguilar, Jeronimo de 276
Ahaggar Mountains 80

Ahvaz, Iran 595, 597
Ainu 40, 42, 105
Air Mountains 71
Akeley, Carl 1-2
Akeley, Delia 1-4
Alabama River 770
Alarcón, Hernando de 270
Ala Tau Mountains 706
Albany, Australia 356-357
Albany, New York 226
Albi 508
Albigensian heresy 95
Albuquerque, Afonso de 291
Aldrin, Edwin "Buzz," Jr. 29, 37-38
Aleppo, Syria 108, 596
Aleutian Islands 266, 600, 612
Alexander 639
Alexander Aegus 13
Alexander Archipelago 63
Alexander I 63, 91
Alexander I Land 92
Alexander the Great 5-13, 218, 808
Alexandretta, Syria 108
Alexandria, Egypt 7, 76, 97, 152, 289, 785, 789
Alfonso (of Portugal) 287
Algerian Memories 862
Algiers, North Africa 281, 737
Algonquin (tribe) 216-217, 765
Alima River 134
Al-Jazira, Syria 416
Al-Kufrah 738
Allahabad 462
Allumette Island 216
Almagro, Diego de 628, 670
Almagro, Francisco 673
Almanzor 571
Alps 87, 408, 450, 475, 654
Altai Mountains 185, 219, 707
Alvarado, Hector de 271-272
Alvarado, Pedro de 176, 275-276, 279, 672
Amazon Basin 337
Amazon River 304, 409-410, 413, 474, 477, 481, 627-629, 631
Ameralik Fjord 606
American Fur Company 82

American Geographical Society 132
American Highlands 339
American Museum of Natural History 2, 3
American Philosophical Society 529
American Revolution 120, 127, 192, 508, 529
American River 760
American Samoa 510
Amirante Islands 392
Amon-Ra 7
Amritsar, India 105
Amsterdam, Netherlands 455, 458, 486
Amu Darya River 8, 808
Amundsen Gulf 17
Amundsen, Roald 14-22, 56, 130, 158, 160, 337, 429, 641, 747, 859
Amundsen-Scott Base 377, 804
Amur 705
"Amy, Wonderful Amy" 492
Anabasis 868, 870
Anadyr River 41
Añasco Bay 248
Andalusia, Spain 287
Andaman Islands 693
Anders, William 28
Anderson, William R. 611, 613
Andes Mountains 99, 101, 157, 174, 299-301, 409, 479, 654, 768
Andrade, Antonio de 23-25
Andronicus II 67
Andronicus III 77
Andros Island 697
Angareb River 45
Angediva Island 390
Angkor, Cambodia 395
Angmagssalik, Greenland 342
Angola 57, 137-138, 313, 500
Angostura 479
Annam, Vietnam 394
Annapolis Royal, Nova Scotia 214
Antarctica 90-93, 158, 160-163, 325-329, 336, 375, 452-453, 744-747, 801, 804, 853, 856

Antarctic Circle 91, 262
Antarctic Peninsula 92-93, 803, 853
Antarctic Treaty 340
Anticosti Island 194-195, 498
Antigua 635
Antioch, Syria 97, 220, 598
Antivari, Yugoslavia 186
Apalachen 769
Aparia 629, 630
Apollo **26-33,** 37, 402, 558
Appalachian Mountains 118, 529, 770
Appenine Mountains 31
Apuré River 478
Aqualung 282-284
Arab Bureauscuba 89
Arabian Peninsula 108, 223, 772
Arabian Sea 435
Aral Sea 78, 597
Arawak (tribe) 248-249
Archimedes Crater 556
Arctic 129-132, 159, 255, 336, 646, 856
Arctic Circle 328, 612, 640
Arctic Ocean 14, 21, 469, 509, 801, 821, 857
Arequipa, Peru 99
Areta (tribe) 384
Arghūn 67
Arguin Island 426
Arias, Pedro 767
Arikara (tribe) 483, 532
Aristotle 5, 9
Arkansas River 83, 372, 497, 662, 663, 761
Arkansas (tribe) 516
Armenia 67, 597, 689, 868
Armstrong, Neil 29, **34-39,** 523, 558
Arnhem Land 812
Around the World in Eight Days 700
Arrillaga, José de 834
Artaxerxes 867
Arteaga, Melchor 100
Artemisia (of Greece) 434
Artocarpus 478
Aru Island 487
Aruwimi River 797

Ascension Island 127, 190, 302
Ashango (tribe) 323
Ashley, William Henry 758-759
Ashquelon, Israel 787
Asian Antiquities Museum (New Delhi, India) 807
Assam, India 752
Assassins 97
Assiniboine River 823
Astin Tagh mountains 706-708
Astor, John Jacob 64, 483-484, 824
Astoria, Oregon 535
Astrolabe 326-328
Asunción, Paraguay 167
Aswan, Egypt 76
Atahualpa (of the Incas) 672, 768
Atbara River 45
Athabaska Pass 824
Athabaska River 823
Athens, Greece 434, 785, 870
Athi Plains 1
Athi River 505
Atlantic Anomaly 352
Atlantic Ocean 4, 210, 407, 472-473, 493, 500, 509, 598
Atlantic Ridge 211
Atlas Mountains 79, 182, 435, 828, 861
Atlasov, Vladimir 40-42
Atlasova Island 40
Attock, Pakistan 434
Auckland, New Zealand 449, 453
Augustus 383
Augustus Grant, James 776
Aujila 738
Aurora Borealis 352
Austin, Horatio 368
Australia 453, 487-491, 493, 510-511, 519-522, 812
Austrian Alps 450
Autolycus Crater 556
Avavares 166, 347
Avila, Pedro Arias de 617
Awdaghost, Mali 416
Axel Heiberg Glacier 20
Ayres, Harry 450
Azemmou, Morocco 566
Azevado, Francisco de 25
Azores 246, 390

Aztec 276-279
Azua, Dominican Republic 275

B

Baalbek, Lebanon 97, 787
Baalbek, Syria 597
Babylon 8, 868
Back, George 366, 367
Back River 368
Bactria 8-9, 219, 461
Badakhshan, Afghanistan 690
Badrinath, India 24
Baffin Bay 368, 603, 645
Baffin Island 525, 640-642
Bafuka, Zaire 4
Bagamoyo 773, 792, 794
Baghdad, Iraq 67, 76, 88-89, 97, 108, 110, 184, 490
Bahía Bariay, Cuba 245
Bahia Blanca, Argentina 297-298
Bahia, Brazil 303
Bahia dos Vaqueiros 312
Bahía San Miguel 616
Bahr-al-Ghazal River 582
Bahr-el-Salam River 45
Baikonur Space Center 380, 778, 818
Baja, California 28, 177, 281, 834
Baker, Florence 43-51, 114, 156, 776
Baker, Samuel White 43-51, 114, 156, 580, 776
Bakongo (tribe) 581
Baku, Azerbaijan 418
Balboa, Vasco Núñez de (see **Núñez de Balboa, Vasco**)
Balchen, Bernt 338
Bali 304, 457
Baliem River 522
Balkan Peninsula 5-6, 44
Balkan Wars 856
Balkh 462
Baluchistan 808
Bamako, Mali 634, 636
Bamian 462
Bancroft, Ann 802
Banda Sea 487

Bangala (tribe) 796
Bangkok, Thailand 491, 666
Bangladesh 575
Bangui 581
Banks Island 601-602
Banks, Joseph 52-56, 91, 257, 262, 360, 575, 601, 632-633, 635, 638
Bantam 456-457, 486-487
Baptista, Pedro Joâo 57-60, 139
Baranof Island 63
Baranov, Aleksandr 61-64
Baranov, Peter 62
Barbosa, Duarte 571
Barcelona, Spain 95, 247
Bari 50
Barka Khan 688
Barker, Frederick 794
Barotse 548
Barrow, John 638-639
Barrow Strait 639
Barrow Submarine Canyon 612
Bar Sauma, Rabban 65-68
Barth, Heinrich 69-74, 737
Bartlett, Bob 430-431, 648, 652
Basel, Switzerland 503-504
Basra, Iraq 77, 89, 416-417
Bass, George 360
Bass Strait 360
Basundi (tribe) 581
Batavia, Dutch East Indies (Djakarta, Indonesia) 64, 261, 733, 810
Bates, Henry Walter 304
Bathori, Sigismund 763
Bathurst, Australia 302
"Battle" of Cahuenga 83
Battle of Coruña 784
Battle of Las Salinas 673
Battle of New Orleans 365
Battle of Okeechobee 83
Battle of Omdurman 583
Battle of Trafalgar 365
Battle of Wounded Knee 532
Battutah, Abu Abdallah Ibn 75-80, 181
Batu 184-186
Baudin, Nicolas 362
Bauer, Ferdinand 361

Baxter, John 356, 357
Bay of Arguin 426
Bay of Bengal 693
Bay of Fundy 213-215
Bay of Guayaquil 671
Bay of San Julián 568
Bay of Santa Cruz 569
Bay of the Horses 165
Bay of Whales 19, 160, 339
H.M.S. *Beagle* 292-294, 296-305
Beagle Channel 297, 299
Bean, Alan 30
Beardmore Glacier 746
Bear Flag Revolt 373
Bear Lake 760
Bear River 620
Beas River 9
Beaufort Sea 600
Beckwith, James Pierson (see **Beckwourth, Jim**)
Beckwourth, Jim 81-85
Beckwourth Pass 84
Bedouin (tribe) 107-109, 111, 786
Beechey Island 368
Beethoven, Ludwig von 474
Beijing, China 65-66, 184, 394, 397, 577, 688, 705, 755
Beja, Abraham de 290
Belcher, Edward 368, 603
Belém, Brazil 304, 410
Belém, Portugal 392
Belerium (Land's End) 710
Belgian Congo 3
Belgica 15
Bell, Gertrude 86-89
Bella Coola River 563
Bella Coola (tribe) 564
Bellingshausen, Fabian Gottlieb von 90-93, 853
Bellingshausen Sea 92
Bena Bena 521-522
Bengal, India 79, 223
Benghazi 738
Benguela, Angola 138
Benin, Africa 157
Benjamin of Tudela 94-97
Bennett, Floyd 160
Bennett, James Gordon, Jr. 789, 792

Benton, Thomas Hart 371, 373
Berbera, Somalia 153, 773
Bering Sea 41, 612, 701
Bering Strait 600
Berlin, Germany 475, 482, 701-703
Berlin Conference (1884-85) 796
Berlin Geographical Society 419
Berrio 387, 390
Bessus 8
Beyond Horizons 339
Bhutan 308, 575, 751
Bibliothúque Nationale 175
Bié Plateau 138
Big Lead 649
Billings, Montana 536
Bimini 696-697
Bingham, Hiram 98-102
Bird, Isabella 103-106, 863
Birú 670
Biscoe, John 853
Bishop, John 105
Bismarck, North Dakota 532
Bitter Root River 535
Bitterroot Range 534
Bjaaland, Olav 19
Black, Campbell 593
Black Death 80
Black Flags 398
Black Sea 44-45, 67, 91, 597, 694, 763, 869
Black, Tom Campbell 591
Blackfoot (tribe) 82, 483, 535
Blaxland, Gregory 55
Bligh, William 54, 189, 264, 359
Blue Mountains 484
Blue Nile River 54
Blunt, Anne 107-111
Blunt, Wilfrid Scawen 107-111
Bobadilla, Francisco de 251
Bobonaza River 411, 412
Boca del Sierpe 251
Bodega y Quadra, Francisco de la 833
Bogotá, Colombia 99, 479
Bolivar, Simon 99
Bolling Advanced Weather Station 161
Boma, Zaire 4, 795
Bombay, India 112

Bombay, Sidi Mubarak 112-116, 153-155, 231, 233, 773, 790
Bomokandi River 4
Bonner, T. D. 84
Bonpland, Aimé 474, 476-480, 482
Book of Ser Marco Polo 687, 694
Boone, Daniel 117-121, 531
Boone, Daniel Morgan 121
Boone, Rebecca Bryan 117
Boonesboro, Kentucky 119-120
Boothia Peninsula 368
Bora Island 733
Bordeaux, France 68
Borman, Frank 28
Borneo 571
Bornu, Nigeria 71
Boston, Massachusetts 227
Botany Bay 260, 360, 510-511
Botletle 546
Bou-Am 736
Boudeuse 123, 127, 190
Bougainvillea 122
Bougainville Island 126
Bougainville, Louis-Antoine de 122-128, 190, 510
Boulogne, France 151
Bounty 54, 188
Boxer Rebellion 584
Boyarsky, Victor 803
Boyd, Louise Arner 129-132
Bozeman Pass 536
Braddock, Edward 117
Brahe, William 145-148
Brahmaputra River 421, 752
Bransfield, Edward 91
Brattahlid, Greenland 343, 524
Braun, Wernher von 27, 352
Brava, Somalia 223
Brazil 455, 510, 838
Brazza, Pierre Savorgnan de 133-136, 581
Brazzaville, Congo 135, 580, 795
Bridgeport, Connecticut 493
Bridger, James 758
Bristol, England 170, 171
British Air League 489
British Antarctic Survey 377

British Hudson's Bay Company 530
British Museum 52, 857
British South African Company 828
Brito Capelo, Hermenegildo de 137-140
Brittany 508
Brooklyn Museum 3
Brooks Army Base 538
Broughton, William 833
Brown, Robert 361
Bruce, James 54
Bruce, Michael 785
Brulé, Étienne 141-143
Bruni d'Entrecasteaux 511
Bryan's Station, Kentucky 121
Bryon, John 123
Bubonic plague 80
Buchanan, James 374
Buchan, David 365
Buddha 462
Buddhism 25, 307, 460, 463, 693, 728
Buenaventura River 759, 760
Buenos Aires, Argentina 99, 157, 296, 299, 482
Bugungu, Africa 47-48
Bukhara River 808
Bukhara, Uzbekistan 78, 184
Bulgars 597
Bulolo River 520
Bumbire Island 794
Bungo 865-866
Bunkeya, Zaire 139
Bunyoro, Africa 46-47, 49-50, 776
Burke, Robert O'Hara 144-149
Burma 862
Burmese Technical Institute 491
Burmese-Thai wars 667
Burns Island 770
Burr, Aaron 662
Burrard Inlet 833
Burton, Isabel Arundell 151, 153, 156-157
Burton, Richard 45, 74, 113-114, **150-157,** 502, 506, 551, 580, 722, 772-777, 792
Bussa Rapids 637

Bykovsky, Valeri 819
Bylot, Robert 473
Byrd, Richard Evelyn 22, **158-163,** 332, 338, 800, 859
Byron, John 187, 785
Byzantine Empire 95, 869

C

Cabeza de Vaca, Álvar Núñez 164-168, 270, 346, 348
Cabo da Roca, Portugal 247
Cabot, John 169-171, 172
Cabot, Sebastian 170, **172-175**
Cabot Strait 194
Cabral, Pedro Alvares 313, 391, 840
Cabrilho, João Rodrigues 176-178
Cache Valley 759
Cadamosto, Alvise da 426
Cádiz, Spain 248, 250, 252, 320, 710, 716
Caillié, René 73, **179-182,** 736
Caillié Travels through Central Africa to Timbuktoo 182
Cairo, Egypt 45, 49, 51, 55, 76, 89, 111, 114, 152, 289, 416, 506, 578, 583, 591, 721, 786
Cajamarca, Inca empire 481, 672, 768
Cajon Pass 621
Calais, France 320
Calcutta, India 421, 491, 575, 577, 755, 807
Calicut, India 78, 222-223, 289, 389-392
California Gold Rush 81, 83
Callisthenes 9
Callisto 848
Caloris 588
Calypso 285
Cambridge Bay 17
Cambridge, England 499
Camden, Arkansas 770
Camelford, Baron 835
Cameron, Verney Lovett 116, 234
Camp VIII 451

Canadian Arctic 361, 364-365, 525, 560
Canadian Arctic Expedition 856
Canadian Arctic islands 858
Canadian Rockies 701
Canary Islands 174, 244, 248, 288, 426, 455, 500, 568, 631
Cannanore, India 289
Canton, China 79, 105, 577, 667, 866
Cañar 481
Cão, Diogo 311
Cap Haitien, Haiti 246
Capara 696
Cape Blanco 426
Cape Bojador 425
Cape Breton Island 170
Cape Canaveral, Florida 26, 28-29, 37, 353, 725
Cape Cod, Massachusetts 213-215
Cape Columbia 430, 431, 650, 652
Cape Cross 311
Cape Dan 605
Cape Delgado 505
Cape Disappointment 832
Cape Fear, North Carolina 837-838
Cape Hatteras 837
Cape Hecla 648, 650
Cape Hood 832
Cape Horn 258, 297, 510, 732, 834, 853
Cape Leeuwin 361
Capelo, Hermenegildo de Brito (see **Brito Capelo, Hermenegildo de**)
Cape Maria van Diemen 811
Cape Mendocino 178
Cape of Good Hope 116, 127, 190, 192, 241, 258, 260-262, 265, 288, 311, 313-314, 319, 386, 388, 390, 455, 566, 666, 832, 865
Cape of Masts 426
Cape of the Virgins 569
Cape Race, Newfoundland 170, 540
Cape Royds 746, 747

Cape Sheridan 650
Cape Town, South Africa 92, 302, 493, 501, 544, 548, 578, 829
Cape Verde Islands 174, 294, 319, 387, 426, 455, 572, 631
Cape Wolstenholme 472
Cape York 647
Cape York Peninsula 487
Caracas, Venezuela 99, 476, 477
Carantouan, New York 142
Cárdenas, Garcia Lopez de 271
Carib (tribe) 248, 838
Caribbean Sea 192, 247, 600, 616, 713, 831, 855
Carlos IV 476
Carlyle, Thomas 358
Carmathians 597
Caroline Islands 326, 328
Caroni River 715, 716
Carpathian Mountains 475
Carpentaria 147
Carpenter, William B. 209
Carpini, Giovanni da Pian del 183-186
Carranca, Andrés Dorantes de 346
Carrel, Alexis 541
Carson, Kit 372, 758
Carson Lake 621
Carstenszoon, Jan 488
Cartagena, Colombia 319, 479, 615, 625
Cartagena, Juan de 567
Carteret, Philip 126, 127, **187-192**
Cartier, Jacques 193-196, 526
Carvajal, Gaspar de 629-630
Casati, Gaetano 797
Cascade Falls 535
Cascade Range 620
Casement, Roger 136
Casiquiare Canal 474, 479
Caspian Sea 13, 97, 185, 418, 435, 597
Cassai River 58
Castillo, Alonso de 165-166, 347-348
Catherine of Aragon 316
Caucasus Mountains 219, 597

Caves of the Thousand Buddhas, 806-807
Cayenne, French Guiana 410, 411, 413
Cayman Islands 253
Cayuga (tribe) 215
Cayuse (tribe) 622
Cebu Island 570, 571
Celebes, Indonesia 190
Central African Republic 135, 581
Centrites River 868
Cernan, Eugene 29, 32
Ceuta, Morocco 425
Ceuta, Spain 79
Chabot, Philippe de 838
Chaffee, Roger 27
Chagga 505, 719
Chaillé-Long, Charles 580
Chalcedon 869
Chalcidice 6
Chaleur Bay 194
Challenger (space shuttle) 39, 467, 725-726
H.M.S. *Challenger* **209-211**, 406
Chalybes 868
Champlain, Samuel de 141-143, **212-217**
Ch'ang-an 460-461
Chang Ch'ien 218-220
Channel Islands 178
Charbonneau, Pompey 532, 534, 536
Charbonneau, Toussaint 532
Charles I (of Spain) 168, 175, 629-630, 768
Charles II (of England) 227
Charles III (of Spain) 123
Charles V (of Spain) 277, 280-281, 567, 570, 573, 671
Charles X (of France) 326
Charlesbourg, Quebec 196
Charlotte Harbor 697
Charlottesville, Virginia 120, 528
Charlton Island 472
Chasseloup-Laubat, Marquis de 395
Chatham 832
Chatham Island 301

Cheirosophus 868-869
Chen Tsu-i 222
Cheng Ho 221-224
Ch'eng-tu 460
Cherokee 118, 119
Chesapeake Bay 142, 470, 764-765
Cheyenne 85
Cheyenne Peak 663
Chiaha 770
Chibcha 479
Chickahominy River 764
Chickasaw (tribe) 770
Chihuahua, Mexico 348, 663
Childersburg, Alabama 770
Children's Crusade 96
Chile 510, 732, 834
Chillicothe, Ohio 120
Chiloe Island 300
Chimbu Valley 521
Chin-liu, China 460
China 461, 463, 469, 484, 509-510, 513, 687, 691-692, 814
China Inland Mission 814
Chinese Turkistan 461
Chira River 672
Chitambo 554
Chobe River 547-548
Choctaw Bluff, Alabama 770
Cholon (Saigon, Vietnam) 394
Cholula, Mexico 278
Cho Oyu 450
Choqquequirau, Peru 99
Chouart des Groseilliers, Médard 225-230
Christian, Fletcher 189
Christmas Island 265
Chryse Planitia 845
Ch'üan-chou, China 79
Chu Chan-chi 223
Chukchi Peninsula 62
Chukchi Sea 611
Chuma, James 116, **231-237,** 552, 554, 826
Churchill River 561
Churchill, Winston 748
Church Missionary Society 503, 505
Church of England 316
Church of Vidigueira 392
Chu Ti, Prince 222

Cilicia, Turkey 88
Cimarron River 761
Ciudad Bolivar 479
Clapperton, Hugh 72, 637
Clark, George Rogers 119, 529
Clark, William 485, 528-537
Clearwater River 534
Cleopatris, Egypt 384
Cleveland, Ohio 702
Clinch River 118
Clinch River valley 119
Clitus 9
The Coast of Northeast Greenland 132
Coats Land 748
Cochin, China 394, 397
Cocos Islands 302
Coelho, Nicolau 387
Cofitachequi 769
Coiba 615
Collins, Michael 29, 37
Collinson, Richard 17, 368, 600, 602
Colombia 479, 615, 625
Colorado River 166, 270-271, 530, 621, 759-760
Columbia 37, 38, 725, 832
Columbia River 372, 483-484, 530, 534-535, 621-622, 821, 824, 832
Columbia River valley 824
Columbus, Bartholomew 239, 241, 249, 251-252
Columbus, Christopher 169-170, **238-254,** 275, 288, 313, 386, 487, 614, 623, 695, 796, 839
Columbus, Diego 238, 240, 251, 254, 696
Columbus, Ferdinand 239, 241, 252
Comanche 761
Comogre 616
Compagnie du Nord 229
Compagnie van Verre 455
Company of One Hundred Associates 217
Compostela, Mexico 270
Concepción, Chile 300
Concepción 567, 571

Condamine, Charles-Marie de La 476-477, 481
The Congo and the Founding of Its Free State 799
Congo Free State 135, 136, 548, 796-797
Congo River 116, 133-136, 138, 580, 792, 796, 798
Congressional Medal of Honor 160
Congress of Vienna 482
Conquistadors 274, 281
Conrad, Pete 30
Conshelf 286
Constanta, Romania 44
Constantinople (Istanbul, Turkey) 44, 66-67, 77, 95-96, 108, 687-688, 694, 763, 785
Continental Congress 119
Contributions to the Theory of Natural Selection 304
Cook, Frederick Albert 429, 645, 650, 652
Cook Inlet 62, 266, 834
Cook Islands 265
Cook, James 52-55, 91, **255-267**, 475, 488, 509, 561, 796, 832, 834
Cook Strait 327
Cooktown, Australia 260
Cooley, W. D. 720
Cooper's Creek 145-147
Coosa River 770
Coos Bay 318
Copiapó, Peru 301
Coppermine River 366-367, 641
Coptic Christians 598
Coquivacoa 624
Coqville 326
Cordillera Mountains 299
Cordoba, Francisco Hernandez de 275, 767
Córdoba, Spain 241, 415
Corinthian War 870
Cornwallis Island 368
Coronado, Francisco Vásquez de 164, 167, 176, **268-273**, 281, 345, 349

Corrective Optics Space Telescope Axial Replacement (COSTAR) 468
Corte-Real, Gaspar 171
Cortés, Hernán 176-177, **274-281,** 669, 672
Cosa 770
Cosa, Juan de la 623
Cosmopolitan 332
Cossacks 40-42, 421
Council of Clermont (1095) 96
The Cousteau Almanac of the Environment 285
Cousteau, Jacques 282-286
Covilhã, Pero da 287-291
Cozumel, Cuba 275-276
Craterus 11, 12
Cree (tribe) 227
Crèvecoeur 514
Crimea, Ukraine 77, 433, 773
Crimean War 153, 773
Crippen, Robert 725
Crocker, George 649
Crocker Land 649
Crooked Island, Bahama Islands 245
The Crossing of Antarctica 377
Crow 81-82, 85
Crown Point, New York 215
Croydon Airfield 490
Crusades 96-97, 186, 424
Cuauhtémoc 279
Cuba 165, 249, 481, 625, 696-698, 768-769
Cubagua Island 630-631
Culiacán, Mexico 167, 270
Cumaná 476
Cumberland 363
Cumberland Gap 118, 119
Cumberland Peninsula 525
Cumberland valley 119
Cunene River 139
Cunningham, Walter 28
Curaçao Island 624
Curtiss Field 539
Custer, George Armstrong 789
Cuzco, Peru 99, 627, 672, 768
Cyprus 96
Cyrene, Libya 434
Cyrus 867-868

D

Dahar-June 787
Dahe, Qin 803
Daily Mail 492
Dakar, Senegal 426
Dalai Lama 307-309, 575-577, 753
The Dalles, Oregon 621
Damascus, Syria 76, 88, 97, 109, 157, 597
Damietta, Egypt 97
Danube River 44
Dardanelles 6
Darién 616
Darien Peninsula 625, 670
Darius I (of Persia) 434
Darius II (of Persia) 867
Darius III (of Persia) 7, 8
Darling River 145, 147
Darling, William 357
Dartmouth, England 472
Darwin, Australia 491-492
Darwin, Charles 292-305, 474
Darwin, Erasmus 292
David, Edgeworth 747
David-Neel, Alexandra 306-310
Davis, John 458
Davis Strait 472, 525
De Long, George Washington 606
Dead Sea 597
Dean Channel 564
Deccan, India 596
Deena 633
Deep Sea Drilling Project 406
Defoe, Daniel
Deganawidah 215
Deimos 587
Delaware Bay 470
Delaware River 470
Delft 487
Delhi, India 23
Denbei 42
Denver, Colorado 84
Derb-el-Haj 76
Derendingen 502
Descartes Mountains 32
A Description of New England 765

Desideri, Ippolito 576
de Soto, Hernando (see **Soto, Hernando de**)
Detroit Arctic Expedition 857
Detroit, Michigan 120, 485, 538
Devil's Ballroom 20
Devon Island 16
Dias, Bartolomeu 241, 288, **311-314,** 386, 388, 426
Dias, Dinis 426
Días, Melchor 270, 271
Dickson, James 633, 635
Diderot, Denis 127
Diebetsch, Josephine 645
Diemen, Anthony van 810
Dieppe, France 837
Dietrich, Rosine 504
Digges Island 473
Dione, moon 849
Discoverie of Guiana 715
Discovery 264-266, 464, 472-473, 830-833
District of Orleans 536
Diyarbakir 77
Djakarta, Indonesia 127, 190
Djenné, Mali 180, 579
Djibouti 580, 583-584
Dnieper River 41
Dolak Island 487
Dolphin 188, 190, 191, 257
Dominican Republic 615
Donnacona 194, 195
Donn River 41
Dorantes, Andres 165-166, 347-348
Doudart de Lagrée, Ernest 396
Drake, Francis 315-320
Druid 296
Druses 786-787
Druze 87
Dry Tortugas 697
Dubois River 530
Du Chaillu, Paul 321-324
Dudh Kosi River 752
Duifken 486-487
Duke, Charles 32
Duluth, Minnesota 142, 823
Dumont d'Urville, Jules-Sébastien-César 325-329, 511, 853

Dundee Island 339
Du Pont, François Gravé 213
Dupuis, Jean 396-398
Dusky Sound 263
Dutch East India Company 454-455, 469, 486, 732, 809-810
Dutch East Indies 328
Dutch New Guinea 522
Dutch West India Company 470, 732
Dwyer, Michael 520
Dza-chu River 706
Dzungaria 707

E

Eagle 37-38
Eagle, Alaska 18
Eaglet 227
Eannes, Gil 426
Earhart, Amelia 330-335, 493
Earp, Wyatt 337
East Africa 502-505, 507
Easter Island 263, 732
East India Company 151, 564, 575, 811, 733
East Indies 454, 456, 458, 633, 812
Ebro River 94
Ecbatana (Hamadan, Iran) 220
Ecuador 671-672
Edmonton, Alberta 701, 703
Edward I (of England) 68
Edward VI (of England) 175
Edwards Air Force Base 726, 742, 872, 874
Edy, Montana 759
Egypt 51, 476, 503, 598
Eielson, Carl 858
Eight Years' Wanderings in Ceylon 44
Einstein Cross 467
Eisele, Don 28
Eisenhower, Dwight D. 428, 542
Elcano, Juan Sebastián de 571-573
El Carmen, Patagonia 298
Elephant Island 748-749
Eletrophorus electricus 477
Elgon, Mount 828

El Haura, Arabia 384
Elizabeth I (of England) 316-319, 712-713
Elizabeth II (of England) 452
Ellesmere Island 159, 647-650, 802-803
Ellsworth Land 336, 339
Ellsworth, Lincoln 21, 130, **336-340,** 859-860
El-Mahdi 580, 582, 583
El Misti 654
Emin Pasha Relief Expedition 796, 799, 828
Enceladus 849
Enciso, Martín Fernandez de 615, 617
Encounter Bay 362
Endeavour 53, 257-261, 467
Endurance 747-748
English Channel 316, 320, 716
The Englishwoman in America 104
Enlightenment 529
Enriquez de Harana, Beatriz 239, 241
Enterprise 600
Epirus 6
Equatorial Nile Basin 43, 49-50
Erebus 368
Eredia, Manuel Godhino de 487
Erhardt, Jakob 721
Erik the Red 341-344, 524-525, 527
Erik the Red's Saga 524
Erik's Island 342
Eriksfjord 524
Erzurum 868
Esperance Bay 357
Espinosa, Gonzalo Gómez de 571, 573
Espiritu Pampa 98, 101-102
Espiritu Santo, Vanuatu 263
Essay on the Principle of Population 304
Essex 35
Estevanico 166, 268, 270, **345-350**
Etah, Greenland 429, 649-650
Eternity Mountains 339
Ethiopia 45, 503, 506, 522, 666

Etienne, Jean-Louis 803
Etoile 124, 127
Eucla, Australia 356
Euphrates River 8, 11, 88, 108, 597
European Space Agency 465
Evans, Ronald 32
Explorations and Adventures in Equatorial Africa 322
Explorer 1 351-354
Explorer 2 354
Explorers' Club 428, 432, 523, 652
Eyre, Edward John 355-358
Eyre Peninsula 356

F

The Faerie Queene 714
Faidherbe 582
Fairbanks, Alaska 701, 857
Faisal I (of Arabia) 87, 89
Falkland Islands 123, 187, 256, 299, 328, 732
Falkland Islands Dependencies Survey 375
Falklands War 123
Falls of St. Anthony 662
Fan (tribe) 323, 500
Fars, Iran 416, 595, 597
Farthest North 608
Fashoda Incident 578, 582-583
Fatiko, Africa 50, 51
Fatimids 416
Fatouma, Ahmadi 636-637
Femme Osage, Missouri 121, 531
Ferdinand (of Spain) 241, 247, 250-251, 386, 616-617, 624, 697
Fergana, Uzbekistan 219
Fernandes, Alvaro 426
Fernando Po Island 157
Ferrelo, Bartolomé 177-178
Fez, Morocco 79-80
Field Museum of Natural History 1-2
Fiji Island 328, 809, 811, 854
Filchner Ice Shelf 376
Finlay River 563

Finley, John 118
The Fiord Region of East Greenland 131
First Steps in Africa 775
Fischer, Gustav Adolf 827
FitzRoy, Robert 293-294, 296-302
Five Nations 215
Flandro, Gary 847
Flat, Alaska 703
Flathead Lake 620
Flathead Post 759
Flathead (tribe) 534
Flinders, Matthew 55, 359-363, 364
Flinders Ranges 355, 361
Flinders River 146
Floyd Bennett Field 703
Floyd Bennett 160-161
Floyd River 531
"Flying Sweethearts" 493
Flying the Arctic 860
F.N.R.S. 2 659
Ford, Edsel 160
Ford, Henry 542
Formidable 508
Forster, Georg 475
Fort Chipewyan, Lake Athabasca 561, 563-564
Fort Clatsop 535
Fort Conger, Ellesmere Island 647
Fort Crèvecoeur 514, 516
Fort Enterprise, Canada 366
Fort Franklin 367
Fort Frontenac 514
Fort Kootenay 824
Fort Mandan 532
Fort New Archangel, Alaska 63
Fort Prud'homme 516
Fort Ross, California 64
Fort St. Louis 518
Fort Vancouver, Washington 761
Foweira, Africa 49
Foxe Basin 640
Fox, Jack 522
Fox, Luke 640
Fox River 496
Fox, Tom 522
Fra Mauro Highlands 31
Fram 18, 19, 21, 607-608
Francia, José 482

Francis of Assisi 183
François I (of France) 193-196, 837-838
Franco-Prussian War 134, 397
Franklin, Jane Griffin 367-368
Franklin, John 14, 361, **364-369**, 599, 639
Franklin Strait 16, 368
Franz Josef Land 130, 607
Fraser River 563
Fraser, Simon 563
Frederick the Great (of Prussia) 474
Freetown, Sierra Leone 180, 500
Freiburg, Germany 475
Frémont, Jessie Benton 371, 374
Frémont, John Charles 370-374
Fremont Peak 372
French and Indian War 117, 122, 508
French Congo 136
French Foreign Legion 736
French Geographical Society 182, 329
French Guiana 717
French Legion of Honor 326
French Polynesia 733
French Revolution 511
French River 142, 216
Friendship 332, 402-404
Frobisher, Martin 344, 472
Frontenac, Count de 496, 513
Frozen Strait 640
Fuchs, Vivian 375-377, 452-453, 801
Funatsu, Keizo 803-804
Furneaux Islands 360
Fury 641-642
Fury Strait 641

G

Gabet, Joseph 814
Gabon, West Africa 135, 321-322, 500
Gades, Phoenicia 710
Gagarin, Yury 378-382, 402, 559, 782, 818
Galápagos Islands 301, 303

Galfridus of Langele 68
Galileo 32, 464
Galla (tribe) 503-504
Gallatin, Albert 533
Gallatin River 533
Gallus, Aelius 383-385
Galveston Island 165, 166, 346
Gama, Paolo da 387
Gama, Vasco da 224, 288, 313, **386-392**
Gambia 55, 635
Gambia River 426, 633
Ganges River 24, 453, 462-463, 598
Ganymede 848
Garhwal, India 24
Garnier, Francis 393-399
Gaspé Bay 194
Gaspé Peninsula 194-195, 214
Gatty, Harold 700-702
Gaugamela, Assyria 8
Gauhati 463
Gaza 7
Gedrosia 12
Gemini 6 28
Gemini 8 36, 37
Genesee River 142
Genesis Rock 32
Genghis Khan 66, 67, 184
Genoa, Italy 95, 694
Geographical Magazine 755
George III (of England) 53
Georges River 360
Georgian Bay 142
Gerlache, Adrien de 15
Ghat, Libya 71
Gila River 271
Gilbert Island 326
Gilbert, Humphrey 712
Gilgit range 807
Ginuha Genoa, Italy 67
Gjöa 16-18
Gjöa Haven 16-17
Gladstone, William 105
Glenn, John 31, **400-405**
***Glomar Challenger* 406-408**
Gloster Meteor 872
Goa, India 25, 289, 636, 666, 667-668, 865-866

Gobi Desert 308, 420, 461, 691, 705, 707
Godin des Odonais, Isabel 409-414
Godin des Odonais, Jean 409-411, 413-414
Godthåb, Greenland 606
Goering, Hermann 703
Goethe, Johann Wolfgang von 475
Golden Hind 318, 319
Gomes, Diogo 427
Gomez, Fernao 291
Gonçalves, Antao 426
Gondokoro, Sudan 45, 48-51, 114, 156, 776-777
Gordon, Charles "Chinese" 51, 580, 796
Gordon, George 358
Gordon, Richard 30
Goree Island 636
Gorgan, Iran 416
Gorges, Ferdinando 765
Goroka Valley 521
Gouda 454
Graf Zeppelin 338
Graham Land 15
Graham Peninsula 328, 375, 859
Granada, Spain 79, 242, 251, 767
Grand Canyon 268, 271
Grand Tetons, Wyoming 484
Grandmaison, Pedro de 411-413
Grandmaison y Bruna, Isabela de 409
Granicus River 6
Grant, James Augustus 45, 114, 156
Grant, Robert 293
Gray, Charles 145-147
Gray, Robert 832
Gray's Harbor 833
Great Australian Bight 361
Great Barrier Reef 125, 260, 362
Great Basin 760
Great Bear Lake 367
Great Dark Spot 850
Great Falls, Montana 533
Great Fish River 312
Great Inagua Island 245

Great Lakes 141-142, 214, 216-217, 496, 514, 518, 600
Great Plains 272, 664
Great Red Spot 848
Great Salt Lake 372, 373, 620, 759
Great Slave Lake 366, 561
Great southern continent 188, 256-257, 487, 731, 810
Great Trigonometrical Survey 751
Great Wall of China 666, 691
Greek History 870
Green Bay, Wisconsin 216, 496-497
Greene, Henry 473
Green Harbor, Spitsbergen 858
Green River 759
Greenland 129, 132, 171, 173, 341-343, 469, 524-525, 527, 604-606, 612, 645-647, 649, 711, 858
Greenland Ice Cap 159, 644
Greenland Sea 611
Greenlanders' Saga 524, 526
Greenville 256
Grenville, Richard 713
Grierson, John 592
Griffon 514
Grijalba, Juan de 275-276
Griper Bay 640
Griper 639-640
Grissom, Virgil I. "Gus" 27, 28, 402
Gros Ventre (tribe) 535
Groseilliers, Médard Chouart des (see **Chouart des Groseilliers, Médard**)
Grüber, Johann 576
Grytviken 749
Guadeloupe Island 248, 838
Guam Island 569
Guaraní 167, 168
Guayaquil 628
Guiana 716, 763
Gulf of California 270, 280, 496, 621
Gulf of Carpentaria 145, 146, 362, 487, 812
Gulf of Guinea 55, 157, 387, 636, 735, 737

Gulf of Maracaibo 615
Gulf of Mexico 496-497, 516-517, 529
Gulf of Oman 434
Gulf of Paria 251, 624
Gulf of St. Lawrence 193, 194, 498, 539
Gulf of Suez 384
Gulf of Taranto 434
Gulf of Tonkin 396
Gulf of Urabá 615, 625, 670
Gulf St. Vincent 362
Gunnbjörn's Skerries 342
Gustav V (of Sweden) 422
Güyük 185, 186
Gwadar, Pakistan 10
Gymnias 868

H

Haakon VII (of Norway) 19, 130
Hab River 10
Hadhramaut, Yemen 384
Hadjui 736
Hagia Sophia 67, 96
Hail, Saudi Arabia 88
Haiphong, Vietnam 398
Haise, Fred 30
Haiti 517
Half Moon 469-470
Halicarnassus 6
Hall, F. C. 700
Hamadan, Iran 8
Hamburg, Germany 16
Ha-mi 461
Hamid, Abdul 751
Hankow, China 396, 397
Hanoi, Vietnam 393, 398-399
Hanssen, Helmer 19
Harana, Diego de 246
Harar, Ethiopia 153
Harbor Grace, Newfoundland 333
Harrison, William Henry 82
Hartog, Dirk 488
Hassel, Sverre 19
Hatton, Denys Finch 590
Hauptmann, Bruno 541

Hawaiian Islands 104, 255, 265, 408, 484, 510, 542, 832, 834, 854
Hawikuh, New Mexico 270, 349
Hawkal, Abu al-Kasim Ibn Ali al-Nasibi Ibn 415-417
Hearne, Samuel 509, 821
The Heart of the Antarctic 747
Hebron, Jordan 97
Hecla 639-642
Hecla Bay 640
Hecla Strait 641
Hedin, Sven 418-423, 728, 807
Heemskerk 810
Heligoland Island 711
Hellenism 5, 12
Henderson, Richard 118-119
Hennepin, Louis 513-514
Henrietta Bird Hospital 105
Henry IV (of France) 213, 215
Henry VII (of Norway) 170
Henry VIII (of England) 316
Henry the Navigator 239, 387, **424-427**
Henslow, John 293, 294, 301
Henson, Matthew A. 18, 158, **428-432,** 645-651
Heraclides 13
Herat, Afghanistan 690
Herbert, Wally 652
Herjolfsson, Bjarni 524, 525
Herodotus 6, **433-435**
Herschel Island 18
Herschel, John 302
Hiawatha 215
Hickok, Wild Bill 789
Hillary, Edmund 376-377, **449-453,** 801
Hilton, James 522
Himalaya mountains 24, 309, 450-451, 453, 522, 751-752, 755, 772
Himyarite (tribe) 384, 385
Hindu Kush Mountains 8, 9, 78, 434, 462
Hingol River 10
Hinkler, Bert 490-491
Hispaniola 245-246, 249, 251, 615, 623
History 433-434

Hit, Iraq 597
Hitler, Adolf 423
Hobart, Tasmania 328-329
M.S. *Hobby* 130
Hochelaga (Montreal, Quebec) 195-196
Hog Cay, Bahama Islands 245
Hokkaido, Japan 104
Hollandia 455
Hollick-Kenyon, Herbert 339
Holston River valley 118
Honduras 253, 280
Hong Kong 105
Honolulu, Hawaii 600
Honorato da Costa, Francisco 58
Hopewell, New Jersey 483
Hopi (tribe) 271
Hormuz, Iran 10, 12, 223, 289-290, 666, 689-690
Hornemann, Friedrich 55
Hornet 39
Hotien 463
Hottentot (tribe) 388
Houghton, Daniel 55, 632-633
Houtman, Cornelis de 454-459, 486
Houtman, Frederik de 455, 458-459
How I Found Livingstone in Central Africa 793, 798
Howitt, Alfred 148
Howse Pass 824
Hsi-ning, Tsinghai 728
Hsiung-nu 219
Hsüan-tsang 460-463
Huadquina, Peru 100
Huascar 671
Huascarán 655-656
Hubble, Edwin P. 464
Hubble Space Telescope 464-468
Huc, Evariste Regis 814
Huckleberry Finn 801
Hudson Bay 173, 225-227, 229, 366, 368, 472-473, 497, 508, 640
Hudson, Henry 469-473
Hudson, John 472
Hudson River 470
Hudson Strait 472

Hudson's Bay Company 225, 227, 230, 366, 564, 618-619, 622, 759, 761, 821-823
Hulagu Khan 688
Humber River 142
Humboldt, Alexander von 293, 474-482, 505
Humboldt, Alexander von (son) 474
Humboldt Current 481
Humboldt River 620
Humboldt Sink 620-621
Humboldt, Wilhelm von 474-475
Humphreys, Jack 492
Hunt, John 451
Hunt, Wilson Price 483-485
Huron (tribe) 141-143, 215-217, 226
Hwang Ho River 707

I

Iberian Peninsula 95
Ibn Battutah, Abu Abdallah (see **Battutah, Abu Abdallah Ibn**)
Ibn Hawkal, Abu al-Kasim Ibn Ali al-Nasibi (see **Hawkal, Abu al-Kasim Ibn Ali al-Nasibi Ibn**) 415-417
Ice Fjord 131
Iceland 239, 341, 525, 613
Ictis Island, St. Michael's Mount, Cornwall 710
Id-al-Khabir 152
Idaho 484, 534, 620
Igloolik Island 641
Iguaçu Falls 168
Î-a-la Crosse 561, 619
Il-Khan Abaga 67-68, 693
Ili River 219
Illinois River 497, 516
Illyria 6
In Darkest Africa 799
Inca Empire 98-102, 174, 627, 669, 671, 768
Independence Bay 429, 647
India 450, 462-463
Indian Ocean 10, 11, 456, 488, 504, 598

Indochina 862
Indonesia 454, 458
Indus River 5, 9, 11, 78, 421, 434-435, 463, 598, 754-755, 808
Indus Valley 9, 596
Innocent IV 183
Inquisition 95
Inside Passage, Alaska 834
International Date Line 573
International Geophysical Year 93, 340, 351, 376, 801
International Trans-Antarctica Expedition 803
International Women's Peace Congress 820
Inuit (tribe) 344, 368, 428-432, 473, 498, 641, 645, 647-648, 650
Investigator Strait 362
Investigator 361-364, 600-603
Iraq Museum 89
Irish Sea 711
Irkutsk 701, 703
Iron Gates 461
Iroquois (tribe) 142, 194-196, 215, 217, 225-227, 513, 765
Iroquois Confederacy 142, 215
Irwin, James 31
Isabela, Dominican Republic 248-249
Isabella (of Spain) 241-243, 247, 250, 251, 254, 386, 616
Isenberg, C. W. 503
Isfahan, Iran 77
Iskander 290
Iskenderun, Turkey 7
Islam 75
Island of Thule 711
Issus, Turkey 7
Issyk-Kul 461
Istanbul, Turkey 96, 490, 687, 869 (see also Constantinople)
Isthmus of Darien 615-616
Isthmus of Panama 317-318, 615, 617
Italia 22
Ituri forest 797
Ituri River 3-4
Ivens, Roberto 137-140
Ivory Coast 579

Iztaccíhuatl 278

J

Jackson, Frederick 608
Jackson Hole, Wyoming 484
Jackson, Thomas "Stonewall" 374
Jaén 481
Jaette Glacier 131
Jahangir, Emperor 23
Jalapa, Mexico 277
Jamaica 249, 253-254, 357-358, 626
Jamaica Channel 253
James Bay 472
James I (of England) 712, 716
James II (of England) 229
Jameson, Robert 293
James River 764
Jamestown, Virginia 763
Jan Mayen Island 469
Janszoon, Willem 486-488
Japan 492, 809
Jarra 633
Jason 490, 492
Jauf, Saudi Arabia 110
Java 222-223, 457, 486, 488, 667, 862
Jeannette 606
Jefferson River 533
Jefferson, Thomas 482, 528-530, 533, 536
Jersey Island, English Channel 716
Jerusalem, Israel 65, 76, 87, 96-97, 597, 786
Jessup, Morris K. 647
Jesuit missionaries 23-25, 494, 498, 512, 668, 866
Jet Propulsion Laboratory 847
Jhansi 491
Jhelum River 9, 11
Jidda, Saudi Arabia 76, 152, 290
Jih-k'a-tse, Tibet 308, 753
Jinja, Uganda 3
Johansen, Hjalmar 607
John Bishop Memorial Hospital 105

John F. Kennedy Space Center 402, 587
John I (of Portugal) 240, 247, 288, 424, 425
John II (of Portugal) 288, 290, 291, 311, 313, 386
John III (of Portugal) 864
John of Monte Corvino 68
Johns Hopkins University 337
Johnson, Amy 333, **489-493**
Johnson, Lyndon B. 404
Johnston, Keith 235, 236, 826
Johore 458
Joinville Land 328
Joliba 636, 637
Jolliet, Louis 494-498, 513, 516
Jordan Valley 597
José, Amaro 57-60 139
Josephine Ford 160
A Journey in Ashango Land 324
"J.T.": The Biography of an African Monkey 2
Juan Fernández Islands 124, 188, 569, 732
Juba, Somalia 223
Juba, Sudan 591
Jumano (tribe) 347
Jungle Portraits 4
Junkers, Hugo 422
Jupiter 464, 468, 847-850
Jupiter Inlet 697
Jur River 582

K

Ka'abah 152
Kabalega Falls 43
Kabara 636
Kabul, Afghanistan 8, 434, 808
Kabul River 434, 462
Kabylia campaigns 736
Kadiköy 869
Ka-erh 754-755
Kafu River 47
Kagoshima 667
K'ai-feng 687
Kai Island 487

Kailas Mountains 421
Kalahari Desert 544, 546
Kalami River 10
Kalgan, China 705
Kalomo River 549
Kalongosi River 553
Kamalia 634
Kamchadals 42
Kamchatka 511
Kamchatka Mountains 41
Kamchatka Peninsula 40-42, 267, 510
Kamchatka River 41, 42
Kamehameha (of Hawaii) 64, 832, 834
Kanawha valley 121
Kanbaya, port 596
Kan-chou River 808
Kane, Elisha Kent 644
Kangaroo Island 362
Kannauj 462
Kano, Nigeria 71
Kanpur 462
Kansas (tribe) 662
Karachi, Pakistan 10, 434, 491
Karagwe 776
Karakorum, Mongolia 184-185
Karakorum Range 862-863
Karankawa (tribe) 518
Karbala, Iraq 88
Karlsefni, Thorfinn 527
Karuma Falls 48
Kasai River 548-549
Kasanje, Africa 58-59
Kashgar, China 419-421, 463, 690, 808
Kashmir, India 24, 105, 462, 755, 807, 862
Kasonia, Gascony, France 67
Kassange 549
Katanga 58
Katmandu, Nepal 452, 753
Katsina, Nigeria 72
Kauai, Hawaii 64
Kazakhstan 778
Kazeh 553, 774, 790
Kazembe, Zambia 58-59, 233
Kealakekua Bay 266
Kearny, Stephen W. 373
Keeling Atoll 302

Kellett, Henry, Captain 602-603
Kemys, Lawrence 716-717
Kennedy, John F. 26, 34, 402, 404
Kentucky River 118-119
Kenya 504, 589-591, 594, 719, 773, 828
Kerguelen Island 265
Kerman 12
Keyzer, Pieter de 455-456
Khabarovsk 701-703
Khadija (of Maldive Islands) 78
Khanbalik 688, 691-693
Khubilai Khan 184
Kharashahr 461
Khartoum, Sudan 4, 45, 49-50, 591, 776
Khawak Pass 8
Khazars 597
Kheidir, Iraq 88
Khojali 582
Khon Rapids 395
Khorasan, Iran 66
Khotan, China 420, 463, 690, 708, 807
Khrushchev, Nikita 381, 779, 818
Khumbu Glacier 451
Khurasan 596
Khuzestan, Iran 416-417, 595
Khwarizm, Persia 78
Khyber Pass 9
Kiangsu 692
Kiev, Ukraine 184, 186
Kikuyu (tribe) 719, 827
Kilimane 551
Kilwa, Tanzania 289, 392
Kim 151
King George Sound 302, 361, 832
Kingsley, Charles 499
Kingsley, George 499
Kingsley, Henry 499
Kingsley, Mary 499-501
Kingston, Ontario 513-514
King William Island 16, 368
Kinshasa, Zaire 4, 581, 795
Kintup 752
Kipfer, Paul 658
Kiribati Islands 733

Kisangani, Zaire 4, 795
Kisulidini 721, 722
Kisumu 3
Kitchener, Horatio Herbert 583
Kitty Hawk, North Carolina 837
Kitui 505
Kivoi, King 506
Klamath Lake 621
Klamath River 620
Kmeri (of Usambara) 504
Knox Coast 853
Kodiak Island, Alaska 62-63
Koko Nor 705, 707, 728, 752
Kolobeng 544, 548
Kootenay (tribe) 824
Korea 106
Korean War 35, 401
Korntal 506, 507
Korolov, Sergei 380, 778-779
Koryaks 41, 42
Kosmos 482
Koundian 579
Kouroussa, Guinea 180
Krapf, Johann Ludwig 152, 502-507, 718, 721-722, 827
Krestovka River 41
Kronshlot, Russia 91, 93
Kublai Khan 65-66, 687-689, 691-693
Kucha 461
Kukawa, Nigeria 72-74, 737
Kukukuku (tribe) 521
Kuldja 706
Kumbum 728
Kun Lun Shan mountains 219, 707, 807
K'un-ming, China 221, 396, 692
Kurdistan Mountains 868
Kuril Islands 40
Kuruman 544
Kuskov, I. A. 64
Kwango River 138, 549
Kyakhta, Russia 420, 705
Kyi-Chu River 753
Kyirong 753
Kyoto, Japan 865
Kyrgyzstan 461
Kyushu 667, 865-866
Kyasha 667

L

La Boussole 509, 511
Labrador 173, 338, 432, 498, 526, 652
Lacerda, Francisco José de 57-58
Lachine Rapids 142, 195, 497
La Concepción de Urbana 478
La Condamine, Charles Marie de 409-410
Ladakh, India 105, 755
La Dauphine 837-838
Lady Alice 794-795
A Lady's Life in the Rocky Mountains 104
Lae, New Guinea 520
Lagos, Portugal 239, 737
Lagrée, Ernest Doudart de 395
La Guajira 624-625
La Hogue 638
Laing, Alexander Gordon 181
Lake Alakol 185
Lake Albert 3, 43, 47-48, 50, 794, 798
Lake Athabaska 822
Lake Bangweulu 232-234, 551-552, 554
Lake Chad 69-72, 136, 737
Lake Champlain 215
Lake Chilwa 550
Lake Courte Oreille 226
Lake Dilolo 548
Lake Edward 798
Lake Erie 142, 513-514
Lake Eyre 356
Lake Huron 142, 216, 496, 514
Lake Illiwarra 360
Lake Issyk-Kul 419
Lake Itasca 662
Lake Kazembe 233
Lake Leopold 796
Lake Malawi 550-552, 826
Lake Manitoba 823
Lake Maracaibo 624
Lake Michigan 216, 496-497, 514
Lake Mweru 552
Lake Naivasha 827
Lake Ngami 544, 546
Lake Nipissing 142, 216
Lake Nyasa, Malawi 112, 231-232, 236, 505, 773, 789, 826
Lake of the Woods 823
Lake Ontario 513
Lake Parima 479
Lake Rukwa 826
Lake Simcoe 142
Lake Superior 142, 225-227, 823
Lake Tahoe, Nevada 104
Lake Tanganyika 113, 115-116, 155-156, 233-234, 236, 551-553, 774, 790, 792, 794, 826
Lake Terrens 356
Lake Victoria 3, 45, 113-114, 155-156, 435, 772, 775-777, 794, 798, 828
Lake Winnipeg 823
Lamaism 574
Lambaréné, Gabon 134, 322
Lamego, Joseph de 290
La Motte, Dominique 513
La Navidad (Limonade-Bord-de-Mer, Haiti) 246, 248
Lancaster Sound 16, 639, 642
Lanchou 691
Landells, George 145
Lander, Richard 637
Land's End, Belerium 710
Langle, Paul-Antoine de 509-510
L'Anse aux Meadows, Newfoundland 526
Laos 667
La Paz Bay 280-281
La Paz, Bolivia 654
La Pérouse, Jean-François de Galaup, comte de 326, **508-511**
La Pérouse Strait 510
La Relación y Comentarios 168
La Rochelle, France 766
La Salle, Illinois 516
La Salle, René-Robert Cavelier de 512-518
Las Conchas, Argentina 299
Las Palmas, Canary islands 244
Lassen Volcanic National Park 83
L'Astrolabe 509-511

Latakia, Syria 787
Lavaca River 518
Lawrence of Arabia (see Lawrence, T. E.)
Lawrence, T. E. 87, 89
Lazarev, Mikhail 91
Le Bourget Field 540
League of Nations 522
Leahy, Dan 521-523
Leahy, Michael J. 519-523
Leahy, Patrick "Paddy" 521
Lebanon 786
Ledyard, John 55, 632
Leech Lake 662
Leeward Islands 357
Legion of Honor 128, 579
Leh, India 421, 755
Leif Eriksson 251, 343, **524-527**
Leifrsbudir 526-527
Leif's Booths 526
Lemhi River 533-534
Lennon, Patrick 296
Leopold II (of Belguim) 134-136, 738, 796-797, 799
Lesseps, Jean de 510
Levant 787
Lewis, Meriwether 458, **528-537**
Lhasa, Tibet 24, 306, 308-309, 421, 574-577, 707, 727-729, 753, 813-815
Liang-chou 461
Liber Tatarorum 186
Libreville, Gabon 135-136
Liegnitz, Poland 184
The Life and Adventures of James P. Beckwourth, Mountaineer, Scout, Pioneer, and Chief of the Crow Nation 84
Lima, Peru 99, 157, 481, 627, 673
Lima, Rodrigo da 291
Lincoln, Abraham 374
Lincoln, Nebraska 538
Lindbergh, Ann Morrow 542
Lindbergh, Charles 160, 492, **538-542**, 592, 743
Linnaean Society 304
Linnaeus, Carolus 53
Linschoten, Jan Huyghen van 455

Linyanti 549
Lippershey, Hans 464
Lisa, Manuel 483
Lisbon, Portugal 239, 241, 312-313, 387, 390, 454-455, 666, 668
Lisiansky, Yuri 63
Little America 160-161
Little America II 338-339
Little Falls, Minnesota 538
Liv's Glacier 160
Livingstone, David 60, 74, 115-116, 134, 231-236, 397, 502, **543-554**, 718, 777, 789-793, 798, 825
Livingstone Falls 795
Livingstone, Mary 551
Llanos 479
Loango, French Congo 581
Loire River 710
Loja, Bonpland 481
Lolo Pass 534
Lombok 304
London Daily Mail 492
London Ethnological Society 323
London Missionary Society 297, 543, 548, 550
"The Lone Dove," 492
Long Island, Bahama Islands 245
Long Island, New York 539
Longfellow, Henry Wadsworth 215
Lono 266
Lop Nor, China 219, 420-421, 706, 708
Lop Nor Lake 807
Los Angeles, California 83, 177
Los Angeles-Chicago Bendix Trophy Race 700
Los Majos Islands 834
Los naufragios 168
Los Patos, Peru 301
Lost Horizon 522
Lou Lan, Tibet 421, 807
Louis IV (of France) 513
Louis IX (of France) 186
Louis XIII (of France) 216
Louis XIV (of France) 474
Louis XV (of France) 123
Louis XVI (of France) 509

Louisiade Archipelago 126
Louisiana Territory 497, 517, 529-530, 536
Louis-Philippe 327
Louis Philippe Land 328
Louisville, Kentucky 119, 530
Louvre Museum 326
Lovell, James 28, 30
Loyalty Islands 329
Lualaba River 134, 233, 552, 553, 792, 794, 796, 826
Luanda, Angola 59, 500, 549
Luang Prabang, Laos 395, 667
Luapula River 139-140
Lucas, Simon 55, 632
Lucma, Peru 100
Lukuga River 116, 826
Luna **555-559**
Luo-yang 460
Luque, Hernando de 670
Lusar 728
Luta N'Zige 46, 47
Luvironza 774
Lyell, Charles 302
Lygdamis (of Greece) 434
Lyons, France 186

M

Mababe River 547
Mabotsa 544
Macao 510
Macedonia 5, 433
Mach, Ernst 872
Machiparo 630
Machu Picchu 98, 100, 102
Mackenzie, Alexander 367, **560-565**, 834
Mackenzie, Charles Frederick 231
Mackenzie Delta 601
Mackenzie Pass 563
Mackenzie River 18, 367, 560, 562, 601, 801
Mackinac 496, 514
Macquarie Island 92
Mactan Island 570
Madagascar 456, 458
Madeira Islands 19, 239, 425

Madeira River 630
Madison, James 533
Madison River 533
Madura 457
Magadha 462
Magdalen Islands 194
Magdalena River 479, 615
Magellan, Ferdinand 174, **566-573**
Magomero, Africa 231
Maharashtra 463
Mahdia, Tunisia 415
Maigaard, Christian 645
Makatéa Island 733
Makololo 546-550
Makran Coast, Pakistan 10-11
Malacca, Malaya 223, 667, 865
Malagarasi River 790
Malaga, Spain 79
Malakal 591
Malange, Angola 138
Malawi 828
Malay Archipelago 327, 459, 666, 742, 865
Malay Peninsula 105, 666, 692
Maldive Islands 78, 223
Malheur River 620
Mali 578-580
Malindi, Kenya 223, 290, 389-390
Malta Island 785
Malthus, Thomas
Mambirima Falls 140
Mana, India 24
Mana Pass 24, 754
Manco 672
Manco II 99
Mandan (tribe) 532, 823
Mandarin 460
Manhattan 470
S.S. *Manhattan* 17
Mankinga (of the Chagga) 719-721
Manning, Thomas 574-577
Manoa, South America 715
Manuel Comnenus 95, 96
Manuel I (of Portugal) 313, 386, 390-391
Manuel II 566
Maori (tribe) 259, 260, 302, 810

lxiii | Index

A Map of Virginia, 764
Mar'ib, Yemen 384
Maragheh, Azerbaijan 66
Marañón River 411, 413
Marchand, Jean Baptiste 136, **578-584**
Marcos, Fray 176
Mare Crisium 559
Mare Imbrium 556
Margarita Island 251, 624
Margarita, Venezuela 630
Mariame (tribe) 347
Mariana Islands 569, 573
Mariana Trench 211, 659
Marias River 533
Marie Byrd Land 160
Marie Galante Island 248
Marina (Malinche) 276, 278
Mariner **585-588**
Markham, Beryl 333, **589-594**
Markham, Mansfield 590
Markland, Labrador 526-527
Ma-Robert 550
Marquesa Island 263
Marques, Manuel 23-24
Marquette, Jacques 494, 496, 497, 513, 516
Mars 586-587, 843-846, 850
Mars 2 587
Marshall Islands 401
Martha's Vineyard, Massaachusetts 214
Martinez, Juan 715
Martin, James 827
Martyr, Peter 173
Marvin, Ross 430
Mary Kingsley Hospital 501
Marysville, California 84
Marzuq, Libya 71, 737
Mas Afuera 188
Masai (tribe) 825, 827-828
Masaki 719
Masasi, Tanzania 235
Mashhad, Iran 419
Mason, James 854
Massa'ot 94, 97
Massassa Rapids 795
Massawomeke (tribe) 765
Mas'udi, Abu al-Hasan 'Ali al- **595-598**

Matagorda Bay 518
Matavai Bay 258
Matoaka (Pocahontas) 764
Matterhorn 653
Matthew 170
Mattingly, Thomas 32
Maud 21
Maui, Hawaii 542
Mauna Loa 854
Mauritius 127, 302, 363, 810
Mauritius 455
Mawson, Douglas 746
Maya 275
Maysville, Kentucky 121
Mbomu Rapids 581
McAuliffe, Christa 726
McClintock, Francis 368, 602
McClure, Robert 368, **599-603**, 640
McDivitt, James 29
McGregor River 563
McMurdo Sound 19, 376, 377, 746
Mecca, Saudi Arabia 75-77, 110, 151, 152, 290, 597
Medal of Freedom 39, 286
Medina, Saudi Arabia 75, 76, 152, 290, 597
Medina, Woolli 633
Mediterranean Sea 11, 67, 108, 282, 286, 408, 476, 591, 596, 735, 774, 786-787, 837
Meknes 736
Mekong 706
Mekong River 393-395
Melbourne, Australia 19, 145, 148-149, 355, 362
Melchior, Simone 284
Melville Island 600, 639-640
Melville Peninsula 641
Melville Sound 601-602, 640
Memphis, Tennessee 516, 770
Mendaña, Alvaro de 126, 189
Mendoza, Antonio de 167, 176-177, 268, 270, 272-273, 280, 348-349
Mendez, Diego 253, 254
Menindee, Australia 145, 147-148
Merchant Adventurers 175

Mercury 481, 587-588, 850
Mercury 31, 401
Mercury 5 28
"Mercury Seven" 401, 404
Mercy Bay 602-603
Méré 582
Meru 3
Meryon, Charles 784-785, 787
Mesawa 503
Mesopotamia 8, 87, 97, 219-220, 808
Messina, Sicily 97
Mestiza 479
Metternich, Clemens von 475
Metzenbaum, Howard 405
Mexico City, Mexico 167, 270, 272, 273, 541
Michilimackinac 216, 496, 516
Micronesia 327
Midjökull 342
Miletus 6
Mill, John Stuart 358
Minab River 10
Mindanao Island 571
Minnetaree (tribe) 532, 534
Mirambo 790
Miranda 850
Mirnyi 91-92
Miss Boyd Land 131
Mission San Gabriel 760
Mississippi River 165, 494, 496-497, 513-518, 529-530, 661-662, 767, 770, 823
Mississippi Valley 517
Missoula, Montana 620
Missouri 483, 533, 662
Missouri River 483, 496, 516, 530-533, 535-536, 759, 823
Missouri (tribe) 531
Mitchell, Edgar 31
Mocha, Yemen 666
Moffat, Robert 544
Mogadishu, Somalia 223
Mohawk (tribe) 215, 225
Mohi, Hungary 184
Mojave Desert 760
Mojave River 760
Mojave (tribe) 621, 760
Mile St. Nicolas, Haiti 245
Mollison, Jim 492, 493, 592

Moluccas (Spice Islands) 127, 174, 318, 457, 567, 570-571, 573, 733, 865
Mombasa, Kenya 3, 113, 223, 289, 389, 504, 718, 828
Möngkhe 184
Mongol Empire 688
Mongolia 704-705
Mongolia and the Tangut Country 706
Mongols 65-67, 77, 97, 183, 185, 576, 687, 691-693
Moniz, Felipa Perestrello de 238
Montana 484, 533
Monterey, California 83, 510, 761, 834
Montevideo, Uruguay 296, 299
Montezuma 274-276, 278, 279
Montgomerie, Thomas George 751
Monticello 482
Montpelier, France 95
Montreal, Quebec, Canada 195, 226, 483-484, 497, 512-513, 516, 518
Monts, Pierre de 214
Moore, John 784
Moors 241-242, 424
Morant Bay 357
Morel, Edmund 136
Moriussaw, Greenland 432
Morocco 106, 287, 736, 763, 861
Morovejo, Evaristo 100-101
Morozko, Luka 41
Morrow, Ann 541
Moscoso, Luis de 771
Moscow, Russia 184, 701, 703
Mossel Bay 312, 388
Mount Aconcagua 99, 101, 654
Mountain Green 620
Mountain men 758
Mountains of the Moon 798
Mount Albert 506
Mount Ararat 689
Mount Brown 361
Mount Cameroon 500
Mount Chimborazo 480
Mount Cook 450
Mount Desert Island 214
Mount Egmont 450

Mount Elgon 828
Mount Erebus 746
Mount Etna 67
Mount Everest 450-451, 752
Mount Fuji 450
Mount Gardner 832
Mount Hagen 521-522
Mount Herschel 453
Mount Hood 833
Mount Hopeless 147
Mount Huascarán 653, 654
Mount Idinen 71
Mount Illampu 654
Mount Kenya 3, 505, 827
Mount Kilimanjaro 505, 718-720, 827
Mount Koser Gunge 862
Mount Olympus 870
Mount Orizaba 654
Mount Palomar 465
Mount Rainier 833
Mount Royal 195
Mount Ruapehu 449
Mount Shasta, California 620, 654
Mount Tapuaenuku 450
Mount Taveta 827
Mount William 506
Mozambique 57-58, 137, 223, 388-389, 392, 505, 550, 865
Muddy Pass 372
Muhammad Tughluql 78
Mukden, Manchuria 106
Mukut Parbat 450
Multan, India 11
Multan, Pakistan 78
Mundus Novus 841
Munster, Ireland 713
Murchison Falls 48
Murray, Mungo 546
Muruj adh-Dhahab 595
Muslims 389, 424
Mussolini, Benito 22
Mustang Island 346
Mutis, José Celestino 479
Mweru, Lake 232

N

Nablus 597

Nachtigal, Gustav 737
Nafud Desert 110
Nagasaki, Japan 866
Nagchu 707
Nagchuka 729
Nain 754
Najaf, Iraq 77
Najran, Saudi Arabia 384
Nalanda 462, 463
Namibe, Angola 139
Nanking, China 222-223
Nansemond River 765
Nansen, Fridtjof 15, 18-19, **604-609,** 645
Nan Shan mountains 707
Naples, Italy 95
Napoléon Bonaparte 474, 528, 784-785
Napoleonic Wars 56, 365, 476, 482, 638, 831
Napo River 627-629
Nares, George 209, 210
Narragansett Bay 838
Narrative of the United States Exploring Expedition 854
Narváez, Pánfilo de 176, 278
NASA (see National Aeronautics and Space Administration)
NASA Space Flight Center 466
Nass River 622
Natchez (tribe) 516
Natchitoches, Louisiana 664
National Aeronautics and Space Administration (NASA) 26, 29, 31, 36, 39, 465-467, 660, 723-724, 726, 780, 847
National African Company 828
National Air and Space Museum 743, 845
National Geographic Society 159, 377, 652
Native American 470, 478, 495-496, 514, 516, 518, 527-528, 530, 532, 534-536
U.S.S. *Nautilus* 610-613, 859
Navárez, Pánfilo de 165, 346
Navasota, Texas 518
Navidad, Mexico 177
Nduye, Zaire 4
Nearchus 10-13

Nearest the Pole: A Narrative of the Polar Expedition of the Peary Arctic Club 652
Necho, King 435
Needles, California 621
A Negro at the North Pole 432
Negros Island 571
Nelson, Horatio 359
Nelson River 229
Nepal 450-453, 751
Neptune 847, 849-850
Nestorians 65, 66
Nestorius 66
Netsilik 16
Neva 63
Nevado Coropuna 99, 101
New Archangel, Alaska 64
New Brunswick 194-195, 214
New Caledonia 264
Newfoundland 53, 171, 194, 256, 332, 713, 526, 540, 701, 837-838
New France (Canada) 141, 212, 216-217, 225, 494, 496, 497, 512-513, 516
New Guinea 3, 127, 190, 328, 487-488, 519-520, 523, 811-812
New Holland 488, 812
New Ireland 127, 190
New London Company 763
Newport Harbor 838
New Sarai, Russia 77
New South Wales, Australia 359, 511, 643
New Spain (Mexico) 176, 280, 517
Newton, Isaac 465
New York 483, 485, 513, 523, 539-541
New York Harbor 470, 837-838
New Zealand 92, 160, 258, 327, 357, 450, 452-453, 746, 809, 832
Nez Percé (tribe) 534
Ngounié River 322
Niagara River 142, 513-514
Nicaragua 627, 767
Nicholas II 420-421
Nicholas IV 68

Nicholls, Henry 55
Nicollet, Jean 216, 217, 371
Niger 53
Niger River 52, 54-55, 72, 416, 579, 632-636, 737, 828
Nikolayev, Andriyan 819, 820
Nikumaroro Atoll 335
Nile River 11, 45-47, 51, 76, 113-114, 150, 152-153, 155, 435, 502, 506, 551, 553, 578, 582-583, 591, 598, 721-722, 772, 774-777, 792, 798
Nimrod 746-747
Niña 243, 246, 247, 250, 487
Nixon, Richard M. 30, 38
Niza, Marcos de 268, 270-271, 348
Njoro, Kenya 590
Nobel Peace Prize 609
Nobile, Umberto 22, 130, 337, 859
Noel, Anne Isabella 107
Noe, Lewis 789
Noga 814-815
Nombre de Dios, Panama 316
Nome, Alaska 18, 21, 701
Noonan, Fred 334, 335
Noort, Oliver van 458
Nootka Convention 831
Nootka Sound 833-834
Nordenskiöld, Nils A. E. 21, 418, 605, 645
Norfolk 360
Norfolk Island 360, 510
Norgay, Tenzing 451-452
Norge 22, 337, 859
Normandy 512, 540
Noronha, Fernando de 58
Norsemen 524-527
Northeast Passage 21, 175, 469
North Frisian Islands 711
North Holland 454
North Island (New Zealand) 259, 302, 327, 449, 811
North Magnetic Pole 15-16, 600, 642
North Pole 18, 21-22, 158-160, 428, 431-432, 606, 608, 610-612, 644, 647-652, 801, 803, 859

lxvii | Index

The North Pole: Its Discovery Under the Auspices of the Peary Arctic Club 652
North Saskatchewan River 823
Northward over the "Great Ice" 652
North West Company 561, 564, 619, 822-824
Northwest Passage 14, 16-17, 52, 56, 170, 173, 214, 217, 264-265, 280, 364, 368, 470, 472, 509, 599, 601, 603, 639-640, 642, 832, 834
The Northwest Passage 18
Norway 469, 525
Nothing Venture, Nothing Win 453
Nova Scotia 170, 343, 470, 539, 589, 592, 593, 638, 660, 838
Novosibirsk 701, 703
Ntem, West Africa 323
Nueva Andalucía 625
Nullarbor Plain 356
Núñez de Balboa, Vasco 253, **614-617,** 625, 670
Nun Kun Range 862
Nyangwe 795
Nyoros 46, 51

O

Oaxaca, Mexico 176
Oberon 850
Ocean of Storms 30, 557
Ocean World 285
Oceanographic Museum of Monaco 285
Oceanus Procellarum 557
Odoric of Pordenone 24, 576
Ogden, Peter Skene 618-622
Ögedei 184, 185
Ogooué River 133-134, 322, 500
Ohio River 119, 496-497, 513, 516, 530
Ojeda, Alonso de 171, 249, 615, **623-626,** 670, 840
Okavango River 139
Okhotsk, Siberia 62-63
Okinawa, Japan 874
Olaf I (Norway) 524

Ollantaitambo, Peru 99
Olympias 5-6
Olympic Games (1936) 423
Omaha (tribe) 531
Oman 77, 490, 596
Oneida (tribe) 215
Onondaga (tribe) 215
Onondaga, New York 226
On the Ocean 709
On the Shape of the World 415
Operation Highjump 163
Opium War 544
Oran 737
Order of Christ 425
Ordos Desert 705
Oregon River 530
Oregon Trail 372, 484, 485
Orellana 628, 629, 631
Orellana, Francisco de 627-631
The Origin of Species 304-305
Orinoco River 251, 476-479, 715-717
Orkney Islands 711
Oromo 503
Orteig Prize 539
Ortiz, Juan 770
Osage (tribe) 662
Oscar (of Sweden and Norway) 608
Oscar II (of Sweden) 419
Oslo, Norway 16, 19
Oswell, William Colton 546-548
Oto (tribe) 531
Ottawa (tribe) 226-227
Ottawa River 142, 195, 216
Ottoman Empire 44, 49
Otumba 279
Ouango 581
Ouessant Island 710
Ouezzane 736
Ovando, Nicolás de 252-254
Overweg, Adolf 70, 72
Ovimbundu 58
Oxus River 416
Ozark Mountains 770

P

Pacific Northwest 483, 535

Pacific Ocean 28, 39, 210, 408, 472, 511, 529-530, 535
Padilla, Juan de 271
Pai River 394
Paiva, Afonso de 288, 290
Pakistan 462, 808
Palau 318, 573
Palermo, Sicily 417
Palestine 597, 689
Palmer, Nathaniel 91-92
Palmer Peninsula 93, 748
Palmyra, Syria 87, 109, 385, 597, 786
Palo de vaca 477
Palos de la Frontera, Spain 240, 243
Pamir Mountains 419, 420, 807-808
Pamir Plateau 690
Pamlico Sound 837
Panama 253, 627, 670-671
Panchen Lama 308, 753
Pánuco, Mexico 165, 166
Papua 520-523
Papua (tribe) 520
Paraguay River 164, 168
Paraná River 168, 174
Paria Peninsula 842
Paris, France 67, 482, 511-512, 539-540
Park, Mungo 55, 632-637
Parmenion 7, 9
Parry Channel 17
Parry Islands 639
Parry, (William) Edward 56, 600-601, 638-643
Parsnip River 563
Pasha, Emin 580, 796
Pasha 316
Pastaza River 413
Patagonia 296, 299-300, 568
Patani 666
Patapsco 765
Patapsco River 764
Patuxent River 765
Paulet Island 748
Pawnee (tribe) 82, 759
Pawtucket 838
Peace River 563
Pearl Islands 616

Pearl River 866
Peary Arctic Club 647
Peary Channel 645
Peary, Josephine 429, 646
Peary Land 645
Peary, Robert Edwin 18, 158, 428-432, 644-652, 654, 800, 802
Peck, Annie Smith 653-656, 862
Pecos River 272
Peel Sound 368
Peel Strait 16
Peloponnesian War 434
Peregrinação 665
Pereira, Gonçalo 59
Persepolis, Persia 8, 595
Persia (Iran) 5-6, 8, 65-67, 77-78, 97, 105, 184, 219, 433, 690, 808
Persian Gulf 10-12, 110, 289, 434
Persian Pictures, A Book of Travels 87
Perth, Australia 403
Peru 337, 481, 627, 653, 767-768
Peshawar, Pakistan 219, 462
Peter I 42
Peter I Island 92, 859
Petherick, John 45-46, 776
Petra, Jordan 385
Petropavlovsk-Kamchatski 510
Philadelphia Academy of Natural Sciences 322
Philip I (of Spain) 173
Philip II (of Macedonia) 5-6
Philip II (of Spain) 317, 319, 570
Philip IV (of France) 67
Philippines 3, 570, 742, 809
Phillip, Arthur, 511
Phobos 587
Phoenix 63
Piacenza 689
Piccard, Auguste 657-660
Piccard, Jacques 657-660
Piccard, Jean 657
Pichincha 480
Piegan (tribe) 822-824
Pierre, South Dakota 532
Pikes Peak 663

Pike, Zebulon 661-664
Pillars of Hercules 710
Pim, Bedford 603
Pindar 6
Piner's Bay 853
Pinta 243-246, 487
Pinto, Fernão Mendes 665-668
Pinzón, Martín Alonso 245
Pir-Sar 9
Pisa, Italy 95
Pisania 633, 635, 636
Pitcairn Island 188, 189
Pitt, William 784, 835
Pizarro, Atahualpa 671
Pizarro, Francisco 99, 481, 615-617, 625, 627-629, **669-673**, 767-768
Pizarro, Hernando 673
Plateau of Tibet 421
Platte River 485, 531, 759
Pluto 850-851
Pnompenh, Cambodia 395
Pocahontas 762, 764
Pocatello, Idaho 620
Pocock, Edward 794
Pocock, Frank 794-795
Podang, India 309
Point Arena, California 178
Point Barrow, Alaska 18, 22, 266, 600, 612, 703, 801, 857-858
Point Conception, California 177
Point Loma Head 178
Poland 492
Polar Star 339
Polo, Maffeo 687-688
Polo, Marco 65, 184, **687-694**, 706
Polo, Niccolò 687-688
Polybias 709
Polynesia 92, 327, 732
Pompey's Rock 536
Ponce de León, Juan **695-698**, 768
Pond, Peter 561
Popocatépetl 278
Popovich, Pavel 819
Porpoise 329, 363
Port Augusta, Australia 361
Port Desire 299
Portland, Oregon 761
Portneuf River 620

Portobelo, Panama 317
Port Sudan 4
Port Suez, Egypt 152
Portugal 455-458
Porus (of India) 9
Post, Wiley **699-703**
Potala 309, 575-576, 753
Potawotomi (tribe) 513
Potomac River 764
Powell River 118
Powhatan (tribe) 764
Press On: Further Adventures of the Good Life 874
Prester John 287-290, 425
Price, W. Salter 116
Prince Edward Island 194, 265
Prince of Wales Strait 601
Prince Regent Inlet 642
Princess Martha Coast 91
Prince William Sound 62, 63
Principles of Geology 294
Project Mohole 406
Project Vanguard 352, 353
Prussia 474-475, 506
Prussian Geographical Society 74
Przewalski's horse 707
Przhevalsky, Nikolay 418-419, **704-708**
Ptolemy 798
Pueblo, Colorado 83, 663
Pueblo (tribe) 347
Puerto de los Reyes, Paraguay 168
Puerto Rico 696-697
Puget, Peter 835
Puget Sound 832
Pundits 751-753
Punjab, India 462, 754
Punta Alta, Argentina 297
Puquiura, Peru 100
Purari River 520
Putnam, George Palmer 332
Pygmies 1, 4, 321, 324, 797
Pyrenees Mountains 872
Pytheas **709-711**

Q

Qagssiarssuk, Greenland 343
Quapaw 497

Quebec, Canada 143, 212, 216, 217, 494-498, 512
Quebec City, Quebec 195, 215, 494
Quebrabasa Falls 549
Quebrabasa Rapids 550
Queen Charlotte Islands 834
Queen Charlotte Sound 259, 263-264, 833
Queen Maud Gulf 17
"Queen of the Air," 492
Queensland, Australia 360, 520, 523
Quelimane, Mozambique 140, 232, 550
Quesada, Gonzalo Jimenez de 479
Quetzalcoatl 276, 278
Qui Nhon, Vietnam 222
Quindio Pass 480
Quiros, Pedro Fernandez de 125
Quito, Ecuador 410, 479-480, 628
Qumis 596

R

Rabai 721, 828
Rabbai Mpia 504-506
Radisson, Pierre Esprit 225-230
Rae, John 368
Raleigh, Walter 712-717
Ram, Hari 752
Ramotobi 546
Ramsay, William 88
Ramu 520
Rangpur, Bangladesh 575
Rappahannock River 765
Rappahanock River 764
Rebmann, Johannes 113, 504-505, **718-722**
Recife, Brazil 174
Red River 396, 398, 662-663
Red Sea 4, 13, 76, 285, 290, 384, 503, 580, 583, 584, 666, 773
Reliance 360
Repulse Bay 640
Resolution 261-264, 266, 830
Resolution Island 472
Restello, Portugal 392
Return Reef 367

Revillagigedo Island 834
Revolt in the Desert 87
Reynier Pauw 454
Rhages, Iran 8
Rhea 849
Rhine River 475
Rhodes, Cecil 828
Rhodes, Greece 289
Richardson, James 70, 72
Richelieu, Cardinal de 217
Richelieu River 215
Ride, Sally 723-726
The Rifle and Hound in Ceylon 44
The Right Stuff 874
Rihla 80
Rijnhart, Petrus 727-730
Rijnhart, Susie Carson 420, **727-730**
Rincon, New Mexico 167
Rio Colorado 298
Rio Conejos 663
Rio de Janeiro, Brazil 59, 91, 93, 123, 296, 568, 841
Rio De Oro 426
Rio dos Bons Sinais 388
Rio Grande 167, 272, 347, 348, 517, 663
Rio Grande Valley 271
Rio Negro 478, 630
Rio Nunez 180, 181
Rio Plata 298
Rio Santa Cruz 299
Río de la Plata 167, 172, 174, 568, 841
Riobamba, Ecuador 411
Ripon Falls 776
Ritter, Karl 70
Riyadh, Arabia 88
Roanoke Island 714
Roberval, Jean-François de La Rocque, Sieur de 196
Robinson Crusoe 359
Robinson, John 662-663
Rock of Aronos, Pakistan 808
Rockefeller, John D. 160
Rocky Mountain Fur Company 761
Rocky Mountains 51, 104, 373, 484-485, 529-530, 663, 758-759, 821, 823-824

Rogers, Will 703
Roggeveen, Jacob 731-734
Rogue River 178
Rohlfs, Friedrich Gerhard 735-738
Rolfe, John 764
Rome, Italy 95
Roosa, Stuart 31
Roosevelt 430-431
Roosevelt, Eleanor 333
Roosevelt, Franklin D. 542
Rosas, Juan Manuel 298
Rose, Louise 452
Ross, Alexander 759
Ross Ice Barrier 160
Ross Ice Shelf 19, 20, 452, 746
Ross Island 746
Ross, James Clark 16, 56, 328, 368, 600, 642
Ross, John 368, 639
Ross Sea 339, 747
Rousseau, Jean-Jacques 127
Rowley, Henry 231
Royal Botanical Gardens, Kew Gardens 54, 363
Royal Geographical Society 48, 55, 60, 105, 112, 114-115, 138, 152-153, 156, 231, 235, 237, 303, 324, 546, 550-552, 637, 652, 747, 750, 754, 756, 775-776, 789, 792, 826-828, 859, 863
Royal Gorge 663
Royal Society 52-54, 209, 256-257, 305, 360, 366, 575, 601, 638
Ruiz, Bartolomé 671
Ruiz, Hipólito 476
Rum Cay, Bahama Islands 245
Russia 482, 484, 510, 597
Russian America 61, 63
Russian Far East 705
Russian Revolution 857
Russo-Turkish War 93
Rustichello 694
Rutan, Burt 739
Rutan, Dick 739-743
Ruvuma River 551, 826
Ruwenzori Range 798
Ruzizi River 155, 553, 774, 792

Ryukyu Islands 223, 667

S

Sabians 597
Sabos (of the Bedouins) 384
Sacagawea 532-536
Sagres, Portugal 425
Saguenay River 195, 213
Sahara Desert 69-71, 79, 416, 435, 455, 861
Saigon, Vietnam 105, 394, 398
Saint Croix River 214
Saint Elias Mountains 510
Saint Elmo's fire 296
Saint Helena Bay 388
Saint-Malo, France 127
Sakhalin 510
Salapunco, Peru 99
Samana Cay, Bahama Islands 245
Samaná Bay 246
Samar Island 570
Samaritans 97
Samarkand, Uzbekistan 78, 461
Samudra, Sumatra 79
San Antonio 567, 569
San'a, Yemen 597
San Antonio Bay 347
San Antonio, Texas 166, 539
San Bernardino, California 621
Sancti Spiritus, Argentina 174
San Diego Bay 177
San Diego, California 539, 760
San Diego Harbor 178
San Domingo, Cuba 319
Sandwich Islands 510
Sandy Hook 470
San Fernando de Apuré 478
San Francisco, California 104
San Francisco Bay 832, 834
San Germain, Puerto Rico 696
San Gerónimo, Mexico 270
Sangre de Cristo Mountains 373, 663
San Joaquin Valley 372, 621, 760
San Jose, Trinidad 715
San Juan, Puerto Rico 671, 696, 698
San Kuri 3

Sanlúcar de Barrameda 568, 573
San Luis Rey 537
San Miguel, California 83, 672
San Miguel Island 177
San Salvador, Bahama Islands 176, 245, 696
Sansanding 634, 636
San Sebastián 615
Sanskrit 462-463
Santa Barbara Channel 177
Santa Catalina Island 177
Santa Cruz 511, 697
Santa Cruz Islands 189
Santa Fe, Argentina 299
Santa Fe, New Mexico 662-664, 761
Santa Fe Trail 83
Santa Maria 243, 245-246, 248
Santa Maria de la Antigua del Darién 615
Santa Maria Island 246
Santangel, Luis de 242
Santiago 567, 569
Santiago, Cuba 275
Santiago Island 572
Santo Domingo, Dominican Republic 165, 249, 251-254, 274, 615, 625, 696, 840
San Tomás 717
Santos, Brazil 157
Sao Gabriel 387, 390
São Jorge da Mina, Benin 239
Sao Rafael 387, 390
Sao Tiago 294
Sargasso Sea 244
Saskatchewan, Canada 561, 822-823
Sasquatch 453
Saturn 464, 467, 847, 849-850
Saturn 37
Saturn V 27
Savannah River 769
Savitskaya, Svetlana 723
Sawyer, Herbert 105
Say, Nigeria 72
Schenectady, New York 225
Schiller, Friedrich 475
Schirra, Walter "Wally" 28
Schmitt, Harrison 32
School of Mines 475

Schumacher, Raoul 593
Schurke, Paul 801
Schweickart, Russell 29
Schweinfurth, Gerog 4
Schweitzer, Albert 134
Scillus 870
Scoresby, William 56
Scotland 484, 493, 525, 711
Scott Base 452, 453
Scott, David 29, 31, 36
Scott, Robert Falcon 19, 21, 453, 744
Scott, Walter 635
Scottish Geographical Society 745
Scylax of Caryanda 434-435
Sealab 286
Seal Nunataks 803
Sea of Crises 557
Sea of Japan 510
Sea of Marmara 6
Sea of Okhotsk 510, 701
Sea of Plenty 558
Sea of Tranquility 37
Seattle, Washington 18, 857
Sebituane 547
Sedgwick, Adam 293
Ségou 579, 634
Seine River 540
Seistan 596
Sekelutu 548-550
Seleucia-Ctesiphon, Iraq 220
Seminole 83
Seneca (tribe) 142, 215, 513
Senegal 180, 579, 632, 636
Senegal River 426
Serpa Pinto, Alexandre Alberto da Rocha de 138
Sesheke 547
Setúbal 666
Seuthe 870
Seven Cities of Cíbola 164, 167, 270, 281, 345, 348, 349, 768
Seven Pillars of Wisdom 87
Seven Years' War 187, 255, 410, 508
Seville, Spain 254
Shackleton Base 376, 452
Shackleton, Ernest 20, 375, **744-749**, 857
Shackleton Ice Shelf 854

Shanapur, India 231
Shang-ch'uan Island 866
Shang-tu 691
Shanghai, China 397, 399, 692, 728
Shaw, T. E. 87
Shawnee (tribe) 118, 120
Sheffield University 489
Shelekhov, Gregory 62
Shensi 692
Shepard, Alan 31, 402
Shepard, Sam 874
Sherpa 451, 453
Shewa, Ethiopia 290, 503
Shi'ite Muslims 77, 88
Shigatse, Tibet 421
Shipton, Eric 450
Shiraz, Iran 77
Shire River 550
Shoemaker-Levy 9 468
Shoshoni (tribe) 532-534
Siam 812
Sian 461, 463, 692
Siberia 267, 469, 482, 492, 509-510
Sicily, Italy 67, 95, 434, 710
Sidayu 457
Siddhartha Gautama 307
Sierra de Quareca 616
Sierra Leone 387, 426
Sierra Nevada 83, 372-373, 621, 760
Sijilmasa, Morocco 416
Sikkim 308, 751, 814, 816
The Silent World 285
Silk Road 218, 220
Silla 634
Silverstein, Abe 26
Simbing 633
Simla, India 105
Simonstown 501
Simpson, George 619
Simpson Strait 17
Sinai, Egypt 290
Sinai Desert 97
Sinai Peninsula 76
Sinaloa, Mexico 281
Sind, Pakistan 151, 434
Singapore, China 105, 491
Singh, Duleep 44

Singh, Kalian 754
Singh, Kishen 752
Singh, Mani 751, 753-754
Singh, Nain 750-756
Sinkiang Uighur, China 66, 704-706
Sino-Japanese War 106
Sino-Swedish Scientific Expedition 422
Sinta, Pedro de 426
Sioux (tribe) 227, 532
Sioux City, Iowa 531
Siple, Paul A. 163
Sitka Island 63
Six Months in the Sandwich Islands 104
Skate 860
Sketches Awheel 862
Skraelings 527
Sky Roads of the World 493
Slave River 561
Slidell, John 854
Smith, Jedediah 620-621, **757-761**
Smith, John 470, **762-766**
Smithsonian Institution 743
Smoky River 563
Snaefellsnes 342
Snake River 372, 484, 534, 619-620
Snook, Neta 331
Society Islands 733
Society of Geography 138
Socrates 867, 870
Sofala, Mozambique 289, 392
Soko (tribe) 796
Sokoto, Nigeria 72
Solis, Juan Diaz de 173, 568
Solomon Islands 126, 189-190, 326, 328, 511
Somali Desert 3
Somaliland 773
Somers, Geoff 803
Somerset Island 16
Son-tay, Vietnam 398
Songkhla, Thailand 491
Sonora, Mexico 167
Soto, Hernando de 164, 167, **767-771**
South 749

South China Sea 222
Southern Alps 449-450
South Georgia Island 91, 749
South Island, New Zealand 259, 263, 327, 449, 810-811
South Magnetic Pole 328, 747
South Orkney Islands 328
South Pass, Wyoming 372, 485, 757
South Peak 451
South Pole 14, 18-20, 158, 160-161, 163, 338, 377, 452-453, 744, 746-747, 804, 859
South Seas 509, 513
South Shetland Islands 92, 93, 328
Soviet Space Commission 818
Soyuz I 382
Space Telescope Science Institute (Baltimore, Maryland) 466
Spanish-American War 158
Spanish Armada 315, 319-320, 714
Spanish Inquisition 241
Spanish Trail 372
Sparta 870
Speke, John Hanning 45-46, 112, 113-114, 153-156, 502, 551, 580, 722, **772-777,** 794
Spencer Gulf 355, 356, 361, 362
Spencer, Herbert 358
Spice Islands 127, 174, 318, 457, 567, 570-571, 573, 733, 865
Spirit of St. Louis 539, 542
Spitsbergen Islands 130, 160, 642
Spitsbergen, Norway 21, 22, 337, 365, 611-612, 858
Spruce, Richard 481
Sputnik 26, 36, 351, 353, 379, 555, 557, **778-782**
Sri Lanka 44, 51, 79, 222-223, 596, 598, 693, 862
Srinigar, India 105, 406
Stadacona (Quebec City, Quebec) 195-196
Stafford, Thomas 29
Stag Lane 489
Stalin, Joseph 779
Stanhope, Hester 783-787
Stanislaus River 760
Stanley Falls 795

Stanley, Henry Morton 115, 134-135, 138, 233, 236, 553, **788-799,** 828
Stanley Pool 134-135, 795
St. Ann's Bay 253
Station Camp Creek, Kentucky 118
St. Augustine, Florida 319, 696
St. Croix, Virgin Islands 248
Stefansson, Vilhjalmur 857
Steger International Polar Expedition 802
Steger, Will 800-805
Stein, Aurel 806-808
Stephen of Cloyes 96
Stewart, James 542
St. Helena 302, 834
St. Ignace 496
Stingray Point 764
St. John's, Newfoundland 196
St. Joseph, Missouri 483
St. Lawrence River 193, 195, 212-213, 215, 227, 255, 497-498, 526
St. Louis, MIssouri 483-485, 530-531, 536, 539-540, 662
Stockton, Robert F. 373
St. Paul, Minnesota 662
St. Petersburg, Russia 420, 705, 708
Strabo 384
Strait of Belle Isle 194, 526
Strait of Georgia 833
Strait of Gibraltar 408, 415, 710
Strait of Hormuz 223
Strait of Juan de Fuca 832, 854
Strait of Magellan 124, 174, 188, 300, 318-319, 327, 458, 569, 600
Straits of Mackinac 514
Straits of Malacca 459
Streaky Bay 356
Stuart, John McDouall 144, 146, 149
Stuart, Robert 483-485
St. Vincent, West Indies 357
Submarine Force Museum 613
Sué River 582
Suffren 394
Sulpicians 513

Sumatra 223, 456, 458, 633, 666, 692
Sunda Strait 456
Surabaja, Indonesia 457, 491
Surveyor III 30
Susa 8, 10, 12
Susi, David 115, 231, 233-236, 552, 554, 790
Susquehannah River 142, 765
Susquehanna (tribe) 141, 142
Sutlej River 421, 754
Sutter's Fort, California 372, 373
Svalbard Islands 469
Sverdrup, Otto 18, 606
Swahili 504, 720, 828
Swallow 188-190
Swan 316
Swan River 356
Swedish Geographical Society 418
Sweetwater River 485
Swigert, John 30
Swiss Alps 450
Sydney, Australia 92, 302, 326, 355, 363, 510-511, 853
Sydney Harbor 362
Sydney, New Zealand 452
Syr Darya River 185
Syria 7, 596, 598
Syrian Desert 108, 109
Szechwan, China 106, 219, 460, 692, 814

T

Tabasco, Cuba 276
Tabasco, Mexico 276
Tabora, Tanzania 113-116, 155, 233-234, 554, 774-776, 790, 792, 826
Tadoussac, Quebec 213-214
Tagus River 247, 387, 390, 668
Tahiti 53-54, 124, 191, 256-259, 263, 265, 302, 328, 359, 832
Taino (tribe) 245
Takla Makan 420, 690, 706, 708, 807-808
Talavera Commission 241
Tallahassee, Florida 165
Taloi Mountains 11

Talon, Jean 496
Tampa Bay, Florida 165, 769
Tamralipti 463
Tana River 3, 506
Tangier, Morocco 79, 426, 736
Tankar, China 420
Tanzania 223, 231, 553, 773-774, 790, 826
Tao-chou 814
Taos, New Mexico 83
Tarim Basin 420-421, 706
Tashkent, Uzbekistan 419, 461
Tasman, Abel 258-259, **809-812**
Tasmania 302, 359-360, 364, 367, 809-810
Tassili-n-Ajjer Plateau 71
Ta-T'ang Si-Yu-Ki 463
Tatars 41, 666
Tatar Straits 510
Tawang 755
Taxila, Pakistan 9, 462
Taylor, Annie Royle 813-816
Taylor, Jim 521-523
Tegulet, Ethiopia 290
Tehachapi Mountains 760
Tehran, Iran 87, 105, 419
Tekeze River 45
Telefomin 522
Tenerife Island 568
Tengri Nor Lake 755
Tennessee River 770
Tennyson, Alfred 358
Tenochtitlán (Mexico City, Mexico) 276-279
Tensas (tribe) 516
Tereshkova, Valentina 723, **817-820**
Terhazza, Mali 80
Ternate, Indonesia 304
Terra Australis 188, 256-257, 487, 731, 810
Terror 368
Tete, Africa 58-59, 550
Teton Sioux (tribe) 532
Thailand 222, 223, 667, 692, 812
Thames River 493, 835
Thar Desert 463
Thebes, Egypt 6, 95
Theodore Roosevelt 648-649, 652

Thessaly 6
Thok Jalung, Tibet 754
Thompson, David 821-824
Thomson, Charles Wyville 209-210
Thomson, Joseph 231, 235-236, **825-829**
Thrace 6, 433, 870
Through the Dark Continent 798
Thucydides, Historian 870
Thurii, Greece 434
Thuzkan, Tuscany, Italy 67
Tib, Tippu 794-795, 797
Tibet 450, 574-576, 704, 727-728, 730, 752-753, 772, 813-814, 815-816
Tibetan Buddhism 307, 576, 689
Tibetan Pioneer Mission 816
Tider, Morocco 426
Tidore Island 571, 573
Tien Shan mountains 419, 461, 706-708
Tierra del Fuego 53, 258, 264, 296-297, 299-300
Tigre 503
Tigris River 108, 110, 868
Tiguex, New Mexico 271
Tiguex War 272
Tikrit, Iraq 596
Timbuktu, Mali 69, 73, 80, 179-181, 634, 636, 737
Timor, Malay Archipelago 189, 491
Tinian Island 192
Tintellust 71
Tinto River 243
Tiribazus 868
Tissaphernes 868
Titan 849
Titania 850
Titov, Gherman 380
Tlaxcala, Mexico 277-279
Tlingit-Haida 63
Tockwough (tribe) 765
Tokugawa 866
Tom Thumb 360
Tonga Island 265, 328, 809, 811
Tongariro National Park 449
Tonquin 484
Tonty, Henri de 513, 514, 516

Toowoomba 520
Töregene 185
Torres, Luis Vaez de 126, 261, 488
Torres Strait 126, 261, 362, 487
Toulon, France 182, 282, 326, 659
Tovar, Pedro de 271
Tower of London 714, 716
Trabzon 694, 869
Traits of American-Indian Life and Character 618
Transantarctic Mountains 20
Transcontinental Air Transport 541
Trans-Siberian Railroad 701
Transylvania Company 119
Trapezus 869
Travancore, India 865
Travels in West Africa 501
Treaty of Tordesillas 386, 567
Trebizond, Greece 67
Trent Affair 854
Triana, Rodrigo de 244
Trieste 659
Trieste, Italy 157, 659
Trinidad 567, 571, 573
Trinidad 251, 276, 624, 715
Tripoli, Libya 55, 70, 71, 737
Triton 850
Trois-Rivières, Canada 226-227
Trondheim, Norway 711
Troy, Greece 6
True Relation of Virginia 764
Trujillo, Peru 627, 481
Truman, Harry S 428
Tsaidam, China 219, 705
Tsangpo River 752, 753
Tsaparang, Tibet 24-25
Tswana 544
Tuakau, New Zealand 449
Tuamotu Archipelago 92, 124, 189, 191, 733
Tuat, Algeria 737
Tübingen 502
Tucker, HL 101
Tudela, Spain 94, 97
Tukulors 579
Tumba Lake 796
Tumbes 671, 672
Tun-huang 691, 807
Tunis, Africa 307

Tunisia 76, 710
Touré, Samory 579
Turtle Lake 823
Tuscaloosa, Chief 770
Tutuila 510
Tuvalu Islands 733
Twenty Thousand Leagues under the Sea 610
Tyre, Lebanon 7, 433

U

Ubangi River 581
Uganda 45, 114, 773, 776, 828
Ugogo 774
Ujiji, Tanzania 115-116, 233, 552-553, 774, 790
Ukambani 505-506
Ulan Bator 705
Ulfsson, Gunnbjörn 342
Ulloa, Francisco de 281
Umbriel 850
Umivik Fjord 605
Umpqua River 761
Umpqua (tribe) 761
Unalaska, Aleutian Islands 62
Unbeaten Tracks in Japan 105
The Undersea Odyssey of the "Calypso" 286
United States Biological Survey 337
Unyanyembe 773
Uranus 847, 849, 850
Urban II 96
Urga 705
Urubamba River 99, 100
Uruguay 482
Uruguay River 174
Usambara 504, 506
Ussuri River 705
Uzbekistan 77

V

Vaca, Álvar Núñez Cabeza de (see **Cabeza de Vaca, Álvar Núñez**)

Valladolid, Spain 254
Valles Marineris 587
Valley of Añaquito 480
Valley of Mexico 278, 279
Valley of Taurus-Littrow 32
Valparaíso, Chile 300, 301, 328
Valparaíso, Spain 318
Van Allen radiation belts 352, 376
Van Diemen's Land 810
Vancouver, George 62, 263-264, 361, 564, **830-835**
Vancouver Island 833
Vanguard 1 351, 353, 354
Vanikoro Island 511
Vanuatu Archipelago 125, 263, 328
Varanasi 462
Velázquez, Diego 275, 277, 278
Velho, Alvaro 390
Venera 781
Venezuela 476, 842
Venus, 256, 259, 585, 587-588, 781-782
Venus de Milo 325-326
Veracruz, Mexico 277
Veranzano, Girolamo da 837
Verkhne-Kamchatsk 42
Verne, Jules 610, 658
Verón, Pierre Antoine 123, 126
Verrazano, Giovanni da 193, 470, **836-838**
Verrazano-Narrows Bridge 836
Ver-sur-Mer, France 160
Veslekari 131
Vespucci, Amerigo 623-624, **839-842**
Vestfold Hills 860
Victoria 567, 571, 573
Victoria Falls 549
Victoria Island 17
Victoria Land 163, 377
Victoria Nile 48, 50, 794
Vidin, Bulgaria 44
Vienna, Austria 184
Vientiane, Laos 395
***Viking* 843-846**
Viking (ship) 604
Viking Lander Atlas of Mars 846
Vilcabamba mountains 99
Vilcabamba River 99-100

Ville de Bruges 581
Ville de Paris 638
Vincennes 853
Vinland 524, 526-527
Virgin River 759
Virginia 529, 713, 763
Visconti, Teobaldo 689
Viscount Melville Sound 639
Visscher, Frans Jacobszoon 810-811
Vitcos 98-102
Vogel, Edward 73
Volga River 77, 184, 688, 818
Vostok 91-92, 380, 402, 559, 781, 818-819
Vostok Island 92
A Voyage of Discovery to the North Pacific Ocean and Round the World 835
Voyage to Terra Australis 363
Voyager (airplane) 740-743
Voyager 1 and 2 847-851
Voyages 227
Voyages to the Frozen and Pacific Oceans 564
The Voyages and Adventures of Fernão Mendes Pinto 668

W

Wabag Valley 521
Wagner, Johannes 721
Wahgi Valley 521
Wainwright, Jacob 234
Wakamba 505-506
Walker Lake 760
Walla Walla, Washington 620-622
Wallace, Alfred Russell 304-305
Wallace Line 304
Waller, Horace 235
Wallis Islands 192
Wallis, Samuel 124, **187-192** 257
Walsh, Donald 659
Walvis Bay 312
Wamba, Zaire 4
War of 1812 64, 365
War of the Austrian Succession 187

Washington, D.C. 466, 536, 538, 764
Watauga Treaty 119
Wateita (tribe) 719
The Water Babies 499
Wau, Sudan 582
Wayne, Anthony 528
Weddell Island 328
Weddell, James 263, 327-328
Weddell Sea 163, 747
Wedgwood, Josiah 292
Wekotani 231, 232
Westall, William 361
West India Company 733
West Indies 213, 316, 831
West Palm Beach, Florida 660
West Road River 563
West with the Night 593, 594
Whiddon, Jacob 715
Whiskey Rebellion 528
White, Edward 27
White, John 714
White Nile River 50, 136, 582, 776, 798
Wilkes, Charles 329, **852-855**
Wilkes Land 853
Wilkins, (George) Hubert 337-338, 749, **856-860**
Wilkins-Hearst Expedition 859
Wilkinson, James 661-664
Willamette River 761
William Henry Ashley's Missouri Fur Company 536
Williams, Roger 838
Wills, William John 144-149
Wilson, Edward 744
Wind River 484, 761
Wind River Range 372
Windward Passage 245
Winnebago (tribe) 216
Winnie Mae 700-702
Wisconsin River 496
Wisting, Oskar 19
Wolfe, Tom 874
Wollongong, Australia 360
Wood, Maria 533
Woods Hole Oceanographic Institution 660
Worden, Alfred 31
Workman, William Hunter 861

Workman, Fanny Bullock 656, **861-863**
The World of Silence 285
World War I 3, 87, 89, 337, 422, 519, 748
World War II 27, 132, 162, 375, 401, 449, 493, 520, 522, 658, 780, 860
Wright, Orville 35, 743
Wright, Wilbur 35, 743
Wright, William 145, 147
Wu-Ti 218, 219

X

X-1 872, 873
X-1A 874
Xanadu 691
Xavier, Saint Francis 497, 667-668, **864-866**
Xenophon 867-870
Xocotla, Mexico 277
XS-1 project 872

Y

Yadkin valley 118-119
Yakutat Bay 63, 510
Yang-chou 692
Yangtze River 106, 222, 396, 692, 728
The Yangtze River and Beyond 106
Yao (tribe) 112, 231
Yaqui 167
Yaqui River 270
Yarkand, China 421, 690, 755
Yatung, Sikkim 816
Yauri, Hausa 636-637
Yeager 874
Yeager, Chuck 871-874
Yeager, Jeana 739-743
Yelcho 749
Yellow River 460, 691
Yellowstone River 533, 536
Yenbo', Saudi Arabia 152
Yenisei River 482

Yeti 453
Yokohama, Japan 106
Yongden 308-310
York 530, 534, 664
York Factory, Canada 366
Young, Brigham 372
Young, John 29, 32
Younghusband, Francis 577
Yucatán Peninsula 275
Yucay, Peru 99
Yüeh-chih 218
Yukagirs 41
Yukon River 18, 801
Yule, Henry 750
Yuma, Arizona 271
Yung-lo 222-223
Yungay 654
Yunnan, China 396, 692

Z

Zaire 1, 774, 826
Zambezi 547, 549-550
Zambezi River 58, 139-140, 232
Zambia 140, 547, 554, 828
Zanzibar, Tanzania 112-116, 153-154, 156, 223, 234-236, 504, 552, 776, 789, 792, 795-796, 798, 826-827
Zanzibar Island 721
Zaysan 707
Zeehaen 810
Zeeland 458
Zeila, Somalia 77, 290
Zelée 327, 328
Zenag 523
Zen Buddhism 307
Zenobia 786
Zimbabwe 140
Zinga 581
Zoar 498
Zond 5 557
Zond 6 557
Zoroastrianism 596
Zumaco 628
Zumbo, Mozambique 140
Zungomero 773
Zuni (tribe) 270, 345, 349-350
Zvedochka 782